THE PEOPLE WE MEET IN STORIES

THE PEOPLE WE MEET IN STORIES

Literary Characters That Defined the 1950s

Robert McParland

ROWMAN & LITTLEFIELD
Lanham • Boulder • New York • London

Published by Rowman & Littlefield
An imprint of The Rowman & Littlefield Publishing Group, Inc.
4501 Forbes Boulevard, Suite 200, Lanham, Maryland 20706
https://rowman.com

6 Tinworth Street, London SE11 5AL, United Kingdom

British Library Cataloguing in Publication Information Available

Library of Congress Cataloging-in-Publication Data
Names: McParland, Robert, author.
Title: The people we meet in stories : literary characters that defined the 1950s / Robert McParland.
Description: Lanham : Rowman & Littlefield, 2020. | Includes bibliographical references and index.
Identifiers: LCCN 2020010025 (print) | LCCN 2020010026 (ebook) | ISBN 9781538130353 (hardcover) | ISBN 9781538130360 (epub)
Subjects: LCSH: American fiction—20th century—History and criticism. | Characters and characteristics in literature. | Social change in literature.
Classification: LCC PS374.C43 M37 2020 (print) | LCC PS374.C43 (ebook) | DDC 813/.540927—dc23
LC record available at https://lccn.loc.gov/2020010025
LC ebook record available at https://lccn.loc.gov/2020010026

∞ ™ The paper used in this publication meets the minimum requirements of American National Standard for Information Sciences Permanence of Paper for Printed Library Materials, ANSI/NISO Z39.48-1992.

CONTENTS

ACKNOWLEDGMENTS

A thank-you goes to Stephen Ryan and Deni Remsberg, who helped set this book in motion, and thanks to Jon Sisk, his assistant Chelsea Panin, and the team at Rowman & Littlefield for bringing it to completion. Previous reflections on James Baldwin's "Sonny's Blues" appeared in the essay "To the Deep Water" in *Interdisciplinary Humanities* (Fall 2006).

1

INTRODUCTION

The People We Meet in Stories

This book is about the literary characters that illustrate social changes in America in the postwar 1950s. From Holden Caulfield to Augie March, dozens of characters became familiar to anyone who opened American novels during those years. These characters entertained thousands of readers while revealing some of the underlying currents of ambition, desire, and concern that were central to the American dream. In the 1950s, literary voices unsettled readers and probed American society. The postwar 1950s brought antiheroes, or flawed heroes, to readers. Stories brought what critic Leslie Fiedler called "the more post-apocalyptic fears and hopes of our blessed but immediately complex times." Poet Robert Lowell dubbed this period "the tranquillized fifties." Literary critic Richard Chase called it a period of "unresolved contradictions . . . seldom absorbed, reconciled, or transcended."[1] Literature responded to life in this era. Ralph Ellison's *Invisible Man* and James Baldwin's *Go Tell It on the Mountain* and *Giovanni's Room* explored matters of identity. Conventional perspectives were challenged by the works of Jack Kerouac, the Beat poets Allen Ginsberg and Gregory Corso, and the clever and creative William S. Burroughs and his *Naked Lunch*. James Bond and Perry Mason were heroes of popular culture.

Why do we care about fictional characters? How do we feel about our relationship to them as we read? Most often we are wondering what they will do and whether they will succeed. We are engaged in curiosity and speculation. Will they win love or lose it? Will they defeat the adversary? Once we take an interest in a character, we may be carried along by the narrative and plot that unfolds the story of their life and adventures. We enter the experiences of fictional characters and their conversations.

When we pick up a novel, we set aside the recognition that these events are fiction, and we hope to be entertained. The reader practices the willing suspension of disbelief and moves in and out of this connection with the text, while still aware of daily reality.[2] If the book is put aside and then returned to, the reader reenters and revives the imaginative encounter. Narrative leads us into identification, or it may encourage emotional responses or ethical judgments. One might become invested in the outcome for this character. When we look at a character as a person, we look at characteristics, or personality traits. Fictional characters become figures in the imagination of the reader. We share in the lives of these "people."

What might fictional characters suggest to us about life and human experience? In a 2016 study conducted at Durham University in Britain, more than fifteen hundred readers responded to questions about their encounters with fictional characters in literature. According to Richard Lea of *The Guardian*, roughly four hundred of these readers offered "detailed descriptions" of their encounters. Lea points out that "19 percent said the voice of fictional characters stayed with them even when they weren't reading and influenced the style and tone of their thoughts." It seemed to some of these readers as if "the character had started narrating my world." Charles Fernhough, a psychologist involved in the study, said: "For many of us, this can involve experiencing the characters in a novel as people we can interact with."[3]

"Stories can inform people's emotional lives," wrote Cody C. Debistraty in the *Atlantic* in 2014. "Stories can be a way for humans to feel that we have control over the world. They allow people to see patterns where there is chaos, meaning where there is randomness. . . . Storytelling especially in a novel allows people to peek into someone's conscience to see how other people think."[4] Literary critic Wayne Booth once wrote, "We care, and care deeply, about Raskolnikov and Emma. . . . Our interest in the fate of Oedipus and Lear . . . springs in part from our conviction that they are people who matter." Their fate matters to us, he says. "We care about them as human beings." How is what will happen in the life of Emma Bovary or the life of Julien Sorel important to me? Wayne Booth observed, "we are not in a position to profit from or be harmed by a fictional character."[5] We know that this is a representation. Yet, we bring ourselves to this. Some part of ourselves observes that we may identify with or be found to have something in common with this character.

Of course, a story must engage us and draw us in to this concern and connection, or identification, with characters. Readers bring their knowledge to the reading experience. When we read, our interpretations are influenced by our past reading experiences and life experiences, our interests, point of view, values, and worldview. The experience of fiction urges us to respond to the character's position. A reader can maintain detachment and not be swept up in identification. (One might see characters as a structuralist like Roland Barthes viewed them: as verbal signifiers, as constructions made from words on a page.)[6] Or, a reader may be drawn by some personal relevance that the text has for his or her life. One may be transported by the text. In any case, involvement in a text creates emotional connection with characters. It may prompt empathy for their goals, needs, and point of view, as well as concern about what will happen to them.

Literature portrays human beings and their relationships. These are imagined people who parallel our human lives, who express their uniqueness. Characters may provide us with information about the world, about the human condition, and about human psychology. For Richard J. Gerrig, a psychologist at Yale University, identification is "a natural consequence of the structure of cognitive processing."[7] Stephen Davies, a distinguished professor of philosophy at the University of Auckland in New Zealand, recalls Aristotle's *Poetics* and the experience of an audience that feels fear and pity for a tragic character. He considers "the role narratives play in our lives, not only via fictions but also more generally in shaping our identities, histories, cosmologies, and genealogies, and to observe that fact-seeking narratives deal as often with what might happen, what did not occur, as with what is actual."[8]

Readers, of course, are unique individuals with personal life experiences and individual ways of seeing the world. Different kinds of texts may produce different responses among readers. Readers make meaning through an experience of fiction, a transaction between the story and themselves. Considering the imaginative power of texts, we may ask if readers are constructed by various discourses or if they are autonomous, independent subjects free to make their own decisions about what a story means to them. We have idiosyncratic emotional reactions to what we read. We have opinions. We may experience difficulties in understanding. Meanwhile, readers like ourselves are situated in different social contexts. We approach texts with different strategies and past reading experiences, as we interpret and evaluate what we are reading.

There have been a variety of empirical studies in recent years that have explored reader empathy for fictional characters. Researchers ask whether there is any causal relationship between an experience of fiction and empathy. Does fiction promote empathy? Or do people who tend to be more empathic read more fiction? Psychologists involved in these studies have suggested that the potential for empathic response occurs when a reader is transported by a story.[9]

While one may be transported imaginatively into a fictional world and the experiences of a fictional character, one always knows, on some level, that this book is a material object and that someone has written it. A story is written at a given point in time and may enlist influences of the culture in which it has originated. For example, Ray Bradbury's *Fahrenheit 451* is the work of a uniquely creative mind, but, even while it is set in a future time, it also may reflect America in the early 1950s. Bradbury's concern with the problems and dehumanizing aspects of modern culture can be seen throughout his stories. In one of them, only the radio and machines are alive in a home after a family and a neighborhood has disintegrated in a nuclear blast. In "The Pedestrian," one's constitutional right to take a walk, rather than drive a car, becomes suspicious in a neighborhood where everyone drives automobiles. These stories reflect contemporary concerns: characters beset by problems in the modern world. In this case, it is a 1950s Los Angeles world in which cars and automotive mobility predominate and the natural act of walking is subsumed. In *Fahrenheit 451*, the provocative act of reading and thinking has been overcome by disinterest and distraction and enforced by bureaucracy and mechanism.

Perhaps one typical figure of 1950s fiction may be seen in Tom Rath in Sloan Wilson's *The Man in the Gray Flannel Suit*. Tom has joined suburban life and nine-to-five working days, commuting to and from his business. There is little to distinguish Tom from W. H. Auden's "The

Unknown Citizen," who is eulogized in Auden's poem for living an undistinguished and ordinary life and contributing five children to the population. (The Bureau of Statistics has found no official complaints about him.) Tom Rath may find dreams in paperback books, but there is gray flannel monotony in his daily life.

Many servicemen, like Tom Rath, brought home with them from the Second World War the habit of reading. They had been issued paperback books while overseas in uniform. The 1950s saw the further rise of the mass paperback from the Armed Services editions of the Second World War through the development of Penguin, Pocket Books, and new paperback publishing of New American Library and Ballantine. There was a greater mix of the literary "serious" modernist novel and middlebrow fiction. This dovetailed with the postwar rise of consumerism and the introduction of television. For popular fiction, it was a time of metamorphosis. Hardboiled crime stories and science fiction adventures emerged from the pulp magazines and assumed new form in paperback books.

In 1950, David Reisman argued that Americans were becoming more "other directed." While this might be good for organizational behavior, it was not good for autonomy. More people were living conforming lives rather than independent ones fostered by inner beliefs and values, Reisman asserted. In 1956, C. Wright Mills argued that a power elite of technocrats, military, and scientists had gained positions of economic and cultural control in American society. That year William Whyte's *Organization Man* observed that America was becoming a world of corporate middle managers. Novelist Norman Mailer insisted that in this context the role of the artist was to be "as disturbing, as adventurous, as penetrating as his energy and courage make possible."[10]

Literature brought a mix of the tragic and the comic, often in the same novel and in the same character. Holden Caulfield was rebellious, salacious, and satirical. Saul Bellow's Augie March was engaged in a restless search. Jack Kerouac's heroes expressed a restlessness and a search for freedom. Male characters were seen more often in public roles than were female characters. Perhaps this was a reflection of 1950s society. Women had filled many jobs during the war. Now many of them turned away from employment in the public sphere and moved back into the home. African American characters emerged in the writings of Ralph Ellison, Ann Petry, James Baldwin, and Richard Wright and the poetry of Gwendolyn Brooks. Yet, for Ralph Ellison his character was an invisible man, and for Richard Wright to be black in America was to be "The Outsider." Some of these characters of the 1950s appeared existentially alienated: Binx Bolling in Walker Percy's *The Moviegoer*, emerging in 1960, was one of these rootless figures. Frank Alpine, who found work in Morris Bober's Brooklyn grocery in Bernard Malamud's *The Assistant*, was another. Ernest Hemingway created the resilient Santiago in *The Old Man and the Sea*. However, he also created the somewhat forlorn Richard Cantwell of *Across the River and into the Trees*.

In this volume, we will look at what Ralph Ellison's *Invisible Man* may have to say to us about contradictions in American life and our moral and civic responsibility for sustaining a democracy. Humbert Humbert will likely puzzle us with his obsession with young Lolita, perhaps leaving us to wonder what we feel about a character like this. There will be stories of adventure: Santiago, Hemingway's old man, will attempt to catch a marlin, and Dean Moriarty and Sal Paradise will head out on the road. Flannery O'Connor's characters may draw us into some reflection on the sacred and the profane. We will ask whether readers are attracted or repelled by these characters, whether they sympathize with them or identify with them. Hopefully, this volume will point readers toward new fictional acquaintances.

We get to know characters gradually, much as we get to know each other. We can be wrong in our first impressions and evaluations. In Fitzgerald's *The Great Gatsby*, Nick Carraway only gradually begins to get to know Gatsby. Fitzgerald's technique leads us toward awareness of this character. That is how we begin any story: open to experience, meeting new characters, and anticipating that we will be entertained. We are transported: brought back into another time and place and into the life of a character.

With stories, we peer into the inexplicable uniqueness of other lives. Literature is a path into the minds and spirits of people different from ourselves. Stories bring us the hopes, dreams, attitudes, efforts, and failings of these representatives of the human condition. As stories toss the spark of imagination our way, a reader is drawn into their world. Moved, amused, puzzled, or appalled, a reader grapples with the question of who one is in relation to these people on the page. By reading the literature of a period and researching documents and other historical-cultural material, one begins to get at the temper of the time. Fictional characters, while imagined, may represent some of the behaviors, attitudes, and responses of people to goals, problems, or events that were present in society.

Certainly, characters in literature may seem believable. A reader may be able to visualize them and to feel with them. A reader like this, entering a fictional world, is involved in a cocreation of a text. There are emotional responses, identifications, recollections, and anticipations as one reads. Lisa Zunshine, a literary scholar who engages with cognitive approaches to fiction, suggests that we invest ourselves in the verbal constructions that we call characters. We bring to them "a potential for a variety of thoughts, feelings and desires."[11] A reader is drawn into a story by storytelling. Umberto Eco has suggested that we read mystery stories to be surprised but also to be reassured about life.[12]

Fiction helps satisfy our inclination "to peer into other minds and even share our minds," Gregory Tague points out in *Evolution and Human Culture*. As a development of human evolution, our cultural representations "mimic what we do in real life" (131). When we read stories, we guess at characters' intentions. Tague cites cultural anthropologist Michael Alvard's observation that "our ability to imagine others and their motives, needs, and desires as we imagine ourselves is what promoted cultural practices."[13] Tague elsewhere points out that readers identify with characters. A stage character provides "a visual impact and immediacy." The novelist can offer "multiple points of view" and perspectives extending across time and space.[14]

Involvement in a text creates emotional connection with characters; empathy for their goals, needs, and point of view; and concern about what will happen to them. Even so, texts may produce a variety of different responses. Readers make meaning through an experience of fiction, a transaction between the story and themselves. We may ask if readers are constructed by various discourses or if they are autonomous, independent subjects free to make their own decisions about what a story means to them. There are idiosyncratic emotional reactions and opinions. There may be difficulties in understanding. Readers are situated in different social contexts. They approach texts with different strategies and past reading experiences, as they interpret and evaluate what they are reading. (Meanwhile, postmodern texts, like those of

Robert Coover, John Barth, and Donald Barthelme, began to attempt to de-center reader responses.)

What are we to make of the fictional representation of human beings? Why would a reader feel for a fictional character? How does fiction stimulate some empathic response? How is a story creating effects that evoke sympathy? How will we process these figures, these signifiers and structures? We encounter the psyche of the characters. We see their sociocultural background. How does a character handle conflict? Why does this character act in that way? We will witness how a character thinks, dreams, desires, wants, or hides from self in rationalizing or defense mechanisms. A reader may ask: Is this character believable? What about when our own experience is quite different from the experience of the character we are reading about? In some stories, realism is challenged. What if we are not dealing with realism?

Given literary representation, generally a reader will assume that the fiction reflects life. The reader will bring personal experience and expectations to a story. As Norman Holland suggests, the "propositional thought modes" we bring to our reading "correspond to the very general way that we navigate reality." We make use of schemas: "scripts for how the events of our world normally work."[15] "I have many schemes about people that I bring to bear to understand literary characters," he writes. Yet, as novelist William Gass has said, "Our imaginings are imprecise and misty."[16] Holland quotes psychologist Victor Nell in this respect. Nell observes that the propositions we are given about James Bond, for example, "liberate the reader from the vagueness of imaginings and allow the use of propositional thought modes which . . . are more readily evoked and more richly evocative than the often colorless and wispy pictures we are able to make in our heads."[17] Holland points out that we make assumptions about identity. We make assumptions about time. We organize space. We have genre expectations: the detective will solve the crime; the heroine and hero of a romance will marry. The Hemingway character will have his manhood tested. We will respond to character stereotypes: "the gangster, the detective, the crazy scientist."[18]

A reader is both "inside" a story and "outside" it. After all, one may enter the fictional dream. However, one can also recognize that this is just words on a page. As Norman Holland puts it: "The thinking part of our brains (frontal and cortical) are separate from the enjoying (subcortical) parts."[19] When we "enjoy" a story, there is "only a minimal making sense" of the text. "We enjoy and then we deliberately and separately think about what we have enjoyed. When we do, we are understanding something about the work as we perceive and understand it in relation to ourselves."[20] That is to say, readers become involved in the process of participating in a story and in imagining and constructing characters. A reader may read in an emotionally engaged way for enjoyment. One may seek, interpret, and make meaning. A reader fills in the gaps in the work. As Holland observes, "we project our conscious and, especially, unconscious goals onto the events portrayed. . . . We ourselves wish to see this or that outcome represented in the literary work."[21] "The literary character is like an optical illusion for our brains," writes Norman Holland. "Why do I think and feel that this character I am reading about is a real human being when I know she is not?"[22] We know that the character is the fictional creation of an author. Yet, we also approach these representations as if they were people. "We have no rational way of deciding between our two perceptions: characters as people; characters as figments of authorly imagination."[23]

Consider our sense of pity for Dickens's Oliver Twist, Stephen Davies suggests. We recognize that most of us can do nothing about international situations we learn about on broadcast news. "It was for the same reason that my pity for Oliver Twist did not move me to action. I could do nothing for him because in this case we inhabit different worlds." Davies writes: "I cannot change Oliver's world, but the story should lead me to oppose real-world policies that tolerate poverty and child-labor." He adds, "We respond emotionally to scenarios that are hypothetical or counterfactual as to ones that are actual."[24] We may be drawn into concern by literature's portrayal of human beings and their relationships. These are imagined people who parallel our human lives, who express their uniqueness. These characters may be embedded in the context of a historical period or subculture. We may recognize that the character is a sign of culturally situated production, an expression of the time and culture in which he or she was first imagined. Even so, characters bring us reading experiences, evoke sympathy, or point us toward something universal, something we share with them. They may provide us with information about the world, about the human condition, and about human psychology.

READING IN THE 1950s

The quiet conservatism of the 1950s must be qualified. Certainly, it was a time of Dwight Eisenhower's steady reassurances, a time of economic development and of relative stability. Yet, it was also a period of some underlying anxieties, given the Cold War, House hearings, and awareness of the new atomic age. Meanwhile, the 1950s increased mobility with cars and expressways. The war initiated this mobility, drawing people from towns. Movement to the suburbs doubled by 1960. There was some shift of women out of jobs when the Second World War concluded. There was a renewed emphasis on home and family. However, the presence of women in the workforce remained a factor in the postwar economy.

The cultural critic Morris Dickstein says that as he worked on his book on the 1950s postwar period, he realized that the 1950s era and the 1960s are "not as sharply distinct" as he had thought.[25] There is overlap. This is true in America's literature. For example, *Catcher in the Rye* and *On the Road* can be associated with the spirit of "the sixties." They anticipate the counterculture. So do nonfiction texts like C. Wright Mills's *The Power Elite* and the critical position presented by William Whyte in *The Organization Man*. Dickstein recognized that postwar prosperity was significant and that economic success set the stage for the 1960s. He recognized an "exploding intellectual culture" of which he was a recipient in the 1950s. (He was a student at Columbia from 1957 to 1961.) He states that he and his peers felt a sense of rebellion against the 1950s culture. They read Norman O. Brown, Herbert Marcuse, Paul Goodman, and Norman Mailer.[26]

Following the Second World War, enrollment in higher education in the United States increased. Assisted by the GI Bill, some 7.8 million veterans became nearly half (49 percent) of the enrollment of U.S. colleges and training programs in 1947. The GI Bill next included Korean War veterans and concluded in 1956. In the 1950s, there were 1,327 four-year colleges in the United States. There were 344 public colleges and 983 private colleges. By 1960, there was a total of 1,422 four-year colleges (367 public and 1,055 private). College enrollment increased with the baby-boom cohort and rose at a rate of about 3.7 annually to some 6 million students by 1988. The female enrollment at colleges rose from .7 million in 1950 to 7.2 million in 1988. Women are now the majority of college students.

Female writers made a significant impact in the 1950s. Margaret Louise Coit's biography *John C. Calhoun: American Portrait* (1950) won the Pulitzer Prize in 1951. Marianne Moore won the Pulitzer Prize for poetry in 1952. Ann Petry's *The Narrows* (1953) probed city life. Rachel Carson's *The Sea around Us* (1951) provided an illustrated look at the life of oceans and opened a path toward her subsequent indictment of DDT spraying and call for ecological responsibility in *Silent Spring* (1962). In France, Simone de Beauvoir published *The Second Sex*, and arriving in New York, Hannah Arendt published *The Origins of Totalitarianism*. Patricia Highsmith wrote chilling mysteries like *Strangers on a Train* and *The Talented Mr. Ripley*. Dorothy Day penned her autobiography, *The Long Loneliness*. Mary McCarthy wrote *The Charmed Life* (1955), and Caroline Gordon wrote *The Malefactors* (1956). Gwendolyn Brooks won the Pulitzer Prize in 1950 for her poetry volume *Annie Allen* and published her only work of prose fiction, *Maud Martha* in 1953. Flannery O'Connor emerged as one of the most psychologically and theologically probing fiction writers of the 1950s and early 1960s. Ann Bauman wrote the lesbian novel *Odd Girl* (1957) and Ayn Rand, in *Atlas Shrugged*, argued for libertarian freedom and the "virtue of selfishness." Ketti Frings (Katherine Hartley) won the Pulitzer Prize in 1958 for her Broadway stage adaptation of Thomas Wolfe's *Look Homeward Angel*. Lorraine Hansberry's *A Raisin in the Sun* won the Drama Desk Award in 1959. Grace Metalious stirred controversy, provided titillation, and achieved extraordinary sales with *Peyton Place*. These women opened new paths for fiction and for other women writers who would follow.

The first National Book Awards were given in January 1950 to William Carlos Williams, Nelson Algren, and Ralph Waldo Emerson biographer Ralph L. Rusk. The *New York Times* observed: "The three writers are serious writers, shy of personal publicity, who have reflected on the meaning of America."[27] Along with these awards, the publishing industry began making use of marketing techniques used by advertising agencies to reach mass popular culture. There continued to be concerns about the diminishment of literary quality as the market expanded. New American Library adopted the slogan: "Good reading for the millions."[28] Television, expanding quickly in the 1950s, sought viewers and sold ads. Publishers realized that the medium could also help sell books. The American Book Association acknowledged that "the book trade's fear of television is unjustified."[29]

Then there was the paperback revolution in book publishing, which increased exponentially in the 1950s. The paperback encouraged the printing and distribution of genre fiction. In 1951, Doubleday was the largest of the science fiction publishers. New American Library and Ballantine reached for the science fiction audience also. Ballantine published some science fiction hardcover editions as well. Science fiction began to emerge from the pulps into book form. Isaac Asimov had written for the science fiction magazines. His novels *Pebble in the Sky* and *I, Robot* appeared in 1950. *The Foundation* trilogy followed, beginning in 1951 and followed by *The Martian Way* (1952) and *The Caves of Steel* (1954). In 1952, readers were treated to *Isaac Asimov Presents the Great Science Fiction Stories*.[30]

SOCIAL COHERENCE AND POSTWAR WRITING

Was the 1950s a period of coherence, as historian George M. Marsden characterizes it? One might point to America's pragmatic liberalism and its scientific rationality as a legacy of the Enlightenment. Books oriented toward self-help and religious faith were circulated in postwar America. Rabbi Liebman's *Peace of Mind* (1946) and Norman Vincent Peale's *The Power of Positive Thinking* (1952) were especially popular. In a Gallup poll, 75 percent of respondents stated that religion was "very important" to them and served as a way to "answer" the day's problems. Between 1950 and 1960, American church attendance increased by around 14 percent. However, while this was an era of family, church, home, and workplace, it was also a time that experienced an undercurrent of anxiety. Postwar economic prosperity and a hopeful can-do spirit of American optimism existed in tandem with Cold War anxiety. In 1950, psychologist Rollo May published his study on anxiety, recognizing that a little anxiety may challenge a person toward personal growth. However, he also observed that postwar America experienced some cultural anxiety. Historian of religion George M. Marsden recognizes the 1950s as a time of "great cultural anxiety and uncertainty."[31] This underscored the search for meaning, which took on a religious tone. Religious books were regularly on America's best-seller lists. Films like *Ben-Hur* (1959) were popular. The nation developed a Judeo-Christian liberal consensus, observes Marsden. It then saw the decline of this consensus later in the century. That cultural consensus shifted amid social change and identity politics. In Marsden's view, the religious right in the 1980s sought to return to a 1950s nexus. Yet, that establishment itself was not always "friendly" to religion and its truth claims, such as a salvation message. Marsden saw this as a reaction by elites and courts to secularize the society and push religion from the public sphere.

Postwar writing was usually not the same as the socially and politically engaged writing of the 1930s. There was a turn of attention to the struggles of individuals. Stephen Schryer's study of postwar American fiction begins by recalling the *Partisan Review* feature "Our Country and Our Culture," in which notable thinkers of the time considered literary culture and democracy and generally favored public intellectual contribution rather than accepting the artist as alienated. (Norman Mailer and C. Wright Mills disagreed and sided with alienation.) America's postwar intellectuals witnessed a rising middle class, the expansion of college education, and the emergence of a new managerial class. There was the formation of what economist John Kenneth Galbraith called "the New Industrial State." Lionel Trilling criticized the "organizational impulse" toward order and rationality in bureaucracy and technicians. His character John Laskell in *The Middle of the Journey* (1947) is a New Deal liberal planner engaged in low-income housing for families. He faces loss and illness and changes his perspective. It now appears to him that the progressives are "projecting their subjective desires on the world."[32]

Fictional characters reflected transformations in American society. Hiram Hayden, editor of the *American Scholar*, gathered writers in a New York apartment for a discussion about American fiction on July 16, 1955. This group included Ralph Ellison, John Erskine, Stephen Becker, Jean Stafford, Simon Michael Bessle, and William Styron. Hayden commented that he had heard suggestions "that the American novel is not very distinguished."[33] Stephen Becker claimed that "a smaller percentage [of readers] cares for the serious novel" than did in the period before Dickens. Ralph Ellison addressed an idea that perhaps that audience, including many newspaper readers, felt a sense of wonder that provided them with "a grasp of contemporary change," "a sense of discovery," and "the newness within the familiar."[34]

Some readers in the 1950s turned to reading books for self-improvement. Louis Menand observes that "[t]here was a major middle-class culture of earnest aspiration in the 1950s."[35] As Tim Lacy points out, there was a claim that reading the Great Books "fosters the critical faculty" and provides questioning of "stock notions."[36] At the center of the Great Books program were men like John Erskine, Robert Hutchins, and Mortimer Adler. Lacy writes: "Adler envisioned a public philosophy rooted in Aristotelean thought and supplementary to the great books idea."[37] He turned to Thomistic and Aristotelean ideas while a secular Jew. He was an *Encyclopedia Britannica* editor and among his writings was the popular *How to Read a Book* (1940). Adler left the University of Chicago in 1952 and began his public intellectual phase. The Great Books of the Western World series appeared that year. He also promoted his educational Paideia Program. His goal was to "enlighten the polis," observes Lacy.[38] A program of reading would assist individuals in their intellectual growth, creating a more empowered public. These readers of the Great Books could deal with the modern world and build a stronger democracy. They would join what Robert Hutchins called "the Great Conversation." Thus, the Great Books would contribute to cultural capital, offer access to ideas, encourage civic dialogue, and foster discourse communities concerned with the transmission of meaning.[39] The Great Books would be more accessible and contribute to communications in the public sphere. To be for the Great Books was to be opposed to anti-intellectualism and to aim at a flexible and thoughtful public philosophy.

For the reading public, to vicariously experience adventure among fictional characters was also a respite from loneliness. "Being alone is also a force in America today," writes Robert Ferguson. "We turn to fiction to recognize something in ourselves and the world around us."[40] Solitariness appears throughout American literature. Herman Melville speaks of the experience of being "isolato."[41] We listen to the interior reflections of fictional characters and are engaged in "the search for a reliable voice."[42] In the 1950s, fictional characters faced existential issues of dread or anxiety and sought freedom of spirit. Speakers turned inward, meditating on change, aging, loss, exclusion, or difference. They sought romance, stories of love and hope, and expansions of the spirit. This contemplation and search for human connection, however, was not new. Ferguson quotes Alexis de Tocqueville's observation from the 1830s that individualism "disposes each member of the community to sever himself from the mass of his fellows and draw apart with his family and friends."[43] This is a separating individualism. A concern of the 1950s was whether community in America could be revived and strengthened, or whether it would be eclipsed by the impact of modernity.

EVENTS OF THE 1950s

The 1950s, mid-century, may be viewed as a transitional time. It was a time of recovery and economic growth, a period during which suburbs grew along with consumer culture. Yet, it was also a time of civil rights struggle, an era in which poverty and racism remained concerns. Beneath the apparent complacency was Cold War tension and concern about the atomic bomb. American literature argued for individualism against the conformity characterized by the organization man and registered a cultural anxiety, reflecting Europe's postwar existentialism. Yet, roads were built, suburban communities formed, the Korean War—never quite resolved—was half-forgotten, and America experienced a time of relative prosperity. Shall we look back upon the 1950s as sane, stable, disciplined, and hopeful, or as anxious, repressive, and conformist? Literature is a resource for our inquiry.

America created suburban culture in the 1950s. Towns grew in population with the construction of new homes, tree-lined streets, roads, and stores. In schools, children practiced air raid and bomb drills, huddling and squirming under desks in impossible poses for implausible safety from the atom bomb. In a Nevada desert, the hydrogen bomb was tested. It detonated in a fireball and thrashed sand and disintegrated land for three miles in all directions. Nuclear power prompted a new age of anxiety.

In Wheeling, West Virginia, on February 9, 1950, Joseph McCarthy (R-Wisconsin) declared that there were communists in the government. He held up a piece of paper that he asserted was a list of communist sympathizers who, he said, were known to the State Department. There was no such list. However, McCarthy's assertion contributed to an era of Cold War anxiety. Tensions between the United States and the Soviet Union had escalated. On January 21, 1950, Alger Hiss, who had been accused of spying for the Soviet Union, was sent to prison for perjury. Weeks later Britain jailed Klaus Fuchs, a physicist, for selling nuclear secrets. The Sino-Soviet Pact was signed in February, making China and the Soviet Union allies. Julius and Ethel Rosenberg were charged with passing atomic secrets to the Russians and sent to Sing Sing Prison to await execution.

In 1950, Estes Kefauver chaired the committee investigating crime in interstate commerce. The Kefauver hearings examined organized crime, money laundering, corruption, and the drug trade across more than a dozen U.S. cities. Television brought public attention to the hearings. President Truman signed an executive order supporting the committee's examination of tax returns. The racketeers created "a cloak of respectability" through charitable donations, noted Daniel A. Bolick, the IRS assistant commissioner. The investigation turned up corruption of some police chiefs and linked politicians to facilitating crime fostered by the Mafia. (Meyer Lansky, Frank Costello, and Abner Zwillman were among those named.) Along with congressional hearings and news, television brought Milton Berle, George Burns and Gracie Allen, "What's My Line?," and a variety of other game shows into middle-class homes. On the radio, listeners heard Frank Sinatra's vocals and Nat King Cole singing "Mona Lisa." Whether listeners smiled like Mona Lisa or not, they knew that events were happening overseas. America went to war.

THE KOREAN WAR

Two significant global issues were of concern to the Truman administration: how to limit communist expansion and how to respond to diminishing colonial enterprises and emerging nationalisms. American foreign policy in the new decade developed a policy of containment, following the George Kennan telegram of some eight thousand words on February 22, 1946, regarding Soviet expansionist "tendencies."[44]

In Asia, Americans were present in South Korea in an advisory capacity. American concern in Korea was focused on the prospects of global communism. In 1950, Joseph Stalin remained at the center of

Soviet totalitarianism. In China, Mao was heralded as the revolutionary leader whose civil war victory brought Marxism to the populous country to create a new era. On October 1, 1947, Mao proclaimed the People's Republic of China at Tiananmen Square. The nationalists under Chiang Kai-shek fled to Formosa, now Taiwan. That Stalin had ruthlessly eliminated opposition and promoted pogroms was yet to be widely revealed. That Mao was a source of widespread "terror he had let loose on his own people" was yet to be seen.[45] Soviet influence shadowed North Korea, where Kim Il-sung had been placed in power in 1945. The new leader looked to China and sought Soviet backing for a military move into South Korea. Stalin resisted challenging the U.S. presence there.

As the tensions of the Cold War developed, the Marshall Plan, the European Recovery Program for reconstruction, was announced in June 1947, and the protective arrangement of the North Atlantic Treaty Organization (NATO) was created in early April 1949. The anxiety of a nuclear world increased as the Soviet Union tested the atomic bomb in the Kazakhstan desert on August 29, 1949. The American public learned of this on September 23. Meanwhile, scientists informed President Truman of their work on the hydrogen bomb. The "super bomb" project would be revealed on January 30, 1950.

The U.S. nuclear arms plan recommended that a civilian agency, not the military, would be placed in charge of supervision of nuclear arms development. Scientists had explicitly cautioned against its use. The administration was aware that the atomic bomb was qualitatively different from any other weapon in the military arsenal. However, now they argued that nuclear force had to exist as a deterrent, a threat, in a standoff against Soviet arms. The United States housed 369 atomic bombs at the end of 1950.[46]

On June 15, North Korean troops crossed the 38th Parallel, using the roads and railway. President Harry S. Truman was home in Independence, Missouri, after having recently dedicated a Baltimore airport. Secretary of State Dean Acheson was at a farm in Maryland. On that Sunday, John Foster Dulles and John Allison suggested that the United States intervene if the South Koreans were unable to stop the North Korean advance. Their concern was that repercussions might lead toward escalation into another World War. Truman was back in Washington, DC, on June 25. The National Security Council recognized the North Korean incursion into South Korea as a violation of the

United Nations charter. The Soviets would only respond to force, the administration concluded. "We had to meet them on that basis," said Truman.[47]

The Korean War began on June 25, 1950, when the North Koreans streamed across the 38th Parallel into South Korea. The United Nations approved a resolution to protect South Korea. President Harry S. Truman sent American troops to halt the North Korean invasion. He did so without congressional authorization. When General Douglas MacArthur engaged his forces in a strategy to foil the North Korean advance, China attacked, decimating American troops and forcing them back south of the 38th Parallel.[48] U.S. and South Korean military forces had to pull back to the south. MacArthur then launched the landing at Inchon in September. (Inchon was to the west of Seoul, along the coast.)

Within the shadow of the Cold War lingered the potential for nuclear calamity. To the president's advisors, it was evident that any use of atomic warfare against China in the Korean War would bring both Chinese and Soviet response. Such a response might engage Europe in a protective move to arm itself against the Soviet Union. Truman ordered MacArthur not to intervene and not to advance to the Yalu River. General Douglas MacArthur was relieved of command for insubordination. General Matthew Ridgway was appointed to lead the forces in Asia. The war was terminated July 27, 1953, but never formally concluded: the armistice was inconclusive. Some 36,568 Americans died in the fighting. As many as two million Koreans, including civilians, perished in the war.

A 1950s TIME LINE

Literary characters entered American consciousness and became part of a broadening popular culture. *Catcher in the Rye* by J. D. Salinger was published in 1951. The story of Holden Caulfield addressed teenage angst and alienation in plainspoken, rough language and offered a sharp rejection of cultural pretentiousness. Herman Wouk's *The Caine Mutiny* and James Jones's *From Here to Eternity* recalled scenes from military service in the Second World War. On stage, Rodgers and Hammerstein's *The King and I* featured Yul Brynner. Lucille Ball appeared in *I Love Lucy* on television. The show attracted a large audience and sparked the aspirations of young women across the country.

American foreign affairs and domestic culture were shaken by surprises. On April 11, 1951, President Truman relieved General MacArthur of his command. The general had set his sights on attacking China if North Korea and China did not sit down for talks to resolve the war. Rather than expanding the war, Truman focused upon containing the fighting and moving toward a settlement. Meanwhile, across the United States, baseball, the national pastime, provided fans with a diversion and an array of near-mythical sports figures. That autumn, sports fans in New York heard an ecstatic radio announcer react to Bobby Thomson's three-run home run in the ninth inning by repeating "The Giants win the pennant!" The 1951 New York Giants won the National League pennant in the ninth inning against the Brooklyn Dodgers with a home run off Ralph Branca. The Dodgers won the pennant in 1952 over the Giants but lost the World Series in seven games against the New York Yankees. The Dodgers and Yankees met in the World Series, with a Yankees victory in 1953. The Giants, with Willie Mays, Don Mueller, Alvin Dark, and Monte Irvin, won the National League pennant in 1954, with the Dodgers six games back.

In 1952, Dwight D. Eisenhower ran for the presidency. Richard Nixon, the vice-presidential candidate, told the nation about his campaign finances. Following *The Milton Berle Show*, he appeared on television with his "Checkers" speech in which he referred to the family dog. "Checkers" was the only campaign contribution that he had kept, he said. The Eisenhower-Nixon ticket was elected to office in November, defeating their Democratic opponent Adlai Stevenson in a landslide vote. America evidently sought the apparent security that a celebrated general with a Republican agenda might provide.

The nuclear arms race was clearly under way. A U.S. atomic test blew up an island in the Pacific Ocean on November 1, 1952. The Soviets exploded a thermonuclear device in the desert on August 12, 1953. The Soviets' first intercontinental ballistic missile (ICBM) was reported on August 7, 1957, and Sputnik made the news on October 4, 1957. Cold War tensions were reflected in the arms race and the space race.

There were a variety of other diversions and sources of hope and consolation for the American public. Norman Vincent Peale's *The Pow-*

er of Positive Thinking was a huge best seller that stayed on the list throughout the year. On the radio, country star Hank Williams sang "Your Cheatin' Heart." In American homes, Ozzie and Harriet and *Dragnet* appeared on the television. The Steel Seizure Case of 1952 was big news. Harry Truman declared a national emergency and claimed that he had to take control of steel factories because of a labor strike. The steel was needed for the Korean War effort, he said. Truman contended that there was in the presidency "inherent powers to meet national emergencies." (One may see a parallel in Donald Trump's insistence that monies allocated by Congress for military projects be redirected to fund the building of a wall on the U.S. southern border.) Truman's action would expand presidential powers. With Executive Order 10340, he emphasized the need for steel production. Recognizing wage and price controls in key industries, the steel companies would not consent to pay increasing demands from workers and their unions. At the end of 1951, a strike was anticipated.

"These are times of crisis," Truman asserted in a speech on April 8, 1952. He responded to Chinese intervention in the Korean War. He also directed his speech at the Soviet Union. The 1947 Taft-Hartley Act provided Truman with authority via court order to suspend a strike if it would affect national security. Truman had vetoed the Taft-Hartley Act but, ultimately, the legislation passed. Truman was pro-labor and would not use this. Instead, he had to claim executive authority.

The Supreme Court heard the case *Youngstown Sheet and Tube Company v. Sawyer*, beginning on May 12, 1952. The court voted 6–3 for the steel companies. Justice Hugo Black affirmed that the president's power "must stem either from an act of Congress or from the Constitution itself" [Youngstown Sheet and Tube Co. v. Sawyer 343 U.S. 579 (1952)]. This case frames the U.S. Constitution separation of powers and was a judicial response to presidential power.[49] The military goal was to hold the line against communism and preserve wartime production. The concern was with the steel companies potentially raising prices. The political goal was to get the industry back to the bargaining table.

In 1952, Senator Joseph McCarthy appointed Roy Cohn chief counsel to government operations.[50] In his checkered career, Cohn represented mobsters Anthony "Fat Tony" Salerno and Carmine Galante as well as Cardinal Spellman and Cardinal Cooke. He was also an advisor to Donald Trump. Cohn attended the Fieldston School in Riverdale, where now stands the Ethical Culture Society. Cohn was disbarred for unethical practices. The term *witch hunt* was applied to the McCarthy House Un-American Activities Committee (HUAC) hearings. Those hearings were news in the early 1950s. Arthur Miller's *The Crucible* is about a witch hunt set during the Salem witch trials but refers implicitly to the stresses of this period. Edward R. Murrow cast light on Joseph McCarthy's practices and the allegations he never substantiated.

World affairs that were reported to Americans in newspapers and on television in 1953 included the death of Joseph Stalin, the appointment of Marshal Josip Broz Tito in Yugoslavia, and earthquakes in the Greek isles. The Soviets put down a strike and riot in East Germany by using tanks and military troops. Other disruptions across the world created peril and concern. In Iran, in 1953, Mohammad Mossaddegh's regime was toppled, and Shah Mohammad Reza Pahlavi was installed with support of the American CIA. Edmund Hillary and Tenzing Norgay climbed the heights of Mount Everest. Samuel Beckett created *Waiting for Godot*, and James Baldwin published *Go Tell It on the Mountain*. The first issue of *Playboy* appeared with a centerfold of Marilyn Monroe, from a photo taken of her in 1949. Film actor Marlon Brando starred in *The Wild One* and *Julius Caesar*. Fictional characters blended with screen images of film actors and actresses, sports figures, and political leaders as mythic figures in the American imaginary.

Harsh realities like segregation and racism remained. In *Brown v. Board of Education* in 1954, the Supreme Court ruled against the "separate but equal" policy of racial segregation. Chief Justice Earl Warren wrote the opinion: "We conclude that in the field of public opinion the doctrine of separate but equal has no place. Separate educational facilities are inherently unequal."[51]

Fiction brought readers to distant, imaginary places in 1954. J. R. R. Tolkien's *The Lord of the Rings* appeared with the publication of *The Fellowship of the Ring*. William Golding's *Lord of the Flies* cautioned about aggression, violence, and group behavior among children in his story set on an island. Television brought *Father Knows Best*, a show that focused on family life situations and expressed a sense that all was well in middle America. In 1954, the United States established the Air Force Academy. Musicians played at the first Newport Jazz Festival. Elvis Presley released his first single, "That's All Right."

In 1955, the American Federation of Labor and Congress of Industrial Organizations (AFL-CIO) was formed as the two labor organizations merged. Rosa Parks courageously refused to move from her seat on a bus in Montgomery, Alabama. Her act was a powerful symbolic assertion of civil rights. Sloan Wilson published *The Man in the Gray Flannel Suit*, casting an image of business conformity and a man's dream of freedom. Jonas Salk's vaccine for polio went through an array of experimental trials. Bill Haley's "Rock around the Clock" initiated an era of rock and roll. Elvis Presley, in 1956, had five number one singles, including "Heartbreak Hotel," "Hound Dog," and "Love Me Tender."

Peyton Place seized reader interest in 1956 with Grace Metalious's assertion of the independent woman and her suggestion of scandal. Some sixty thousand copies of the novel were sold in the first ten days after publication. *The Organization Man* by William Whyte told a story about American society and the business organization. Actress Grace Kelly married Prince Rainier of Monaco and became a princess. On the movie screen, Charlton Heston became Moses and Yul Brynner became the Pharaoh in *The Ten Commandments*. John F. Kennedy's *Profiles in Courage* was published and would receive the Pulitzer Prize. Americans saw Elvis Presley on the *Ed Sullivan Show*, and they listened to Harry Belafonte's calypso songs on their radios. Suburban homes welcomed Teflon cookware, Crest toothpaste, Pampers diapers, and blue-green Comet cleanser. Overseas in Europe, there were crises in the Suez Canal that involved Egypt, France, Britain, and Israel. In November 1956, the Soviet Union suppressed a rebellion in Hungary. The United Nations expressed a policy of nonintervention in Hungary, as they had in East Germany in 1953. The soap operas *The Edge of Night* and *As the World Turns* began to air on television. Don Larsen pitched a perfect game for the Yankees in the World Series.

Around 4.3 million Americans were born in 1957. They were among the twenty-nine million children of the baby boom. Dr. Seuss stimulated childhood reading, beginning with *The Cat in the Hat* in 1957. Ayn Rand would have now been able to compose her novel *Atlas Shrugged* on a portable Smith-Corona typewriter if she had chosen to. William Faulkner continued his story of the Snopes family in his novel *The Town*. Brooklyn Dodgers fans were heartbroken as their team announced a move to Los Angeles. The New York Giants would be moving also: to San Francisco. Teenagers danced to the music on *American*

Bandstand with Dick Clark. Jerry Mathis was *Leave It to Beaver*, and Raymond Burr solved cases as Perry Mason. Significantly, the Russian Sputnik launched the space race on October 4, 1957.

Some writers and scientists faced political and social pressures. In 1958, Boris Pasternak won the Nobel Prize following the publication of his novel, *Dr. Zhivago*. However, he was evidently pressured to refuse the prize. Poet Ezra Pound, charged with treason, pleaded insanity. Some nine thousand scientists signed a petition to stop nuclear testing. The European Economic Community was formed, a precursor to the European Union.

In January 1959, Alaska became the forty-ninth state. Hawaii followed on August 21. In Cuba, Fidel Castro's guerillas forced Fulgencio Batista to resign. February 3 was the day the music died, as a plane carrying Buddy Holly, Ritchie Valens, and J. P. Richardson (the Big Bopper) went down in Iowa. Later that year Richard Nixon (in July) and Nikita Khrushchev (in September) exchanged state visits and engaged in a debate. As if that were not strange enough, this was the year that Rod Serling created *The Twilight Zone*. Lorraine Hansberry's *A Raisin in the Sun* won the Drama Desk Award. Charlton Heston was back on the film screen in *Ben-Hur*. Rodgers and Hammerstein produced their hit musical *The Sound of Music*. The Guggenheim Museum opened in New York. American girls got their first Barbie dolls. As Hawaii became the fiftieth state, James Michener's *Hawaii* was a huge best seller.

BOOKS AND CULTURAL CONCERNS

Books and reading in the 1950s were inseparably linked with cultural concerns, as they are now. Books provoke thought; they move hearts and instigate change. Science fiction writer Ray Bradbury asserted this in his arresting novel *Fahrenheit 451*. In a chapter on Bradbury in his book *A Novel Marketplace*, Evan Brier points to the context of publishing in the 1950s and reminds us that Bradbury's topic in *Fahrenheit 451* is the importance of literature and the book. Brier points out the increasing production of paperback books in the 1950s. He recognizes the growing market for books and the developing popular culture in America during the time when Bradbury's novel was written.[52] Popular culture and media have a grip on society in Bradbury's story. The novel predicts a world in which wall TVs are overcoming the book. The very decline of western civilization is linked to the demise of the book.

In our age of electronic accessibility, television or film or the internet will not necessarily overtake the book. Films lead people back to books. Computers make books available. Indeed, it is amid the pace of contemporary society and its wide array of distractions that deliberate reading can contribute to mindfulness. Reading can encourage focus, intentionality, and perhaps empathy. The print book of the 1950s, in hardcover or paperback, supplied a human encounter for the patient reader. It communicated light and darkness and the spirit of civilization.

In the 1950s, there were a variety of different readers, as there are today. Serious readers may like to read unpredictable stories and of unfamiliar worlds, as Shirley Brice Heath has observed.[53] They may not read stories that are merely validating or comforting. A reader might also read aesthetically. Dwight Macdonald's "Masscult and Midcult" (1959) suggested that with the diffusion of middlebrow books there might be some decline in the reading of works of literary quality. The educated reader may prefer the middlebrow to the difficult modernist text. In Macdonald's view, we would thus have a diluted high culture when "everything becomes a commodity." Maintaining the distinction between literary fiction and middlebrow is difficult to do without sounding elitist. Even so, it is possible to read high and low, to view media as well as read in our own age of accessibility. Janice Radway shows in *A Feeling for Books* (1997) that a class of worthy fiction was promoted by the Book-of-the-Month Club.[54] These books, from Herman Wouk's *The Caine Mutiny* (1951) and *Marjorie Morningstar* (1955) to Harper Lee's *To Kill a Mockingbird* (1960), captured a great deal of reader interest in the decade between 1950 and 1960.

America's literary fiction engaged imaginations and influenced public discourse in the 1950s. It introduced readers to fascinating characters. Those characters, with their idiosyncrasies, became part of social conversation and the imagination of thousands of readers. Readers today can open the pages of the novels of the 1950s and encounter these characters again. Stories do not necessarily make us compassionate or brave, but they can broaden our view of the world and human personality. Fiction may lift us from the dirt road of cynicism. For fiction welcomes us into the worlds of imagined people who intrigue us, or perhaps challenge us. Through them we are reminded, often in eloquent terms, of things that we may already know in the heart. In the 1950s, fictional characters lived amid the transformations of the novel. They expressed unique personalities. They reflected social changes in America. Most of all, they lived in imaginations. This is an inquiry into the drama of their lives.

2

WISTFUL WARRIORS

A hero's welcome awaited the returning veterans of World War II. So did the challenge of readjustment. World War II boosted the American economy, and there was an effort to bring 15.7 million veterans back into society with the GI Bill. Some $500 million was dedicated to constructing facilities, to job placement, and to college education and technical training. Home ownership became increasingly possible for veterans. In 1950, the Veterans Administration added the benefit of home loans to the widows of fallen soldiers. There had been severe loss, but there had also been honor. The war was a memory still held closely, but now it could be written about, addressed in stories, and memorialized.

On June 5, 1954, Associated Press journalist Don Whitehead returned to the Normandy beaches from which he had filed his D-Day report ten years earlier. He began his article by describing a gray-haired man and woman walking among the crosses and pausing at one of them. "Beyond the beach rises the bluff where the Germans built their first line of defense," he wrote. Now "slowly the signs of war are disappearing." However, he observed that with the Cold War there was "another brand of tyranny rising from the ashes of World War II."[1]

Whether a new Cold War with Russia or China was on the horizon in 2019 was a matter of speculation. The image of Dwight Eisenhower, architect of the D-Day invasion and America's president in the 1950s, appeared on the face of the dimes jingling in some pockets. On June 6, 2019, world leaders stood respectfully at the American cemetery at Colleville-sur-Mer to mark the seventy-fifth anniversary of D-Day. Aging veterans seated on folding chairs or in wheelchairs recalled the danger, valor, and pain of that day as they looked out across the rows of white crosses on the wide lawn above the beach. Standing with Emmanuel Macron and other European leaders, Donald Trump referred to the "exceptional spirit" of those who had fought for freedom.

That exceptional spirit appears in the postwar novels of the early 1950s. In 1948, Norman Mailer's *The Naked and the Dead* began the procession of American novels that reimagined the struggles and human strength of a generation at war. The American journalist John Hersey followed his stirring account of *Hiroshima* with an equally poignant and disturbing novel about the Holocaust: *The Wall*. James Jones and Herman Wouk told stories of life amid the war in the Pacific. Ernest Hemingway wrote no war novel; rather, he portrayed a forlorn ex-soldier and his dreams. Mailer returned with the story of an amnesiac, one of many veterans who had difficulty readjusting. William Faulkner turned back time with *A Fable*, to the First World War. His story of a Christlike corporal and a proud "old General" was decidedly antiwar but also recognized how the violence of war repeatedly returns.

NOACH LEVINSON IN JOHN HERSEY'S *THE WALL* (1950)

The prologue to John Hersey's *The Wall* introduces us to the discovery of the Levinson Archive. These are records that have been buried in seventeen iron boxes and a number of small parcels wrapped in rags. The question that is immediately set before us is whether such an archive could exist. The rediscovery of lost records is a frequently used plot device that launches us into a new story. In this case, the annihilation of Jewish books, writings, and records was a stark and dismal reality that mirrors the destruction of Europe's Jews during the Holocaust. Hersey sets his novel, *The Wall*, amid recent tragic events in the Warsaw ghetto. Like *Hiroshima*, this novel is a work of empathy. The story ranges across individual characters, regarding the resistance of Polish and Jewish men and women against Nazi force and occupation. He sets forth his story with the frame device of the prologue: An editor has edited the Levinson papers, and these will now be shared with us in the form of a chronologically dated journal.

In several respects, *The Wall* is a stronger novel than Hersey's *A Bell for Adano*, which won the Pulitzer Prize. Writing a story that he has vividly imagined, Hersey moves further away from the journalistic style of his works of the 1940s. With *The Wall*, he is a storyteller who takes on the role of a contemporary historian and builds a novel that is, in its own way, as humanistic as his best seller *Hiroshima*. We are introduced to a curious character, Noach Levinson, who has devoted his life to preserving the Jewish culture of the Warsaw ghetto. He is a little man who obsessively gathers materials, books, stories, poems, news clippings, and letters, which he secrets away. Levinson is a bit of nuisance to neighbors who do not understand his preoccupations. He writes in Yiddish and snoops and pries into everyone's business in his effort to record their stories. He is always scribbling notes, driven by his obsession and belief that only he would be able to pass along their history and their legacy. So, he becomes their historian: a man whose concern is with their individual, personal lives. An acquaintance, Rachel Apt, says: "He was a queer man, but we loved him." He squinted through eyeglasses that made his eyes look odd. He would suddenly blurt out statements like, "I am a coward." He must have been a lonely man, the editor concludes, a man of "timid warmth" who was always writing and tucking away his notes. So, there are stories, observations, and portraits of people that end in blunt phrases like, "Menachem Bavan was taken away today."[2]

Survivors and relatives of survivors and victims of the Holocaust have returned to the place where suffering and torment occurred. With their solemn journeys, they have reasserted their solidarity with those who were lost and reaffirmed their Jewish identity. There were an estimated eight million Jews in Europe in 1939, and about six million of them were killed in the Holocaust. Following the revelations of this systematic slaughter, writers immediately affirmed that memory must be preserved. The American Joint Distribution Committee received a letter from journalists in Poland on March 24, 1947: "We consider it a mission of particular importance that these Jewish writers provide, for the future generations, prose and poetry which will portray and document the recent experiences."[3]

Adolph Eichmann was placed in charge of Jewish "resettlement." In the expulsion from Cracow on August 1, 1940, eighty thousand people, or one-third of the Jews in the city, were driven to other towns. By

October, some fifty thousand of them had been deported. On October 25, the General Government gave notice that there would be no more visas for Polish Jews for this would result in a renewal of Jewry in the United States.[4] There were at that time four hundred thousand Jews in the Warsaw ghetto. The Warsaw ghetto wall was built in November 1940.

Jews attempted to flee from central and Eastern Europe's cities and towns. Refugees from central Europe who had gotten as far as Czechoslovakia could board a ship to travel down the Danube. They might try to reach Palestine. At the Jewish Agency for Palestine, Richard Lichtheim reported on the calamity in Europe. In Belgium and in Holland, the Nazi occupiers were attempting "to eliminate the Jews from public life." There were six thousand refugees in Switzerland but twenty-six hundred of them were destitute. In Poland, the situation was "even worse than in Germany itself."[5]

John Hersey's *The Wall* takes place in the Warsaw ghetto. At the meeting of the Judenrat, the Jews are informed that the Nazis will be setting up "a residence area" for them. Ostensibly, this measure is being taken to quarantine the area against typhus. (Dr. Breithorn is coerced into verifying that the people can get typhus in the summer.) The working of the proclamation is formal, heavy, and dull, but it will carry much weight. Dolek Berson sees the jurist Benlevi's face become "taut, hateful, and somehow crafty."[6] Those who are assigned as "deputy councilors" will be confined to Pawiak Prison. They are taken away by SS soldiers. Berson is completely puzzled when he is approached. He cries out that his presence there is accidental. With eight men—Levinson, Schpunt, and Dr. Breithorn among them—he is placed in a small holding cell. It is his wedding anniversary and feeling dismayed he wants to get a message to his wife. Can Levinson spare a page from his notebook?

The problems of the Warsaw population are brought to us. The narrator alternates scenes between the men in the prison and Symka Berson's experiences, as she waits for her husband. The men with her are imitating Dolek Berson, and she imagines that her absent-minded husband is merely lost on Sienna Street. The home is filled with friends and relatives who have arrived to celebrate the wedding anniversary. Regina Orlowsk plays mazurkas on the piano. But Dolek and his own fine piano playing is missing. Symka wishes to save the lox for him.

Where can he be? The note from him arrives, and she breaks down in tears as she reads: "Taken by bureaucratic error to Pawiak." The guests try to console her. Cousin Meier helps himself to some slices of lox.

Symka misses Dolek Berson but cannot visit him. She can only gaze up at the walls of the Pawiak Prison from across the street. She goes to the police station on Niska Street and is sent away. The Bersons are caught within a Kafkaesque quandary. Tensions are building in the Judenrat. There are Socialist calls to "fight against the ghetto idea."[7] Zionist organizations gather to call for both resistance and patience. The Nazi authorities have made it clear that there will be a ghetto confinement and the hostages will be shot if this is not carried out. An appeal is made to the German commandant: "A City is a living body. How can you sustain a body if one fifth of it, at its entrails, is suddenly tied off without circulation or sensation?"[8] Remarkably, the men are released from Pawiak Prison. Symka hurries to greet Berson. He emerges smiling, telling her that they had a great time. The consequential events of the Holocaust are yet to come.

The story proceeds toward the April 1943 uprising of the Warsaw ghetto. This was the first insurrection, which demonstrated the Jewish people's willingness to fight despite having no chance of success. In September 1941, Noach Levinson (N.L.) notes that an estimated half million Jews now live inside the ghetto wall. There they are compressed within one hundred city blocks. Some seventy thousand refugees have arrived from small towns near Warsaw, several from across the Vistula River. Another forty thousand have come from further away in Czechoslovakia or Germany. The result has been this crowding.

N.L. records the words and actions of Rachel Apt and Mordecai Apt, Pavel Mendes, and the piano playing of Dolek Berson. The men's religious service is interrupted by Nazis who pound at the iron storefront.[9] Three soldiers ask which one of them is the rabbi. Fischel Schpunt stands in for Rabbi Goldflam, and he is ordered to dance. The Nazis demand that there are to be no public meetings. Levinson's journal then skips to March 23, 1940. Walking with Rachel, he recalls how he and the men had laughed because Schpunt was no rabbi. However, even if the phylactery bounding over his forehead looked absurd, it was a distinct reminder of their faith: "our religion which sets us apart." They laughed not at the clown but that the Nazis gained some odd pleasure from the antics of a "harmless little scapegoat." He was also their own little group's scapegoat, and he had the courage to "elect himself to that honorable post."[10]

In April 1940, Levinson asks what the wall that he sees will mean. "Some pattern is forming, I'm sure," he writes. Is this a quarantine area, like they say? The area has a wall three meters (nine feet) high. He concludes that the wall is not simply "a fence or a marker. This wall is actually intended to keep human beings from passing."[11] As life goes on in the Warsaw ghetto, we begin to see additional signs of danger. Levinson records the discrimination against the Jews. They are not to ride trolleys or buses, or purchase gold. They must always wear armbands. Travel is restricted, and bank accounts have been frozen. Shops are occasionally looted. Rachel is building a school, and she recruits Regina Orlewska. She approaches Benlevi who will not allow any "illegal" school. He adds his observation that such schools are "springing everywhere" and the operation of them is perilous.[12]

Hersey continually underscores the moral issues and the problems that beset this community. Berson asserts that there is a difference between being against something, as the Nazis are, and being *for* something, such as ethics.[13] Berson visits Jabloski, who has converted to Catholicism but is still considered a Jew. Kucharski, the custodian, cannot work in a Jewish establishment. He encourages Rachel: "You are special. . . . You seem capable of taking care of everybody."[14] As of October 16, 1940, all Jewish establishments are to move to a location within the district. Part 1 ends with a blockade. They are locked within their wall.[15]

Part 2 begins in December 1940. The wall has been completed. There are eleven gaps in it. Each one is an entrance, not an exit. "We Jews are shut together; that is evident," Levinson writes. Levinson wonders what it will mean to live in a ghetto amid crowds.[16] "Groaning was our music," he writes. People in the ghetto bargain and argue and whine. Berson has joined the police. Wearing a uniform—a cap, a belt, and insignia—he directs traffic. Emotionally, Berson is like a cup filled with hot liquid that must be poured out before he cracks. Schpunt visits the eleven gates and tips his hat in greeting to the Nazi soldiers. This is his new game. He will again play the clown. Meanwhile, Rachel and Benlevi, the Nobel Prize winner, meet again at a Passover seder. Recalling their previous meeting, he shakes his head and says: "foolish girl." She says: "I think I was foolish to tell you . . . of all of you in the

Judenrat to be blind to what was happening here in Warsaw."[17] She charges them with having hidden behind an unjust law. It "should have been [their] business to make sure that every Jewish child received the proper training."[18] Levinson says that Rachel "has a strange impersonal magnetism." He is fascinated by her. Meanwhile, the Polish Jews cling to "their habits of life."[19] We see Ruthka, who goes to an industrial school, which has been created to support the practical industrial arts. Halinka Apt is pretty and dresses modishly, Levinson thinks, as he sees her with many boyfriends. But Halinka, Rachel's sister, has a bad temper.

In another scene, Levinson is assisted by men, including Berson, who dig their way into the Bronislaw Grosser Library, which is outside of the ghetto walls. They excavate and remove bricks and squeeze into the library basement. Once inside, Levinson begins to lead them in collecting books and boxes of official records. They will preserve their cultural treasures and memories. Levinson's abiding regard for literature and for the people of the book and their heritage emerges as he and Berson have a conversation. Berson says that he wishes to sell his own books. Levinson asks him if he would sell his wife. Berson replies that he needs money and had read the books. Levinson responds: "Did you marry Symka to make love to her only once?" The preserver of books and culture, Noach Levinson, encourages Berson to sell something else and to keep his books. "You'll want continuity," he says. "You'll want your books."[20] Levinson represents devotion to the written word. It is through his sincere efforts that the memories of these people and their lives appear for us. It is why we have this record: a lively, truthful, and all-so-human account of life behind the wall. It is a history of life: the story of our humanity.

The rising of 1943 must be distinguished from the August 1, 1944, Warsaw Rising. This involved resistance groups as well as some homegrown fighters. A storm troop commanded by the SS moved in to suppress the revolt, and fifty thousand civilians were massacred. The Nazi decision to commence "the Final Solution" can be traced to the time before January 1942, when the Wannsee Conference met. Transportation of Jews had begun in October 1941. In April 1943, the SS cleared the Warsaw ghetto. Joseph Goebbels provided the news that the dead bodies of forty-five hundred Polish officers murdered by the Soviet NKVD (People's Commissariat for Internal Affairs) had been found in the Katyn Forest in the vicinity of Smolensk. He did not report as loudly about the barbarity of the Final Solution.

Levinson's gathering of records preserves the memory of a community. Likewise, the story of courage in the diary of Anne Frank (1929–1945) is one contemporary account of the dilemma. She was the daughter of German Jewish refugees hiding in Amsterdam. In August 1944, she was discovered by Nazi troops and was sent to her death at Bergen-Belsen. Her diary, published after the war, became a famous account of her endurance. In 1945, there were thirteen million orphaned or abandoned children in Europe. Around one million of these children were in Poland. Recalling the Warsaw Rising, John Hersey's novel is a remarkable testament to a disturbing chapter of human experience.

ROBERT "PREW" PREWITT IN *FROM HERE TO ETERNITY* (1951) BY JAMES JONES

James Jones, one of Maxwell Perkins's late discoveries, was a restless, angry, hungry force: one as punchy as his military boxers in his novel *From Here to Eternity*. Amid a large cast of characters, Prewitt, a bugler and former boxer, stands out as Jones's chief protagonist. Early on in the novel, one already suspects that the virile, difficult sergeant, Milt Warden, is going to have an affair with Karen, the feisty, attractive wife of Captain Holmes, the boxing coach. It looks inevitable. They just don't expect her kid to come home early from school while Mrs. Holmes is somewhat unclothed. *From Here to Eternity* has to break out of the barracks—and it does.

In *From Here to Eternity*, Jones lets some sentences rip without attention to grammar. It becomes a matter of style, a way to catch the earthy vernacular. He drops the apostrophe at times in conversations. Sentences bang along like the fists of boxers, accumulating energy. Jones sometimes rambles along in high-octane bursts of energy. The voices sound convincing. Ernest Hemingway, however, let Charles Scribner know that he was not a fan of the novel. "It is not great, no matter what they tell you," he wrote.[21]

Prewitt is identified as an excellent boxer who can return the crown to G Company's boxing team. He wants to remain on straight duty, to be a regular and to not be pushed into boxing.[22] Prewitt is repeatedly harassed by Warden because he refuses to reenter the boxing ring where he once nearly killed a man. Warden places him on KP duty, forces him to mop floors, climb hills, dig ditches, and perform tasks in an attempt to get him to relent and agree to box. Prewitt surprises the men with his dazzling trumpet playing. He looks forward to getting away to see Violet Ogure. The issue of marriage brings out her concern about her family's response to that. It also brings out some nasty protest from Prew. Why did he get into the army? It wasn't to sweat in mines and pineapple fields for a bunch of snot-nosed, dark-faced n-word brats in the coal dirt. He fumes: "What the hell do you dames want? To take the heart out of a man and tie it up in barbed wire and give it to your mother on Mother's Day?"[23] She yields, as patient as an Asian martial artist, letting him expend his energy until he apologizes. We read: "And it seemed to him then that every human was always looking for himself, in bars, in railway trains, in offices, in mirrors, in love, especially in love, for the self of him is there someplace."[24] And with that meditation, Prewitt returns to base and so ends Book One.

One of the challenges of the film version of *From Here to Eternity* was to escape the censors. In Jones's rewrite, Mrs. Karen Holmes becomes Captain Holmes's sister rather than his wife, thus changing the adultery plot. Screenwriter Daniel Taradash was given the task of condensing the novel, modifying its controversial scenes, and giving focus to a large cast. In the film, Burt Lancaster plays the sadistic heavy, and Montgomery Clift is Prewitt, the man of integrity. Warden and Karen Holmes (Deborah Kerr) have a romance that is paralleled by one between Prew (Montgomery Clift) and Alma (Donna Reed). Warden's torchy beach scene with Karen Holmes includes the famous photo frame of a crescendo of waves and their passionate embrace on the sand. Maggio (Frank Sinatra) and Judson (Ernest Borgnine) mix it up in a lethal fight. Fred Zinnemann's directing launched the film to its Academy Award for Best Picture. Taradash received the award for Best Screenplay.

Jones's novel received the Pulitzer Prize, but most of his characters probably would not have read his long novel in the barracks. They were not readers of literature. Angelo reads comic books. Prewitt points out that he has mixed up the comic book's title. Readall Treadwell reads movie magazines. Maggio knows that Jack London "bummed around," and he has read Steinbeck's *Of Mice and Men*. The men talk about movies and about cowboys, like Gene Autry and Roy Rogers, that "have to be musicians now because they're not Westerns anymore, they're musicals." Book Two begins with the company in Hawaii, in the Schofield Barracks. The regiment insists that the boxing trophy "shall return," just like Douglas MacArthur. Holmes recommends a promotion for Bloom for being a good boxer. The story moves along toward the Pearl Harbor invasion.

CAPTAIN PHILIP FRANCIS QUEEG IN *THE CAINE MUTINY* (1951) BY HERMAN WOUK

Willie Keith has been placed on the minesweeper USS *Caine*. He is the viewpoint character through which the events of *The Caine Mutiny* are presented. However, the dilemma of Captain Queeg, onstage and in film, has received the most attention and public comment. Herman Wouk, whose *War and Remembrance* (1971) and *The Winds of War* (1983) became hugely popular best sellers, was a communications officer on a minesweeper. *The Caine Mutiny* (1951) was his fictional story of a mutiny against a ship's commander. The novel explores the tension between necessary military order and freedom. Queeg has become the ship's highest authority, but he is clearly not equipped to be an officer. He focuses upon petty matters, and when a serious one arises, a tornado, he does not change course to save the ship. Maryk, who is second in command, calls for a response, and Willie Keith joins in the mutiny. However, Willie eventually realizes that the mutiny was not appropriate because the structure of military life requires discipline and obedience of command.

Philip Francis Queeg is forced to give up command of his ship. The mutiny's defense attorney attempts to prove that this was just. Queeg points at the disloyalty of the crew. However, can he blame everyone else and not take responsibility? This is a story about power, authority, and failings in leadership. *The Caine Mutiny* addresses obedience and respect for authority, the individual and group, and loss of respect. Military historian John Keegan points to the military as a "system of subordination and authority."[25]

The Caine Mutiny is Willie Keith's story. However, it is also a story about leadership and the dilemma faced by Captain Queeg. Willie Keith, emerging from studies at Princeton, is a son of privilege. This is the story of his growth, development, and transformation. This is also a moral allegory that regards military justice, the responsibilities of leadership, and respect for the military chain of command. (The U.S. Navy was quick to point out that there had been no mutinies.) The ship is a minesweeper-destroyer in the Pacific. Lieutenant Keefer views their lives aboard the *Caine* as similar to that of prisoners. "We're all doing penance, sentenced to an outcast ship manned by outcasts and named after the greatest outcast of all." They are troubled brothers-at-arms in a Hobbesian world. Queeg insists upon strict military discipline. Yet, the ship does not appear orderly. Rather, it is a broken world. For DeVries, the *Caine* is "a beaten-up tub." Queeg asserts that they must be a functioning family bound by loyalty. He declares his sense of duty and requirement of effort: "Aboard my ship excellent performance is standard performance . . . and non-standard performance is not permitted to exist." Keefer dislikes Queeg intensely and infects the others with his distrust.[26]

The typhoon reflects the tension that is to come. Queeg appears fearful of the storm. The ship gets through the storm. However, Queeg's command is now in jeopardy. *The Caine Mutiny* examines issues of respect for authority or the loss of that respect. It considers the relationship of the individual and the group. Queeg appears to have declined into paranoia. Some of the men reason that something must be done. Queeg has a concern with control; he is paranoid and neurotic. He appears petty. We discover that he ordered an investigation of those who ate a quart of strawberries that was in the kitchen and created a search for a key to the icebox. Executive Officer Stephen Maryk decides that Queeg is "a sick man." Queeg is regarded as unstable. Maryk writes: "This log is being started because . . . the commander of this ship may be mentally disturbed." Maryk is court-martialed for removing Queeg from command. He is put on trial for mutiny and is acquitted.

What would undermine Queeg's authority? The sanity questions begin. Queeg is referred to as "a Freudian delight." By Article 184 of the Naval Code, Queeg might be relieved of his command. A trial emerges at the center of the story and is featured in stage productions and film. The film shows Queeg (Humphrey Bogart) on the witness stand.

Greenwald points out "Rigidity of personality, feelings of persecution, unreasonable suspicion, a mania to perfection, a neurotic certainty that he is always right." Queeg insists that he ran the ship "by the book, but they fought me at every turn." He repeats: "They were all disloyal." Queeg breaks down and falls apart on the stand.[27]

The Caine Mutiny raises the question of what incapacity or disability may mean in relation to leadership. During the 1950s, Dwight Eisenhower was ill three times. Woodrow Wilson and Franklin Delano Roosevelt also experienced disability while in office. Proposed by Congress in 1965 the Twenty-Fifth Amendment was adopted February 10, 1967. The drafting of the amendment provided an alternative to impeachment. If serious questions about competency arose, the cabinet and the vice president would decide if the president was no longer able to serve in office. Those who approached this issue did not want any vice president to usurp presidential authority. The amendment is not a place to go to respond to the unpopularity of a president. It is employed only when the majority of the cabinet and the vice president determine that the president is "unable to discharge the powers and duties" of the office. The president may submit an assertion of having the power to discharge those duties to the President Pro-Tempore of the Senate and the Speaker of the House of Representatives. If agreed, the president can reassume the duties of office.

In a 2018 *Washington Post* article, Meghan Flynn points out that Harvard law professor Arthur E. Sutherland recognized that *The Caine Mutiny* affected his understanding of the problem. He read the novel until 2 a.m. The next day he told the committee he had done so and affirmed that "the committee's deliberations have the same theme as the one in *The Caine Mutiny*." Flynn's article quotes Emmanuel Celler (D-New York) saying, "It's an excellent analogy." There is agreement that an "unfortunate person [is] stricken." "It is an "insult to men's intelligence—the suggestion that his intelligence is gone." Attorney John Freerich echoed this with the American Bar Association in a 1964 Washington, DC, conference for drafting the Twenty-Fifth Amendment.[28]

The Caine Mutiny also raises questions about moral authority and leadership. The central focus of *The Caine Mutiny*, according to *New York Times* military issues editor Hanson W. Baldwin, is "the issue of unreasoning, unquestioning acceptance of orders."[29] Wouk's novel was supportive of military order while Norman Mailer's *The Naked and the Dead* had been critical of conformity. Yet, his story prompts psychological inquiry and questions about leadership and responsibility.

The novel provides a scenario that some believe offers lessons that professional leaders can learn from. Lieutenant Commander Thomas J. Cutler in *U.S. Naval Institute Proceedings* saw *The Caine Mutiny* as instructive. He pointed out that Wouk was a sailor, an officer, who knew what it was like to be on board a ship during wartime, "in a self-contained world." He recommended that the novel "offers simulations" and could be used as a "leadership and followership lab." This would prepare future officers for command decisions, so they could "do these things before our lives and those of others depend on it." Jeffrey L. Butler in *Academic Leader* offers the novel as an example for academic leaders. *The Army Lawyer* (February 2010) examined *The Caine Mutiny* and placed it with *Judgement at Nuremberg* as essential reading. Others have considered the novel useful for reflection for psychotherapists. Richard D. Chessick has suggested that the novel helps practitioners consider the psychodynamics of paranoia and whether an individual should get labeled at all. He points out that psychiatrists can be made to look awkward by clever lawyers. Can a 1953 message of military order and honor be applied to a current audience? The question was raised by David S. Machiowitz in 1983 in the *American Bar Association Journal*. He believes that it can. He asks how we view legal ethics, military conduct, and psychiatry.[30]

The Caine Mutiny is most likely to be remembered through its film version. The screenplay that Herman Wouk wrote for the film was put aside by Stanley Kramer, the film's producer. He hired Edward Dmytryk to direct and Stanley Roberts to come up with a new script. Then Michael Blankfort was assigned to do rewrites to tighten the film to less than two hours. Consequently, the story of Willie Keith's military training and rise in the ranks is eliminated, and the script zeros in on the mutiny. Humphrey Bogart offers a memorable performance as Queeg. The film was nominated for seven Academy Awards and was a box office success in 1954. Wouk's novel won the Pulitzer Prize and was also adapted into a play for the stage, which ran for 415 nights on Broadway. Herman Wouk's contacts in entertainment, including his stint as a writer for the Fred Allen radio show, contributed to his writing of popular fiction. *Marjorie Morningstar* is the story of a young woman who aspires to be an actress and ends up as a housewife. Wouk, who died in 2019 at the age of 103, kept a journal that he began in 1937. There are more than one hundred volumes of his journal.[31]

RICHARD CANTWELL IN *ACROSS THE RIVER AND INTO THE TREES* (1950) BY ERNEST HEMINGWAY

Richard Cantwell is a colonel stationed in Trieste in Ernest Hemingway's *Across the River and into the Trees* (1950). He seeks romance with an eighteen-year-old Italian woman named Renata, although he is past fifty. Cantwell first arrived in Italy when he fought in the First World War on the front near the Vento. He returned there during the Second World War following D-Day in Normandy and the push through Belgium that included the Battle of the Bulge. However, mistakes in following other people's orders caused his demotion from brigadier general to the rank of colonel. The past is surely behind him and he is unable to recapture his youth, even with his new romance. He has a heart condition and is dying. Renata would heal him if she could. She asks him to talk about his war experiences. Cantwell is forced to realize that he is no longer a soldier. He is a man who has undertaken a commitment to this woman. Hemingway's fictional soldiers have not found their return to society easy. If watching a character change and grow is one of the delights of fiction, a reader is likely to be disappointed by Richard Cantwell. He remains stuck, caught in his memories, and repeating his habits. There is no epiphany, no new awareness that will come to him. He does not gain knowledge. He remains ineffectual and appears a bit foolish, trying to recapture youth and aliveness with an eighteen-year-old woman.

Malcolm Cowley saw Cantwell as "the most fully realized of Hemingway's heroes."[32] Richard Cantwell is a divided self, vaguely seeking renewal, while dying. He is like Hemingway's character in "The Snows of Mt. Kilimanjaro" facing disease and demise. He reflects the aimless sense of alienation of his character in "Soldier's Home." As in *A Farewell to Arms* and *For Whom the Bell Tolls*, this is a man who is perhaps finding love in the middle of a century of bloody conflict. With time, Cantwell's life is slipping away. The first sentence of the novel refers to starting out before dawn in the Vento of Italy. It refers to time, the impending break of a new day. Cantwell travels to Venice: a place that may be associated with romance but rests insubstantially on water, rather than being grounded on dry land. Cantwell drifts in the twilight between night and day, the present and memory, life and death. (Venice may recall Thomas Mann's story "Death in Venice.) There is a recollection of war and an experience of facing the press of time and perhaps waning virility. When Renata encourages Cantwell to engage in talk therapy, to pull out repressed memories, this does little to heal him.[33]

Across the River and into the Trees takes its title from the final words of Confederate Civil War general Stonewall Jackson. Wounded grievously in battle, he told his comrades: "let us cross over the river and rest under the shade of the trees." Cantwell is a deeply flawed hero of wartime, now an observer of life more than an engaged participant in it. He has been a tough, masculine fighter with a code of honor and now has become a shadow of his former self. Literary critic Jackson J. Benson, in 1969, suggested that for a reader the lack of recognition that Cantwell is accorded may be turned to pity for him, or by the reader toward himself.[34] He may have been thinking of Aristotle's *Poetics* as he reflected on the pity a reader might feel for a tragic character. Benson writes: "When an act of courage is performed in literature, the reader often is the only witness, the only person who can accord the protagonist proper recognition and appreciation."[35] If the reader identifies himself too closely with this story's protagonist, the reading may dissolve into self-pity and sentimentality. One might add that Cantwell does not appear deserving of this. He is rather self-absorbed and is not as kind toward Renata as she is toward him.

Hemingway had not written an extended work of fiction for ten years. He began writing *Across the River and into the Trees* in Cortina d'Ampezzo in northern Italy in March 1949. For a time, perhaps he was persuaded that it was time to write his own novel of World War II. After all, Norman Mailer had produced *The Naked and the Dead*, James Gould Cozzens published *Guard of Honor*, and *The Young Lions* by Irwin Shaw was quite popular. Thousands of men had returned home from war and were potential readers of a good war novel. Even so, Hemingway never produced that novel. He provided a few glimpses but if his audience eagerly anticipated a novel of war, it was not to be this one.

Cosmopolitan serialized the novel in five consecutive issues between February and June 1950. The story appeared in book form on September 7. It was on the best-seller list for twenty-one weeks and at number one for seven of those weeks. However, critics reviewed the novel harshly. Maxwell Geismer called it "Hemingway's worst novel." Alfred Kazin wrote that he felt pity and embarrassment for Hemingway with his publication of this "confused and vituperatively revealing self-portrayal." Hemingway had engaged in self-parody, he suggested. Philip Rahv considered Renata a "love object" and claimed that the novel was so "egregiously bad" that he could barely comment on it. Subsequent critics have provided other notices. Michael S. Reynolds, for example, has pointed out that this novel, more than any other novel by Hemingway, is filled with "more allusions and arcane references."[36] Some apologists for Hemingway's novel recognize that it is not as compelling as *A Farewell to Arms* or *For Whom the Bell Tolls* but ought to be viewed as part of Hemingway's overall production of fiction.

Hemingway asks for ethical judgment of his characters from us, not just what Jackson Benson refers to as "sympathetic admiration."[37] While he tends to emphasize control, courage, and commitment, his characters approach this code of integrity through different points of view. While not among Hemingway's strongest works, *Across the River and into the Trees* presents an interesting character study. Richard Cantwell is a rather static, unsympathetic, and not entirely likeable character. However, this portrait of an alienated, ineffectual former soldier grasping for a last chance at romance is a story worthy of consideration within the extraordinary corpus that has emerged from Ernest Hemingway's fictional creativity.

THE CORPORAL AND THE GENERAL IN *A FABLE* (1954) BY WILLIAM FAULKNER

A Fable is unlike other William Faulkner novels. It is not set in the American South but, instead, is set in France in 1918, in the last months of the First World War. Its central characters are a corporal and an "old general": the marshal who commands the troops. The corporal is a saint, rebel, and martyr, a simple man with some luminous energy who creates community among the troops. The general is structure, law, bureaucracy, and military order, fighting for honor and perpetuating war. Yet, this is not a war novel as were the stories of Henri Barbusse or Erich Maria Remarque. Faulkner's first novel, *Soldier's Pay*, was set during the First World War, as was *Flags in the Dust*, his third novel to be published. However, *A Fable*, begun as a film script during World War II, is about the ongoing, repeating dilemma of human violence and efforts at peace. The story is less realism than fable and myth, framed by symbol and biblical allegory. While the corporal and the general are central to the story, these characters are part of a broader collective experience: the conditions of war that they all are embedded in. This is "a vast tongueless brotherhood of dread and anxiety."[38] No battle is featured or described: only the aftermath of a pause in the violence that disturbs the commanders.

Seemingly, *A Fable* also operates outside racial considerations. Set in France in the final months of World War I, on the surface it appears remote from such concerns. However, the outsider, a corporal who is a Christ-like figure seeking peace amid devastation, is the scapegoat, the outcast other, and two African American characters also enter the story. Faulkner interpolates the story "Notes on a Horsethief" in which black preacher Tobe Sutterfield and his grandson set free a thoroughbred racing horse and bring the horse through the American South.

This corporal is the peacemaker who has been involved in an action to suspend the fighting, a pause of one day that is called a mutiny. Later, his body is brought to a burial site at the Tomb of the Unknown Soldier. *A Fable* appears to interrogate unjust structures as well as wartime violence, not only those repeating patterns of human aggression that are found in the muddy trenches of battle but also intransigent problems like racism and cultural violence.

As the story begins, the "mutiny" has already occurred. The war has paused for a day. Both Allies and Germans have laid down their arms. Now the corporal and his twelve disciples have been arrested. The corporal will be tried, found guilty, and executed. This Christ will be crucified again. The war will go on, as if this peaceful pause in the fighting had never occurred. The violence of the world persists. Yet somewhere among the crowd, as the story ends, the corporal Jesus figure, like a man on sentry duty, stands inconspicuously on the margins.

The corporal is Jesus Christ, effectively reincarnated: a quiet, nondescript, ordinary man. The corporal is not defined psychologically, as Quentin Compson is in *The Sound and the Fury*. He is an anonymous human in existential crisis: "a face merely interested, attentive, and calm, with something in it none of the others had: a comprehension, understanding, utterly free of compassion."[39] This is the crucified Christ, one who has been miraculous for a day, like a brief lifting of the chalice in consecration. Yet, even after his execution he remains a presence in the novel. The story focuses on the general: a man who is an aristocratic militarist, a well-off Machiavellian authority. The corporal and the general face each other in chapter 8 of *A Fable*. The marshal says that he is "champion of this mundane earth."[40] The corporal is "champion of an esoteric realm of man's baseless hopes and his infinite capacity—no: passion—for unfact." The marshal is reason and order. The corporal is hope and faith, or "unfact." The general asserts that these elements "are not inimical reality . . . they can even exist side by side."[41]

The trial of the corporal parallels the Gospel passion story. The corporal faces the general as Jesus faced Pontius Pilate, or as he encountered Satan, who tempted him on the mountaintop. The corporal's heroism has been a fleeting gesture. His half-sisters Martha and Marya look on along with a former prostitute from Marseille (Martha, Mary, and Mary Magdalene) as he is executed on a Friday. The corporal is idealistic, but it is unclear whether his act and his demise have been redemptive.

Faulkner's writing of *A Fable* began as a film script in 1943 while he was in Hollywood. The story was based on an idea from Henry Hathaway, a director, and William Bacher, a producer. Jesus Christ would be reincarnated as a corporal in France, an unknown soldier who was to be a peacemaker. In a 1943 letter to Harold Ober, Faulkner described the project. He called it "a fable, an indictment of war." If Christ returned, would we crucify him again? He added that the script might not be popular now that America was at war.[42]

Faulkner's *A Fable* won the 1955 Pulitzer Prize and the National Book Award. Yet, it is not as frequently discussed by critics as *The Sound and the Fury*, *Light in August*, *As I Lay Dying*, *Absalom Absalom*, or other major works by the author. Critical perspectives vary. Keen Butterworth believes that the text supports the marshal rather than criticizes him. Joseph Urgo views *A Fable* as reflecting the apocryphal gospels and asserts that the corporal "is not a symbolic Christ" but *is* Christ. Giorgio Mariani observes that there is "an allegorical dimension" to the text but it also "unmasks the readings of the Scriptures that have historically sustained the Western martial ideology." *A Fable*, he concludes, "forces the reader to rethink the Gospels of tradition from the point of view of the critique of war and violence."[43]

A Fable draws upon Henry Cobb's *Paths of Glory* (1935), which is best known through Stanley Kubrick's 1957 film. Both the novel and film underscore the absurdity and horror of World War I trench warfare and the pressures imposed by inept and bungled leadership. Faulkner writes of characters facing "the scarlet and brazen impregnability of general staffs."[44]

In his preface to the novel, Faulkner writes: "This is not a pacifist novel." However, what Faulkner appears to mean is that he views pacifism as too passive. Turning away from war is not the same thing as making an active effort to rid the world of war. Faulkner writes: "Pacifism does not work, cannot cope with the forces which produce wars." To be for peace is an active disposition. Faulkner says, "To put an end to war man must either find or invent something more powerful than war and man's aptitude for belligerence and his thirst for power at any cost."[45]

MIKE LOVETT IN *BARBARY SHORE* (1951) BY NORMAN MAILER

A room is rented in a Brooklyn boarding house by a man who wants to write a novel. He was wounded in the Second World War and now has amnesia. He has forgotten his own past. Mike Lovett's amnesia is a response to the trauma of war. The soldier had experienced the war's intensity, felt a sense of purpose, and established a bond with others in a common goal. Now he had to readjust and might experience feeling disoriented or feeling alienated.[46] The experience of the war years called for a readjustment and called for "retrospective narratives to explain the trauma."[47] The postwar years offered new possibilities for society to reinvent itself. Mailer's novel joined a host of novels and films that inquired into the postwar experience of veterans. For example, in the award-winning film *The Best Years of Our Lives*, Homer Parrish is a disabled veteran. He is bothered by being dependent. "All I want is to be treated like everybody else," Homer says. Willard Waller contends that these veterans felt like "immigrants in their native land." He added that "many may only feel comfortable with other veterans."[48]

Norman Mailer received more critical attention than his fictional character. Most critics observed that *Barbary Shore* fell short of the power of *The Naked and the Dead*. Alfred Kazin "showed that Mailer was not interested in being an 'acceptable' novelist." He recognized that Mailer was ill at ease with the "moral failures of socialism" and the growth of authoritarian power in the United States. He was reaching for a moral statement that his fiction did not elucidate well. *Time* magazine was less kind. "Norman Mailer has a bad case of moral claustrophobia," its reviewer wrote. "The only juice in *Barbary Shore* is embalming fluid." Mailer's novel had been "hauled from the literary graveyard of the 30s" when "social consciousness was in vogue."[49] Perhaps the review reflects the temper of the times in which a cautious conservatism prevailed.

Of *Barbary Shore*, Alfred Kazin wrote that it was "only distractedly a novel." Mailer was "stridently a moralist," Kazin observes, as he reviewed Mailer's *Armies of the Night* in 1968. However, *Barbary Shore*, in Kazin's view, did not work effectively as a novel.[50] Mailer ought to have drawn upon his own personal experience, his life in Brooklyn, says his biographer J. Michael Lennon.[51] Within this was the novel he was meant to write. Instead, he followed up his popular war story, *The Naked and the Dead*, with *Barbary Shore* and *The Deer Park*. While *Barbary Shore* was perhaps better crafted, it did not have the vigor and appeal of the first novel. William Barrett, writing in *Commentary* in 1951, suggested that the war had helped the young novelist by offering a solution to the problem of how "to cope with the vast formless and heterogeneous welter of American life and American characters." The war, Barrett observed, provided the occasion for "throwing all kinds of people together" into a military unit. *Barbary Shore* simply could not do what *The Naked and the Dead* did, even if the new novel was a "smoother, technical performance" with "better control of pace" and fluency of narrative. The character's inability to remember had consequences: a search for identity. However, as an ideological novel that juxtaposed an ex-Bolshevik and a government intelligence officer, the story fell flat, in Barrett's view. He wrote that "the book evaporates into ghostly unreality."[52]

Mike Lovett's condition is the existential situation of modern humanity. "He looks at a sign, but it is printed in an alphabet he cannot read."[53] This is something more than the Dickens character, Jo the sweeper, who is illiterate and destitute. It is here that the modern milieu has diminished the individual, suppressing the soul into amnesia. As the writer McLeod says in the novel, "There is the worker and the machine and as the machine grows larger the man is diminished."[54] Lannie, Lovett's Marxist neighbor in the boarding house, represents this ineffectual existence. We hear him refer to the Narcissus myth to characterize the modern condition of the individual: "the closer you come to the water the more you adore yourself until your nose touches and then you're alone."[55] This is a prescient note for the age of the selfie and Facebook self-indulgence. Mailer is arguing that there is a trend toward conformity, consumerism, and the loss of creativity. Of *Barbary Shore*, Mailer wrote in *Advertisements for Myself* that "it has an air which for me is the air of our time."[56]

Mailer's concern about postwar America is linked with his interest in psychoanalysis and with a search for a liberating ideology in socialist political thought. "*Barbary Shore* was really a book to emerge from the bombarded cellars of my unconscious," Mailer wrote in *Advertisements for Myself*.[57] His character Mike Lovett gets entangled in political conspiracy. In his study of Mailer's fiction and psychoanalysis, Andrew Gordon contends that *Barbary Shore* is "an autobiographical novel in disguise." Lovett reflects Mailer's situation: he is cut off from his past. For Mailer has moved from his interest in Freud and Wilhelm Reich toward existential psychology.[58] The therapist has become a figure who attempts to heal the client by encouraging him to adjust and to conform. These are the very things that Mailer opposes. Mailer seizes the day with a declaration of individualism and self-assertion, a narcissism that opposes the consumerist paradigm and conformist aspects of postwar America. Mike Lovett is situated in a boarding house in a Cold War atmosphere. Mailer wrote in a letter to A. J. Muste in November 1953 that "the hope of socialism . . . can come neither from the U.S. nor of course the Soviet Union."[59] In an earlier letter, he wrote that the United States and the Soviet Union are "driven by insoluble problems toward war . . . a war which may destroy civilization."[60]

The anxiety provoked by this potential confrontation between the United States and the Soviet Union lingered in the air of the 1950s and was a root of the psychological anxiety and sense of drift that lies behind Mailer's novel. In *Barbary Shore*, Mailer was writing "a psychological romance," Andrew Gordon points out. He cites Diana Trilling's observation that "Sigmund Freud and his disciples became the target of some of his sharpest attacks on the modern dispensation."[61] Mailer's interest in his characters' alienation reflects the thought of existentialists, religious thinkers, and the development of psychology and what would later be referred to as "the therapeutic culture."[62]

When Rollo May published *The Meaning of Anxiety* in 1950, he recognized that, while anxiety was a difficult experience that was becoming more widespread, the encounter with anxiety and its treatment could assist in the development of one's life. Also, in 1950, Erik Erikson's developmental perspective appeared in his book *Childhood and Society*. *The Collected Works* of psychoanalyst Karen Horney were published in two volumes in 1950 by W. W. Norton, along with her book *Neurosis and Human Growth* (1950). There were many other developments in psychology. Abraham Maslow's humanistic psychology was further addressed in his book *Motivation and Personality* (1954). Viktor Frankl, who had endured imprisonment in the Nazi concentration camps, wrote the text that would be titled *Man's Search for Meaning*, and his publisher circulated his study *The Unconscious God*. Carl Rogers developed his client-centered therapy and published *On Becoming a Person* (1956). Behaviorism's ascendency in the 1950s was marked by work from Clark Hull, B. F. Skinner, Edward Tolman, Kenneth W. Spence, and Neal Miller's attention to neuroscience. The work of Melanie Klein prompted the development of object relations theory, practiced by D. W. Winnicott. In France, Jacques Lacan reread Freud and provided seminars in Paris.

There were thinkers who contested psychological models. In 1953, R. D. Laing worked at the Glasgow Mental Hospital and in 1956 in London at Tavistock Institute. He entered his anti-psychiatry phase and further explored schizophrenia, which he attributed to the environmental situation rather than biological causes. Gregory Bateson explored a "double bind" theory of family situation and investigated schizophrenia as an expression of distress. Thomas Szasz questioned social control and was critical of the medical model. A critique was presented by Michel

Foucault in *Madness and Civilization.* Philip Rieff completed a dissertation in 1959 titled *Freud: The Mind of the Moralist* and followed this with an exploration of psychology's cultural influence, published in 1966. Mailer's fascination with Freud seems to have blended with his cultural criticism and his own brand of narcissism in *Advertisements to Myself.* Sociologist Christopher Lasch in the 1970s suggested that a therapeutic ethos had "displaced religion" and replaced the Protestant ethos in America. Historian T. J. Jackson Lears in the 1980s and 1990s pointed to consumer culture and changes in religion giving rise to a focus on self-actualization in this world rather than an ethos of conduct befitting a view of salvation and afterlife. Rachel Mykkanen points to cultural concern with maintaining the war economy via consumerism in her 2014 dissertation from the University of California–Irvine. Mailer's novel indicates concern with "social erosion" and with "instability and corruption," observes Maggie McKinley.[63]

Mailer's character Mike Lovett is one of the alienated dreamers of the period. He wishes to write his novel but, given his amnesia, is unable to draw effectively upon his own experiences. Lovett joins the political conspiracy for something to latch onto. He is a bit like the disaffected intellectual of Colin Wilson's British best seller *The Outsider* (1956). Or, perhaps it is Mailer himself who is America's version of the angry young man, asserting artistic individuality against conformity. The "Outsider" is a man who rejects conventional ways of life. He becomes aware of a "world-will" that drives men and women. Wilson moves through existentialist works from Sartre, Kafka, Dostoevsky, and others to affirm the necessity of individuality. One must regain the will to life and Nietzsche's will to power and adopt a vigorous anarchism. In Mailer's work, this assertion of the self becomes increasingly evident as he moves through his next novel, *The Deer Park*, to his essays and *Advertisements for Myself* (1959).

3

ALIENATED DREAMERS

HOLDEN CAULFIELD IN *THE CATCHER IN THE RYE* (1951) BY J. D. SALINGER

Holden Caulfield in *The Catcher in the Rye* sounded some of the first notes of social criticism in 1950s fiction. Troubled and cynical, Holden became an adolescent folk hero. His unique narrative voice drives J. D. Salinger's *The Catcher in the Rye*. Holden questions "phonies" and the hypocrisy of the adult world. Yet he is prone to lying and distortions. He is a trickster figure who is nostalgic for a more innocent time.

Holden's story has been distributed to adolescent readers for more than a half century. *The Catcher in the Rye* is among the most assigned texts in high school classrooms and among the most often banned. Holden, at the age of seventeen, recalls his life from a year earlier. Like Charles Dickens's David Copperfield, whose story he dismisses, Holden gives us an autobiography. Like Dickens's character, he is a young person who rebels against the conventions of his environment. He appears to have a moral interest in society, although his perspective is a cynical one. He thinks of the brother he has lost. His parents linger in the background of his story. Holden insists that his personal history is "lousy" and people are phony. Sally Hayes, in particular, is "quite a little phony." Mr. Ossenberger's "corny speech" is also phony. The world is filled with hypocrisy, and the school he has attended is run by phonies.[1]

Holden has been variously interpreted: as hero and as antihero. He appears to be telling his story to an analyst in a sanitarium. Evidently,

Holden's voice wants to stir his listener. He wants to brag and to critique. He has been expelled from prep school and is now looking backward. Holden is depressed, and he casts the world as wrong and filled with hypocrisy. He wishes to get away from the phony world.[2] He tells us a story that moves across three days that is linked with his past, his family, and society as he perceives it. Holden does not see adult life clearly. Nor does he have much trust. Holden is cynical and defiant. S. N. Behrman in the *New Yorker* was among the critics who recognized the wit and the disillusion in Holden Caulfield. Behrman saw Holden as self-critical and "overwhelmed."[3] One may ask if the tribulations in Holden's personal experience overwhelm him. Or is there something in the larger context of the 1940s and 1950s that Holden is aware of and responding to? A reader may wonder how much of this narrator's depiction of the lives of people around him is a matter of this character's projection. Or is Holden alienated by a society in which he feels he does not fit?[4]

Child psychologist Robert Coles once commented that his patients introduced him to the novel. "I've been told for years about this *Catcher in the Rye*," Coles wrote. "I got to know Holden Caulfield by hearsay before I read him as a reader. My analytic patients spoke of him as if they'd actually met him. They used his words, his way of speaking."[5] When Coles and psychologist Anna Freud discussed Salinger's character, Freud's daughter wondered why adolescents identified with him. Salinger's readers appeared to view Holden as heroic. Anna Freud saw only narcissism, impudence, and a lack of trust in Holden Caulfield. Coles identified humor and vulnerability in the character, alongside self-absorption and a lack of trust. He observed the public response to Holden Caulfield: "Many of us who took to it, embodying his laid-back words, his wisecracks, his cool, worried about him."[6]

Holden is often characterized as the ever-cynical, disaffected teen, and his story has been directed toward young adult readers. However, *Catcher in the Rye* was not intended for teenagers. Nor was it treated in early reviews by literary critics as if it was. Holden Caulfield became one of the more notable (and perhaps notorious) characters of the 1950s. He was imitated. He was censored. The literary critic Alfred Kazin, in 1961, observed that *The Catcher in the Rye* had become "the favorite American novel on the required or suggested reading lists of American colleges and secondary schools."[7]

Why did Holden Caulfield become an adolescent folk hero? It is, in part, because he describes flaws in our society, some psychologists have suggested. Holden has drawn the interpretations of commentators in psychological journals who have focused on distress among adolescents. R. John Huber and Gail Ledbetter see him as typical of "maladjustment" and engaged in "compensatory striving for grandiosity." The first lines of the novel are noted by Benjamin Priest, who observes that "the defiance in the first line has resonated with adolescents through the generations to the present day." Priest turns to psychologist Donald Winnicott's views on adolescent development to analyze Holden.[8] He reminds us that Holden narrates the story of his breakdown and that the "you" in the book is his therapist. Winnicott compares adolescence to an illness, and time is its cure. Priest asks if Holden is providing a self-defensive narrative. He asks if Holden's very critique of the adult world is not an attempt to validate himself and to assert his own potency.

In her book on *The Catcher in the Rye*, Sarah Graham claims that the interest in Holden Caulfield includes readers from all backgrounds. In her view, these readers "recognize Holden's world as comparable to their own." "There is a strong dialogue between the book and teenage experience; they are mutually shaping," she writes. Letters written to Salinger by his readers demonstrate that many of those correspondents identified with Holden Caulfield.[9]

Several critics have taken a theological stance toward Holden. Bryce A. Taylor reads the novel as a religious quest.[10] Taylor addresses Christian sources and themes and Holden's conflicted attitude toward Christianity. Holden views the Christian framework with which he is familiar as hypocritical and ostentatious. He believes that it creates cliques and conformity. Yet, says Taylor, this reference to the defects of organized Christianity in society may suggest some attraction to it. He refers to Legion, the demoniac in the synoptic gospels. He sees the carousel scene as parallel with Dante, being guided through Inferno. Holden is led by his deceased brother Allie and sister Phoebe. "I felt like praying or something when I was in bed, but I couldn't do it." "I'm a sort of atheist," he adds. He asserts that the disciples "annoy the hell out of me."[11] For Louis Menand, in his essay "Holden at Fifty," this results in what he calls "fuzzy Christian thematics about salvation, redemption, and rebirth." Other critics make connections with Zen Buddhism, or with Gnosticism. Dennis McCort has analyzed the novel in terms of

Zen koans. Harold Bloom has suggested that the novel reflects Gnostic Christianity and a refusal of time.[12]

Meanwhile, *The Catcher in the Rye* has frequently been banned in schools. (There was a particularly strong wave of this censorship between 1966 and 1975.) Some of this echoes inclination to ban the novel altogether as inappropriate reading material in nineteenth-century America. Yet, there are more recent concerns about the presumed power of the novel to influence and contaminate young readers. This perspective grants the text a great deal of persuasive power and appears to suggest that its reader is a passive, innocent subject.

The Catcher in the Rye is not only about teenage angst but also reflects the postwar era, including the experience of adults in suburbs and cities, as well as veterans returning to daily American life. That a novel features an adolescent does not necessarily make it exclusively young-adult or teen literature. The implications of *Catcher in the Rye* are broader than this. David Rachels points out that *The Catcher in the Rye* is one of the novels "left behind" on the college level.[13] *To Kill a Mockingbird* and *Lord of the Flies* are also, since they often appear in the high school curriculum. No doubt, *Lord of the Flies* appears there because of the naive assumption that if a book has adolescent characters it must be reading for adolescents. Of course, Harper Lee's novel embodies a cry for justice, and Golding's novel is a scathing inquiry into aggression and violence in humanity: a disturbing reflection on scapegoating, groupthink, and civilization and its discontents. *Catcher in the Rye* is equally significant for an adult reading audience.

The critic Clifton Fadiman asserted that Holden Caulfield had come to life in the pages of Salinger's novel. He wrote that "a human being has been created out of ink, paper, and the imagination."[14] J. D. Salinger gives us Holden's voice, in idiomatic speech. These were "cadences of flat, colloquial prose," observed Virgilia Peterson in the *New York Herald Tribune*. That this novel was published during a conservative time in American culture may have highlighted it as controversial. While Nash K. Burger, in the *New York Times*, referred to it as "an unusually brilliant first novel," Anne L. Goodman found Holden "so completely self-centered" that the other characters lack his "authenticity." "The book as a whole is disappointing," she wrote. In Holden she saw depression, nervous breakdown, vulgarity, and erratic behavior. Holden "is an extraordinary portrait," she added, but "there is too much of him." He is not as sensitive and perceptive as his creator seems to think he is. Paul Engle in the *Chicago Tribune* saw an "authentic teen . . . emotional without being sentimental." However, the *Christian Science Monitor*'s reviewer found the novel distasteful: "swearing and coarse language" made his characters "monotonous and phony." Others expressed a moral concern for American teenagers. "Our youth today has no moorings, no criterion beyond intellect," Virgilia Peterson insisted. There were no guardrails to hold onto along that "steep ascent to maturity."[15]

The Catcher in the Rye was reviewed on July 15, 1951, by Mary McGrory in the Washington, DC, *Evening Star*. "Novels about adolescents can be very facetious, or very excruciating," she wrote. "*The Catcher in the Rye*, which is both funny and painful, is still not like any other fiction about teenagers you ever read." McGrory referred to the novel as the "inside story of an overage 'problem child' who bristles with opinions, nerve ends, complexes, who is half-knight and half-boor." She concluded that "Holden is pitiful and absurd." He is "a terrific liar," and "his nature has not jelled yet." He mourns the death of his brother and rejects the phoniness he sees in the adult world around him. In 1952 in *Commentary*, William Poster wrote: "The ennui, heartburn and weary revulsions [are] actions not of the character but of the novelist." He called Salinger "a well-paid satirist."[16]

In 1959, George Steiner in the *Nation* critiqued "the Salinger industry." He applauded Salinger for having "a marvelous ear for the semiliterate meanderings of the adolescent mind." Granville Hicks, in the *Saturday Review* (July 25, 1959), observed that there were "[m]illions of young Americans who feel closer to Salinger than to any other writer." However, when Alfred Kazin referred to Salinger in 1961 as "everybody's favorite," he was not complimenting the author. Salinger was not by any means Kazin's favorite. Several more recent critics have been kinder in their assessments. Arthur Heiserman and James E. Miller Jr. have asserted that *The Catcher in the Rye* is part of the tradition of the quest novel. The American reader, they observed, "seems fascinated with the outcast, the person who defies tradition in order to arrive at some pristine knowledge, some personal integrity." (They point to Natty Bumppo and Huckleberry Finn and see Holden as James Joyce's Stephen Dedalus and Leopold Bloom "rolled into one crazy kid.") Literary critic Warren French viewed Holden as sick physically and not gaining the understanding he seeks.[17] Defiant, drifting through reverie and guilt feelings, Holden is an artist in the making.

If Holden is indeed this artist, we might wonder if *The Catcher in the Rye* is written for adults rather than for adolescents. Often when teenage characters appear in a novel it gets tagged as a young adult novel or it gets assigned to high school classes. Yet, *Huckleberry Finn*, for example, is more a novel for adults than it is one for adolescents. (Likewise, Oscar Wilde's satirical fairy tales are for an adult audience, not for children.) Salinger's *Nine Stories* appeared on April 6, 1953. Salinger then withdrew from public life into seclusion in Westport, Connecticut, and then in Cornish, New Hampshire. With his major work completed, Salinger became something of a mystery: writing but not publishing, refusing interviews and all biographers, and ever maintaining his privacy.

INVISIBLE MAN (1952) BY RALPH ELLISON

Ralph Ellison's *Invisible Man* explores displacement, identity, and existential struggle in the modern context. He sets his story back more than a decade, in the 1930s. Ellison's themes are poignant for the 1950s: identity, existential issues, the plight of modern man, race, the rural South and the industrial North, communism, black nationalism, and quest. The form is picaresque and episodic, as are Saul Bellow's *Adventures of Augie March* and J. D. Salinger's *Catcher in the Rye*.

From a southern town, the Invisible Man intends to go to an all-black college. He is asked to drive a board member and donor of the college, Mr. Norton. The automobile takes Mr. Norton, "the white benefactor, shrewd banker, skilled scientist, director, philanthropist," to the countryside.[18] Ahead of them they see a former slave cabin, and they visit. Once they are inside, Jim Trueblood tells them a story. Trueblood is a storyteller at heart. However, we may ask if he is a reliable narrator. Is his story true? Or does it suggest a tall tale? He speaks the blues of his life "taking on a deep, incantatory quality, as though he had told the story many, many times."[19] The Invisible Man tells us, "Mr. Norton was listening to Trueblood so intensely he didn't see me."[20] Again, he is invisible.

To Mr. Norton, the story that Jim Trueblood tells is a harrowing one. For in his story Jim Trueblood tells Mr. Norton and the Invisible Man that he has impregnated both his wife and his daughter. Disturbed by this, Mr. Norton needs a drink. The Invisible Man delivers him to a bar in a black neighborhood that is frequented by prostitutes and mental hospital patients. When Mr. Norton is injured there, the Invisible Man gets him out of the bar and returns him to safety. The college administration is not pleased. Dr. Bledsoe has the Invisible Man expelled from the school.

The Invisible Man traverses from the rural South to an industrial northern city. He goes to New York with letters of introduction from Dr. Bledsoe. However, he struggles in New York, and the city is filled with conversations. He attempts to work at a paint factory. He goes to a basement where doors are labeled "Danger": a hell out of Dante's Inferno where he encounters Lucius Brockaway, who declares: "We are the machines inside the machines."[21] The Invisible Man seeks ways to approach his existential condition: "Given the persistence of racial violence and the unavailability of legal protection, I asked myself, what else was there to sustain our will to persevere but laughter? And could it be that there was a subtle triumph hidden in such laughter that I had missed, but one which still was more affirmative than raw anger?"[22]

The Invisible Man faces the dehumanization of the machine as he works at Liberty Paints with Lucius Brockaway. The industrial machine silences and covers over the individual. It places him in a condition of servitude. The Invisible Man joins a political organization, the Brotherhood. However, he does not gain any greater freedom in the Brotherhood. It is a substitute religion, a place of belonging, nationalism, and pseudo-community. The Brotherhood uses the Invisible Man and is focused on self-interest and sustaining the organization. The larger world does not recognize him.

The Invisible Man tells us that for a time he was dominated by the idea of the organization, which "had given the world a new shape and me a vital role."[23] Ellison's anonymous invisible man protests an elderly black couple's eviction from their apartment. He is drawn to the old couple by "a warm, dark, rising whirlpool of emotion," which he says that he "feared."[24] The Brotherhood claims to be for the dispossessed but turns on the Invisible Man, asserting that he may be among the "dead limbs that must be pruned away."[25]

Tod Clifton arrives in the final third of the novel. He is a youth director in the Brotherhood in Harlem. Tod separates from the Brotherhood, which the Invisible Man has joined. Ras, from the Brotherhood, claims that Clifton is a puppet of white masters. This angers Clifton, and there is tension between Clifton and Ras. Ras and the Brotherhood believe that Tod has betrayed their cause. "And before I could answer Clifton spun in the dark and there was crack."[26]

Tod Clifton soon is gone. He reappears selling Sambo dolls in Midtown: little black plastic doll figures held by a thread. A policeman challenges him for peddling without a license. He pushes Tod Clifton, who reacts with a punch. Clifton is then shot. News of the incident circulates. The Invisible Man arranges for a funeral for Tod Clifton, and race riots follow. Tod Clifton is a martyr figure, one whose passing raises questions about social justice. He is also a reflection of the Invisible Man. The Invisible Man passes through an angry mob that wants to hang him.

Traces of jazz and sound pulse through the narrative. The Invisible Man listens to a Louis Armstrong recording while in his basement. He hears "what did I do to be so black and blue?" The narrative includes his high school address, his speech upon the couple's eviction, his eulogy-farewell to Tod Clifton. The riot is one of sound: voices, sirens, guns, interior monologue, flashbacks. The sounds of looters yelling pierce the environment.

Ellison wrote in "The Novel as a Function of Democracy" that a work of fiction can be engaged in advancing a public democratic voice. He writes in "The World and the Jug" that he thought of the *Invisible Man* as "a social action in itself."[27] Ellison drew upon a wide range of writers, white and black: from James Joyce and Ernest Hemingway to Gertrude Stein, Sherwood Anderson, Marcel Proust, and Richard Wright. He drew upon African American oral tradition. Ellison later pointed out that he reflected on the work of Joyce and Eliot, who gave attention to ritual. This novel was an American *Ulysses*, observes Morris Dickstein, one "rich with folklore, verbal improvisation, mythic resonance, and personal history." The story immediately suggests a parallel to Fyodor Dostoevsky's *Notes from Underground*: the Invisible Man lives in a basement. A transition of oral storytelling appears immediately. "I am an invisible man," the narrator declares, and he tells us that he is "not a spook like those who haunted Edgar Allan Poe." His principle action is to tell this story to all audiences who will read and reflect upon the problems of modernity. The Invisible Man is a narrator caught between a folk storytelling culture and the modern age. Despite being invisible and living "in a hole," he affirms he is quite alive.[28] His story will be an affirmation of the human spirit.

Horace A. Porter identifies the novel as "a retrospective and episodic tale" and calls it a "jazz text." Eric Sundquist sees in this novel a construction of history as if that history itself was "a jazz composition or performance."[29] The novel is viewed as a series of statements or jazz solos, riffs, and recollections, improvisations and variations on a theme. Henry Louis Gates refers to this as a "talking book" in which these voices join other African American voices.[30] Ellison is signifying, using the blues and jazz to express this story, and creating an episodic pattern.

There is jazz in *Invisible Man*: the syncopated phrasing of saxophone and trumpet-speech. As a boy, Ralph Ellison played the trumpet and was exposed to military and Western classical music. He recalled that he felt torn between a tradition that was telling him to play "strictly according to the book" and one in which he "was supposed to feel." In his reading, T. S. Eliot's poem "The Waste Land" echoed for him both jazz and this classical tradition. Jazz, Ralph Ellison says, is "individual assertion within and against the group." It is an art of "moments" in which each player challenges the others, as if in a contest: "each solo flight, or improvisation, represents . . . a definition of his identity as individual, as member of the collectivity and as a link in the chain of tradition."[31] *Invisible Man* plays a lament not only solely for the African American person's humanity but for everyone's humanity. Ellison's vision is universal, unfettered, a Gospel spiritual that expresses the soul of humanity.

In *Shadow and Act*, Ellison writes of "the rough-edged tones and broad vibratos, the high, shrill and grating tones which rasp one's ears like the agonized flourishes of flamenco, to the gut tones, which remind us of where the jazz trombone found its human source." Jazz music "is an art which employs a broad rhythmic freedom and accents the lyric line to reinforce the emotional impact," Ellison writes. Words dissolve in music, in a jazz that "utilizes half-tones, glissandi, blues notes, humming and moaning." Jazz may be precise, with "a pronunciation which is almost of the academy one instant and of the broadest cotton field the next." Ellison's novel dwells not only in basements and existential angst but also dwells in this idiom.[32]

Adam Bradley observes that Ralph Ellison's second untitled novel ends as Alonzo Zuber Hickman takes a "quick look at the glowing 369 on the fanlight" and hurries from a townhouse in Washington, DC. He points out that in the prologue to *Invisible Man* the protagonist used a lightbulb to light his underground hiding area. "In my hole in the basement, there are exactly 1,369 lights." Bradley encourages us to read *Invisible Man* as a novel in progress and to include that second novel in our consideration. Ellison was ever revising. Bradley says that "the second novel was his life's work."[33] The first novel responded to Richard Wright. Bradley describes the two novels as evolving in an antiphonal pattern. The first novel is a call, and the second is an answer response. He points out changes in American culture, seeking multiracial democracy. He regards this almost-novel as one that "may prove more pertinent to the challenges facing us in the Twenty-First Century."[34]

AMANTHA STARR IN *BAND OF ANGELS* (1955) BY ROBERT PENN WARREN

Amantha Starr asks the question "Oh, who am I?" as the historical melodrama *Band of Angels* (1955) by Robert Penn Warren begins. Matters of identity arise from Amantha's discovery upon her father's death that she is part white and part black: her mother was a slave. Amantha was raised in Kentucky and was sent north to school. Later, identified as a Negro, she is sold into slavery and becomes slave and lover to Hamish Bond, whose real name is Alec Hinks. So, what are names, racial categories, or human appearances? Amantha is an African American who may be "passing." She marries the transcendentalist Tobias Sears, and they move to St. Louis and then on to Kansas.

Amantha tries to work out her identity, and she passes through self-pity. She claims, "You do not live your life, but somehow, your life lives you, and you are, therefore, only what History does to you."[35] Yet, Amantha gains the willpower and vision to claim her uniqueness. Her struggle with circumstances raises the issue of racial passing. We see parallels in Eliza Harris in *Uncle Tom's Cabin*, Harriet Jacobs in *Incidents in the Life of a Slave Girl*, James Weldon Johnson's *Autobiogra-*

phy of an Ex-Colored Man, Nella Larsen's *Quicksand* (1928) and *Passing* (1929), and Janie Crawford's quest for identity and voice in Zora Neale Hurston's *Their Eyes Were Watching God*.

Amantha tells her story. She must contend with gender and race. In a 1977 interview with John Baker, Warren called *Band of Angels* an "investigation" of "the nature of freedom."[36] Amantha is given voice by a southern white conservative writer.

Robert Penn Warren uses history to attempt to come to terms with America's past. His first major book was his critique of John Brown's raid. Across the years as poet, critic, and novelist, he also attempted to come to terms with slavery and its legacy. In the early 1930s, he was a contributor to the Agrarians' "I'll Take My Stand." The diverse industrial society was not akin to the Southern Agrarian vision for the South. They embraced a notion of the fruitfulness of the land and home. Robert Penn Warren supported the idea of a humane regional life without industrial pace and materialism. He sought harmony in "the life pattern of the community." Warren's essay "Briar Patch" recognizes the development of African American life in the South. He wrote that the southerner found it "irreplaceable in his society and he hopes to maintain its integrity in the face of industrialism . . . he must find a place for the Negro in his scheme."[37]

In the 1950s, Robert Penn Warren was increasingly reflective about the issue of slavery and its legacy. After *Brown v. Board of Education* in 1954 and the Montgomery boycott brought public reactions in the South, the author sought to study the problems. *Band of Angels* was published in 1955. In 1956, Robert Penn Warren wrote *Segregation: The Inner Conflict in the South*. He followed this with *The Legacy of the Civil War* (1961) and *Who Speaks for the Negro* (1965). During this time, Robert Penn Warren's contact and conversations with Ralph Ellison and James Baldwin were important for his thinking about the issues.

Robert Penn Warren left Memphis by plane in 1956 to explore segregation. When we read his essay, it is as if we are there on that plane with him, as it glides over the river, tilting toward Mississippi. Looking down, he guides our vision across a road he once drove toward Natchez and writes a passage reminiscent of the opening of his novel *All the King's Men*: "It seems like a thousand years since I drove down that road."[38] Like the roads of his novel, this one is a passage that soon leads further into the past: recalling Shiloh and then Corinth and "young men in gray uniforms stepping toward the lethal spring thickets of dogwood and redbud."[39] America's history is here; its ghosts dwell in the landscape, as much as in any Eudora Welty story or James Lee Burke novel one has ever read. Robert Penn Warren senses them and their importance for the modern era. History and meaning and the passion and legacy of America's ancestors are never quite gone.

Yet, we are still on the plane. A man originally from New York is handing Warren a newspaper. He is suggesting that people ought to be "more fair thinking" and "affable," so that all the troubles can be "worked out in time."[40] Like a reporter, Warren wants to discover the story firsthand. That image of a newspaper on an airplane in motion seems to suggest the animating action of the news of the day. He is going to Mississippi, and a Tennessee accent was not "good enough credentials there."[41] Experiences trigger memories as he collects the voices of people commenting on segregation: a taxi driver in Memphis, a school superintendent in central Tennessee, a lawyer who has organized segregation groups. He recalls a boy who has hitchhiked from Atlanta to Nashville, who responds with "automatic violence" to the mention of blacks and his mention of "a little trouble down your way."[42] At a motel near Clarksdale, he overhears a conversation in which William Faulkner, never read by the speaker, is compared with Hemingway, a writer he has read. Both are "Gory and on the seedy side of life."[43]

Warren displays evident attentiveness to language and how people speak. That image of the newspaper on the airplane repeats. Similarly, he explores how news is being constructed or suppressed, and he listens for opinions, perspectives, and cues as to what is going on. Warren's essay is filled with an array of people, who are described sharply, with details. He conducts interviews, and we hear dialogue as he asks why people want to keep segregation. We hear from a mulatto grade-school teacher, a charming and articulate forty-five-year-old lady who supports segregation, an official of a segregation group born in Kentucky who asserts, "it ain't right to have mixing."[44] He asks a local NAACP secretary how change will come. Another man there says that they don't "want to aggravate the violence. We have all got to live together. It will take time."[45]

Warren carefully follows an incident in which the television cameras are on, and a black businessman in a blue suit comes forward and the interview is slanted to support segregation. A black working man is told to say some good things on behalf of segregation, but much of what he says breaks through the imposed Uncle Tom role. No, he says. The ultimate goal is not just to go to white schools or to "travel with white people on conveyances over the country." Mobility and charge are something else, he declares: "the negro, he is a growing people and he will strive for all the equalities belonging to any American citizen."[46] One can imagine the television producer starting to sweat, seeking to hush up the man and to get him off camera.

Warren is told by an African American scholar that the most persistent problem for a black individual is that "[h]e is denied human dignity."[47] Integration is not an easy proposition in 1956, the man says. There are African Americans who tell him, "I don't want to socialize."[48] There are white pundits, like a local minister who urge some changes in "the moral level" of some blacks. Warren repeats across several pages the question: "What is coming?"[49] The answers are as varied as a dozen different blues songs, or the vegetation of the Mississippi Delta and the Atchafalaya basin further south. The responses range from "dead backs," "somebody's butt will be busted," and more violence, to: "Fifteen years and they will all be blended in."[50] "Why get so worked up?" says one. Another says: "Democracy is just a name for whatever you like. It has lost its local integrity."[51]

Not much is said by this speaker about national integrity, or about human integrity. From Warren's interviews, it is easy to recognize that people are clearly concerned about their homes and neighborhoods, and they are not quite ready to integrate. However, the day is coming, and the journey continues. Warren writes: "Out of Memphis, I lean back in my seat on the plane, and watch the darkness slide by." He speaks in the voice of a southerner who seeks broader vistas, ones not contained by xenophobia, strangled and confined by the barbed wire of history. He speaks of the southerner who feels "going out of the South, the relief, the expanding vistas."[52] He listens to the soft purr of the engines bearing him through the night.

"Our Twenty-First-Century America" is in motion, filled with signs and voices and reflected back to us on the evening news, on little blurbs appearing on our computer screens. Our journalists, our novelists, and our people who create the social theater of a new century are recalling the roads we have gone down. Perhaps, a few summon us to face realities as we hope for further transformation. Like Robert Penn Warren looking down from that airplane window in 1956, they consider the long road along the river. We are still on the plane next to that man with the newspaper. He suggests that people ought to be "more fair thinking," so that this thing might be "worked out in time."[53] But the road is long. The road is long.

SONNY IN JAMES BALDWIN'S "SONNY'S BLUES" (1957)

The blues evoke the struggles and dreams, the affirmations and sorrows, of people who are confronted with hard uncertainties in life. Played by Sonny, the jazz pianist of James Baldwin's "Sonny's Blues," the blues convey an "inexpressible longing."[54] "Sonny's Blues" explores the struggle of an individual and the inheritance of life that jazz makes available to listeners. In his essay "The Price of the Ticket," James Baldwin writes of a new experience of music that emerged from his meeting the artist Beauford Delaney: "I walked into music. I had grown up with music, but, now, on Beauford's small black record player, I began to hear what I had never dared or been able to hear." Baldwin's character, Sonny, begins to hear and feel in new ways.[55] Yet, Sonny remains isolated in what Baldwin has recognized as "the aloneness in which one discovers that life is tragic, and, therefore, unutterably beautiful."[56]

Sonny's brother, the story's narrator, recognizes that Sonny's life is enhanced by jazz. In the story's penultimate scene in a jazz club, Sonny finally breaks through. He launches into a piano solo flight in which there is a "passing across a threshold" and "a passage from a lower to a higher order of vision."[57] Jazz and blues connect Sonny's eccentric and gifted spirit with humanity. When Sonny finds his groove, he is no longer separate. In becoming the music and expressing emotion, the members of the jazz ensemble become more than separate selves. There is no longer a Cartesian world of separation or isolation at the jazz club, which suits the largely isolated Sonny just fine. When jazz players connect in the music, their synchrony creates a social space in which there is a "coupling of their nervous systems," or "a muscular bonding of rhythmic group connection" occurs.[58] Sonny's musical extension of his spirit reflects that moment in a musician's performing life that Benzon describes: "Something happens to performers, then, at rare moments—something they did not plan or will."[59] The communal dimension of this has been referred to by neuroscientists as the linking of subcortical and cortical systems among musicians and their audience. Antonio Damasio describes this in *Descartes' Error* (1991). The "sharing in the same pattern of neural activity" is observed by Nils Wallin in *Biomusicology* (1991).[60]

Sonny's blues ultimately are about community. In the penultimate scene at the jazz club, the narrator, Sonny's brother, is brought into a realization that music making is about collective dynamics. In jazz, Sonny lives in a world of rhythms, ritual, and spontaneous feeling. Jazz music acts as a means of collective intentionality. The narrator of "Sonny's Blues," a member of the audience, senses that something emotional is going on in music making, just as Leonard Meyer put his finger on it in *Emotion and Meaning in Music* (1956), at about the same time that Baldwin was writing this story.[61]

Baldwin begins his story rhythmically, with cadenced sentences broken by commas that give a staccato start-and-stop effect to the first paragraph. These lines reflect the repetition of the narrator who is reading, then rereading, a newspaper note about his brother, Sonny. In Baldwin's opening, the stutter of prose repetition may reflect a narrator who is trying to emotionally hold together life amid memories and loss. A poetics of repetition marks out "Sonny's Blues." Repetition is a common feature of the blues and its original twelve-bar structure. The three-line stanza of the blues is built upon two lines that repeat and echo each other and express a sentiment that is developed with variations by the third line.

Rather than proceeding in a linear fashion, Baldwin's narrative moves like music, in time that bends back upon itself. The story is not told in chronological time. Instead, as in musical time, it is structured in sections that evoke memory. Music itself is "saturated by time" and translates time into form. This story, likewise, is deeply concerned with change, movement, and subjective inwardness. Sonny himself is an expression of what Lawrence Kramer has described as transitivity.[62] That is, Sonny appears to be always coming apart, or coming back together again. Sonny is a "rootless intensity" for whom time in music brings wholeness or fragmentation, identity or dissociation.

In the story's first reference to music, the unnamed narrator, a schoolteacher, is inquiring about Sonny. The pervasiveness of music and its effects on his life is immediately suggested by the street scene in which music sounds from a tavern: "the juke box was blasting away with something black and bouncy." We see the barmaid keeping time to the music. The narrator says, "I listened to the music which seemed to be causing the pavement to shake."[63] The idea that music causes trembling in the material world and in the human psyche is reinforced by the final image of the story in which a glass of scotch and milk is set on the top of Sonny's piano.

The portrait we are given of Sonny comes to us through his brother, whose winding narrative and distinct point of view is our lens upon Sonny and the action. His narrative, at several points, appears to ask, "Who is Sonny? What has my brother become?" Sonny is a character who represents what Lawrence Kramer has called "romantic repetition," in which the state of mind and feeling evoked by repetition is usually one of distress.[64] The blues so well captures this repetition, reliving, and transformation of pain. Sonny's blues are shadowed by Thanatos at every turn. There is in Sonny's blues a dissolve of personality, or what Kramer refers to as "the transit of identity" in his chapter "Romantic Repetition" in *Music and Poetry* (1984). Sonny, who appears caught between Thanatos and the pleasure principle, reflects Sigmund Freud's view of "repetition compulsion, the living-over of a painful action in defiance of the pleasure-principle [. . .] as a product of the death instinct."[65]

Sonny's life, like his music, is a process of expectancy and patterns of tension. Sonny's consciousness is a dynamic force, the expression of a rhythm. His emotional life is linked with a structural rhythm that unfolds. In psychoanalytic terms, this is the process by which a subject invests psychic energy in an object, making the object meaning for itself. Freud's term *Besetzung* means "occupation" and "electric charge." Sonny reaches for ec-stasis: a movement of consciousness out of self. His investment of psychic energy into the music, his effort to make meaning, charges it with psychological and emotional energy. There is a feeling of distress before Sonny breaks free. This corresponds with what Kramer has said of "romantic repetition," which "usually involves distress, disturbance, or turbulence."[66]

Sonny is also a gifted artist. Baldwin points to the artist and his jazz as an ecstatic fusion between subject and object. Sonny's blues are a search for transformative power, and his drug use, in the hazy intervals of his life, is a substitute and a craving for this experience. In contrast, the narrator has chosen the family life of a schoolteacher. Sonny's life parallels the tragic life of their father's brother, a guitar player, who was the victim of a hit-and-run accident. Mama hums "an old church song" at the window, just before she discloses that "[y]our daddy once had a brother" and the sad tale of his demise. Mama recalls their father's story, much in the manner of a sad ballad. She says, "he was whistling to himself and he had his guitar slung over his shoulder." We see the uncle's lone figure at the roadside and see the father of Sonny and the narrator looking on. Then the sharp image comes of a car filled with drunken white men that hits the guitar player. As he falls, we hear the rhythm of Mama's telling of the story, vividly recalled to her by their father's auditory memory: "and he heard the wood of that guitar when it give, and he heard them strings go flying, and he heard them white men shouting, and the car kept on a-going and it ain't stopped till this day."[67]

The narrator is unprepared for a jazz education, or for Sonny's lifestyle. He watches as Sonny buys a record player and listens as Sonny plays piano to the records. He tells us how Sonny studied the recorded music: "Or he'd play one section of the record, one chord, one change, one progression, then he'd do it on the piano. Then back to the record. Then back to the piano."[68] Sonny is not easily understood by his brother; by Isabel, the narrator's wife; or by others in the society outside the jazz ensemble. For Isabel, "it wasn't like living with a person at all, it was like living with a sound." She thinks that he moves in a different atmosphere: "as though he were all wrapped up in some cloud, some fire, some vision of his own; and there wasn't any way to reach him."[69]

The brother senses that "Sonny was at that piano playing for his life."[70] Indeed, he is. For Baldwin makes it clear that there is the tension of a struggle for life with death in Sonny's music. The narrator wants to rescue Sonny from this, but perhaps only music can be salvific for Sonny. Aware that Sonny suffers, his brother says, "I don't want to see you—die—trying not to suffer." He can see Sonny slowly "killing" himself. Music is Sonny's response to what is otherwise inexpressible.

"It's terrible sometimes, inside," he said. "The streets are cold and there's a storm inside. . . . You can't talk it and you can't make love with it, and when you finally get with it and play it, you realize nobody's listening. So, you've got to listen. You got to find a way to listen."[71] Music—jazz, the blues—is a resistance against "going to pieces." Observing a gospel group singing at a makeshift "revival" meeting on the street, Sonny reflects on suffering. The narrator asks: "But there's no way not to suffer—is there, Sonny?" Sonny responds, "I believe not . . . but that's never stopped anyone from trying."[72]

Gospel music enters this story as an answer to the blues and dwells for a time in tension with it. The gospel message is sung, but it falls short of having any real saving effect. Outside the living room window on Seventh Avenue is a "revival meeting" with "three sisters in black and a brother" with Bibles and a tambourine, into which goes donations. The theme of rescue is underscored. The song is familiar to everyone, the narrator tells us, and "not one of them had been rescued." At best "the music seemed to soothe a poison out of them."[73] The memory of their mother's gospel music comes back to Sonny and his brother. Yet, it is not so much their mother that Sonny recalls but the effect of the drugs that he has been taking. The maternal, the voice of music, and the drug that brings solace, escape, and a sense of control mingle in him. "When she was singing before," said Sonny abruptly, "the voice reminded me for a minute of what heroin feels like sometimes—when it's in your veins. It makes you sort of warm and cool at the same time. And distant. And—and sure."[74]

Sonny wants the feeling of being in control. "Sometimes you've got to have that feeling," he says.[75] Yet, jazz asks for a flexibility, a control that paradoxically is also a letting go of control as well. Sonny's brother sees Sonny looking at him "with great, troubled eyes." Sonny makes it clear that his involvement with music is what sustains him. "It's not so much to play. It's to stand it, to be able to make it at all. On any level. In order to keep from shaking to pieces."[76]

Sonny's suffering reflects what Baldwin, in "Down at the Cross," called "the depths out of which much ironic tenacity comes." In "Down at the Cross," Baldwin suggests a tension and interaction between gospel music and the blues. Yet, in both, he implies, is a search for freedom: "This is the freedom that one hears in some gospel songs, for example, and in jazz. In all jazz, and especially in the blues, there is something tart and ironic, authoritative and double-edged. . . . Only people who have been 'down the line,' as the song puts it, know what this music is about."[77]

Sonny clearly represents for Baldwin the struggle of the artist in society: the creative person who he describes as being in a lover's war with his or her society. In "The Creative Process" in *Creative America* (1962), Baldwin wrote of the artist: "he is his own test tube, his own laboratory, working according to very vigorous rules" to "discover the mystery of human being." The artist knows that "all our action and all our achievement rests on things unseen." Baldwin's essay gives a sense of the creative artist as explorer. It extends the image of Sonny's glass of scotch and milk balancing on his piano to a wider view of society. "A society must assume that it is stable, but the artist must know, and he must let us know, that there is nothing stable under heaven." The artist must seek "the heart of every answer and expose the question the answer hides."[78]

The social critique implicit in "Sonny's Blues" is made explicit in Baldwin's later essay, "On Catfish Row," in *Commentary* (1959). Baldwin is sharply critical of the society that "produced and destroyed" Billie Holiday. He speaks of a "brutally indifferent world" and writes, "We are altogether quick to disdain responsibility for the fate which overtakes—so often—so many gifted, driven and erratic artists. Nobody pushed them to their deaths, we like to say. They jumped."[79] The question in "Sonny's Blues" is whether Sonny will dissolve into drug addiction and death or take the leap of faith into life. Sonny is learning the blues with his life, and the music challenges Sonny to follow Charlie Parker and the other great players who swirl in his thoughts into "the deep water."

Sonny is like a blues note bending toward dissonance. Yet, he will not yet fall to pieces. He meditates on needing a fix, seeking a place to lean. "I needed a clear space to listen," he says. His brother needs a space to listen, too—and so do we, the readers who listen to his story. With Baldwin's narrator, we visit a nightclub and meet Creole, "a coal black cheerful looking man, a musician friend of Sonny's, built close to the ground."[80] We are in that club in the climax of the story. Baldwin brings us there to where we watch and listen to the jazz ensemble from a table in a dark corner.

Sonny obviously has difficulty getting started, finding his groove, launching into his solo. It is in this tension, before Sonny can find his musical voice, that Baldwin gives us an extraordinary meditation on music from the listening narrator's point of view:

> All I know about music is that not many people ever really hear it. And even then, on the rare occasions when something opens within, and the music enters, what we mainly hear, or hear corroborated, are personal, private, vanishing evocations.[81]

We are reminded that the creator of music is hearing "something else" and imposes order on the composition. Baldwin, no doubt, recognizes that this is much like the art of the writer. However, it is "more terrible because it has no words, and triumphant too, for that same reason."[82]

Sonny, facing the void, is an existential character held back in a duet with Creole, who is listening to him and challenging him. "He was having a dialogue with Sonny. He wanted Sonny to leave the shoreline and strike out for the deep water. He was Sonny's witness that deep water and drowning were not the same thing—he had been there, and he knew."[83] The deep water of innovation awaits the assertion of a self in a leap of faith. Baldwin leads us dramatically into this decisive moment for his character poised at his piano. Sonny will take the risk and make the leap into the unknown, where a musical structure shifts and one has to find one's way. It is a moment when "a piano is just a piano" but "[h]e has to fill it, the instrument, with the breath of life, his own."[84]

We see Sonny facing an existential challenge. Baldwin's prose returns to halting staccato sentences broken by commas. "He and the piano stammered, started one way, got scared, stopped; started another way, panicked, marked time, panicked again, got stuck."[85] With the semicolon, we pause, but then we plunge forward. With the ending period we are stuck. We watch Sonny in "the fire and fury of the battle" within him, within the music. It is in the tune "Am I Blue," the narrator senses, that Sonny began to play with heartfelt abandon. "Something began to happen." The players answer, draw apart, come together. Sonny has returned to the community. "He seemed to have found, right there beneath his fingers, a damn brand-new piano."[86]

Baldwin's story suggests that the blues dwell in liminality. They exist in peril of ruin or death, or in anticipation of a life-giving power, to stretch out human capacity for feeling. Creole and the musicians communicate the blues. "He and his boys up there were keeping it new, at the risk of ruin, destruction, madness and death, in order to find new ways to make us listen. For, while the tale of how we suffer, and how we are delighted, and how we may triumph is never new, it always must be heard. There isn't any other tale to tell, it's the only light we've got in all this darkness."[87]

It is this overcoming of the darkness, the opening up of possibilities, that Sonny, the artist, is about. In his communal rhythm and connection, Sonny has gone into his own space. When Sonny makes the music his own, it becomes a gift. In his spirit and in his music "that life contained so many others." Sonny has reached a point of breakthrough and he is giving his life back in music. Here Baldwin provides a beautifully lyrical passage suggesting generation and memory, as Sonny plays. Sonny's music restores to the narrator memory, community, and family. "I saw my mother's face again [. . .] I saw the moonlit road where my father's brother died [. . .] I felt my own tears begin to rise." Yet there is an awareness that "this was only a moment, that the world waited outside, as hungry as a tiger, and that trouble stretched above us, longer than the sky."[88]

The blues live in Baldwin's story as a respite from disaster. They suggest a space of suspension between the trouble of life and that breakthrough to wholeness that is temporary, much like the moment of rest in Schopenhauer's will. Clearly, life plunges on like the next tune the band will attempt. In that final image of the story, a glass of Scotch and milk set on Sonny's piano is described as "a cup of trembling." Fear and anxiety on the edge of piano and soul await the music that will shake and mix that drink. Sonny is that cup and its contents, mother's milk and song of life, the heat, sting, and swirl of hard liquor. These are Sonny's blues.

4

HEROES AND ANTIHEROES

SANTIAGO IN *THE OLD MAN AND THE SEA* (1952) BY ERNEST HEMINGWAY

In *The Old Man and the Sea*, an old man, Santiago, establishes a friendly and supportive relationship with a boy named Manolin. Once a fine fisherman, Santiago appears to some of the townspeople as a somewhat odd, slightly daft, eccentric older man. He is resilient and determined: a man of bravery and absurdity, like Cervantes's Don Quixote. Santiago will set forth on a quest, a fishing boat journey to the sea, and there he will wrestle with God and with nature.

Santiago's principal effort is to overcome his doubt, his damaged pride, and sense of limitation. Santiago is within the natural world, not against it. He is experiencing his connection with the marlin that he has hooked on his fishing line. Santiago identifies with the marlin and is in connection with the stars, the fish, and the sea. He is, like the marlin, suspended at sea, struggling for freedom and control, internally and externally. He recognizes that he is bound to this sea and to this adventure. Santiago's ethic is one of communion with the sea. He displays a reverence for the natural world and interacts with sea and sky. He is glad that he does not have to kill the stars, which are his brothers. As sweat and the glare of light on the water affect his vision, he tries to see clearly. He confronts his own hubris, questioning his motivation for catching and killing the fish.[1]

We enter Santiago's mind, drifting like clouds upon the water. Santiago has followed the birds and the currents of the water.[2] He has no radio, and his guidance system is internal. The natural world of the sea appears as a location for both the friendly flying fish and porpoises and the threatening sharks and Portuguese man-of-war. Santiago is on a quest for wholeness and restoration. To bring in the marlin is a work of honor and self-fulfillment, not of conquest. He does not approach the threats of the sea with terror and ferocity, as Ahab in *Moby Dick* did in his demonic effort to subdue the whale. Rather, Santiago experiences the sea and regards its marine life with respect. At the end, Santiago is like Sisyphus rolling the rock uphill only to have it fall; he is one who gains a pyrrhic victory and then loses his catch. When Santiago feels a twinge in his chest, this may suggest that his own death is not far off. The story concludes with Santiago's dream of lions on the beach: fierce creatures at rest. He has come from the sea of the unconscious to the primal land of dreams, to a return in the cycle of life. The lions represent an atonement with nature. Although at rest, they are luxuriant creatures, whose violent energy could rise at any time.

The text is marked by Hemingway's smooth transitions from narrative to interior monologue and by his use of repetition. As Santiago begins his journey, we enter his experience and the open *a* of *lay* meets with the consonance and assonance of "worn wood of the bow," describing the boat. Santiago has become solitary. The struggle awaits. His voice breaks in with a meditation upon the fish as friend and upon a night of stars. Hemingway displays a sure knowledge of baits, hooks, scents, and light on the water, as well as an understanding of human resolve and courage. He offers us a portrait of Santiago's endurance, his overcoming of failure, and experience of the fragile shifts of triumph and loss. In Santiago, we may see Hemingway's sense of code, his tragic sense of life and death, and the importance of applying this code of courage, discipline, and honor to life. While the critic Jeffrey Meyers claims that Hemingway's story carries "forced and obtrusive" Christian symbolism and is weighted by sentimentality and self-pity, or Kenneth Lynn argues that it is "a book that lapses into lachrymose sentimentality," one may read *The Old Man and the Sea* as a sympathetic portrait of a determined individual. Santiago is not merely a reflection of Hemingway himself, as Harold Bloom has argued.[3] Rather, he is an everyman, a universal character of pride and persistence who endures in the face of natural forces and the vastness of sea and sky. The story parallels the existentialist view of the individual struggle and assertion of freedom and will against fate. Santiago has chosen to take determined action against despair and has set out to engage with experience.

Santiago's connection with the boy, Manolin, becomes a recollection while he is at sea. He recalls telling the boy to not worry about him and to enjoy playing baseball. When baseball comes to mind, it is a way to stay focused, like a pitcher gazing steadily at home plate. He has told the boy that Joe DiMaggio's father was a fisherman. The Yankee ballplayer persists despite a bone spur. The boy is an enthusiastic New York Yankees' fan. Baseball was significant in Cuba during the time Hemingway was writing this story. After 1947, a Major League Baseball agreement with the Cuban league served as a basis for player development. Nine Cubans were active in Major League Baseball at the time that Hemingway was writing *The Old Man and the Sea*. (Curiously, the *Madera Tribune* reported on February 19, 1951, that Dom DiMaggio's fishing boat encountered difficulties in waters near San Francisco. Another boat tragically spilled in the surf off the Golden Gate in San Francisco that same day.[4] The Yankees won the 1951 World Series, and Joe DiMaggio retired from baseball in December 1951, before Hemingway's story appeared.)

A reader may observe the pace of this novel. The first section telling us of his journey is leisurely. Santiago is venturing, "going far out."[5] To be a fisherman is what he was "born for."[6] He soon realizes that he has a potential catch, as something tugs on the line. Holding onto it with thumb and forefinger, he is patient. As the movement of the hooked fish becomes clear, the narrative pace quickens. The marlin breaks the surface of the water mightily, and the struggle begins. A line connects man and fish, the human and the natural world. Santiago wonders if he has not gone out too far. Has man exceeded his limits, like Icarus on fragile wings reaching up into the sky? Santiago identifies with his prey; harpooning it he feels concern ("He knew that half of him had been destroyed").[7] As sharks move in on their prey, the "ay" that comes from Santiago's lips is a sigh, a note of concern, untranslatable but true to the gut. He feels a helpless anxiety and horror at what is to come.

The Old Man and the Sea is a story with a mythic dimension, as G. B. Wilson has pointed out.[8] Santiago is Joseph Campbell's hero with a thousand faces. Santiago becomes Christ crucified, his fishline-tortured palms burning as with nails in the flesh of his hands. The fish, a Christian sign, has been stripped bare. He carries the ship's mast, like a cross, ashore. He then lies arms straight out on the bed, abandoned and broken, yet realizing an achievement. Santiago has faced a universe that is indeed stark, a vast sea that might be overwhelming. However, this sea is not merely "changeless and bare." It is, rather, a sea of life that is full of process and change. A man is taken up in the flow of the universe, in the role he must play. Within this situation are always choices. Santiago's intention, his affirmation and embrace of his isolation, has everything to do with the outcome. In his brief achievement of success, his own resourcefulness meets with some grace. His effort and strength have faced the nihilistic void and discovered that the universe is alive and relational. For "man is not made for defeat."[9] Santiago is redeemed in a world where heroic deeds are possible.

GUY MONTAG IN *FAHRENHEIT 451* (1953) BY RAY BRADBURY

The fireman Guy Montag is at the center of Ray Bradbury's critique of aspects of American society. *Fahrenheit 451* addresses concerns with media, McCarthyism, and Cold War attitudes, as well as with machines and depersonalization. *Fahrenheit 451* urges that one ought to resist and reject conformity. Be an individual, it declares. Do not be absorbed or submerged by mass media. This is a dystopian world in which technology is used for social control. Bradbury does not focus on the government in his fictional society, as in Orwell's *1984* (1949), but on public passivity.

We enter the thoughts of Guy Montag as he changes from being a dedicated fireman to a member of the resistance. At first, he is a follower, a passive character, and his life is described in passive voice. He is a faceless, anonymous person who shares in complicity of the book burning. Montag and his wife are both unhappy. Mildred is addicted to her television. She is enclosed by the walls of her television. She cannot relate to or understand Montag's books. It is only as Montag develops his opposition to the work of the firemen that he becomes a unique individual. He emerges as an active character who embraces a sense of purpose. He becomes a preserver.

When Montag as fireman looks in a mirror at the firehouse, he sees his double: "he might wink at himself, a minstrel man, burnt-corked, in the mirror." This is an unintentional blackface, an image that occurs because of exposure to smoke. The "fierce grin" is his mask, a persona. Conformity is a "mask of happiness."[10] At the firehouse Montag works the night shift. This is a midwestern setting. Montag met his wife in Chicago, and his house is in the suburbs.

Two helper figures enter his life: Clarisse McClellan, to whom he is attracted, and Faber, a retired former English professor. Faber resists book burning. He is afraid of being identified and does not actively resist. Clarisse loves nature and night walks. She is unconventional. Clarisse represents freedom, nature, individuality, and independence. She can be Montag's route to self-discovery. She may move him toward childhood memory, so he may be like Wordsworth returning to a sense of soul. Both Clarisse and Faber do not favor the role of the firemen in their society.

Montag's wife Mildred and Captain Beatty oppose him. Like Aldous Huxley's Mustapha Mond in *Brave New World*, Beatty knows the literature of the past. He recalls and quotes authors from Alexander Pope to Samuel Johnson.[11] Beatty suggests to Montag that he burn his house and his books. The "Mechanical Hound" will supervise the burning. Mildred intends to have the books burned. Montag takes four books that Mildred has missed and escapes. He hides those books in firemen's houses, implicating them. Then he goes to Faber's house. Faber tells him that a war has been declared. Montag seeks to get away. He dresses as Faber, in Faber's clothes, to elude the authorities. At this point, "he would not be Montag anymore. . . . He would become Montag plus Faber, fire plus water."[12] He will become like O. J. Simpson in his white Ford Bronco followed in a television spectacle. When he crosses the river, he is baptized by water and has left fire behind.

In a rural area, he encounters men who have gathered together to share their memories of their reading of books. Granger leads the bookmen who live outside the city. They will head to the north. They plan to one day share their memories of books. The city will disintegrate into apocalypse. Nuclear war is presented in symbolic form. However, society's replenishment and renewal may lie in the bookmen who have traversed to the north. The compass of future hope points true north.

Ray Bradbury's *Fahrenheit 451* predicted the further development of technological culture and mass culture. Cold War threats and anxiety about the atom bomb connected with the science fiction genre as writers explored the topic. (This concern appears to have increased book sales.) Bradbury is different than the science-driven Isaac Asimov, or other sci-fi writers who are enthusiastic about technical developments. Bradbury cautions about extensions of science and technology into the minds and lives of people. He is more like the iconoclastic social critics that extend from J. D. Salinger and Jack Kerouac in the 1950s to Kurt Vonnegut in the 1960s. He creates outsiders, as Evan Brier points out. He predicts where current trends may be leading us, and he challenges societal conventions. Bradbury's characters in Fahrenheit 451 are absorbed in watching wall TVs in a supine stupor. Those television screens today take up our public spaces, ever sounding and flashing images in our bars and family restaurants. They are mounted in SUVs. They inhibit reading in doctor and dentist offices, despite the array of periodical subscriptions that are also available in their waiting rooms.

In the society of *Fahrenheit 451*, books have been banished. They have become obsolete. This is the anti-intellectual world forecasted by historian Richard Hofstadter. Faber, the English professor, tells Montag: "There's a lot of Harvard degrees on the tracks between here and Los Angeles."[13] Professor Granger tells Montag that they have read the books and then felt obliged to burn them, "afraid they'd be found." He says, "All we want to do is keep the knowledge we think we will need intact and safe."[14] If such an effort in preservation is successful, there may be a future society that embraces reading and book knowledge. One might think of Stephen Vincent Benet's "By the Waters of Babylon." The resuscitation of culture may begin because the protagonist has dared to venture on a vision quest into the forbidden territory of the ruins following a nuclear holocaust. There he collects the shards of language and culture, fragmented letters like "Wash" that signal Washington, or other foundational elements of American culture.

In Bradbury's future world, most people have given up on the book and on reading. Beatty the fireman and Faber are Montag's teachers. Granger has memorized passages from books. Books could vanish because of totalitarian suppression, of course. However, in this case they were overwhelmed by popular culture forms and disinterest. "If there were no war, if there was peace in the world, I'd say fine, have fun. But all isn't well with the world," says Faber to Montag.[15] The book was a resource, a ballast against ignorance, a guard against all the tribalism and authoritarian powers that Hannah Arendt declared troubling in *The Origins of Totalitarianism* (1951). Yet, people chose to stop reading. Only later did the government choose to make reading books illegal.[16] How, then, could print media exercise its revolutionary power?

Fahrenheit 451 is about more than censorship, or McCarthy-era anxieties. Bradbury appears to advance the thesis that public education is upended, and civilization is undermined when people don't take the time to read. Bradbury's topic in *Fahrenheit 451* is the importance of literature and the book. The novel predicts a world in which wall TVs are overcoming the book. This society relies on distracting technologies. The decline of society in *Fahrenheit 451* corresponds to loss of literature and an increase of mechanism. The very decline of western civilization is linked to the demise of the book. There is a search for values in this techno–Cold War framework. Jonathan Eller defines the theme of *Fahrenheit 451* as "[t]he decline of literature and human values in an increasingly rational society."[17] The society of *Fahrenheit 451* appears to have adopted a forlorn attitude: Why bother distributing texts to people who probably could not understand them anyway? After all, these would-be readers might soon be destroyed in a nuclear war anyway. (This would leave perhaps the lone reader played by Burgess Meredith in the *Twilight Zone* episode "Time at Last" who sadly breaks his reading glasses.)[18]

Leonard Mead of "The Pedestrian" is a character behind Leonard Montag in "The Fireman." He wishes to walk at night: to breathe the night air and to see the stars. However, he lives in a dull and conforming society where to slow down, walk, and meditate is regarded as deviant. Montag takes a walk and feels like he is "the only pedestrian in the entire city." He is stopped. "So, he walked alone, aware of his loneliness, until a police car pulled up and flashed its cold white light upon him. "What are you doing?" "I'm out for a walk."[19] "The Pedestrian" was published August 7, 1951, in the *Reporter*. The story immediately preceded Bradbury's writing "The Fireman." When going for a walk is viewed as abnormal, there is an abridgement of human freedom. In Los Angeles in 1950, as now, much of the movement of people from place to place is via cars. Stopped by police while taking a walk, Bradbury took his own experience to heart and cast it as a social commentary. Similarly, Montag, not knowing what he is looking for, goes out to the streets at night.

In *Fahrenheit 451*, Montag is isolated in a largely deserted city after nightfall. The workday has emptied out. It is an "empty boulevard" of "stilled vehicles." Public space is controlled. There is streetlight, not natural starlight and moonlight. It is a cold white light, like the harsh flashlight beamed into Tom Joad's face in *The Grapes of Wrath*. The urban and the natural is split. The TV light is artificial. Mildred is empty and alienated. Montag feels alienated and separate from her and society.

Other Bradbury stories lay behind his social critique in *Fahrenheit 451*. In Bradbury's "The Veldt" (1950), George and Lydia have recently moved into their house with their children Wendy and Peter. This suburban house has a room that becomes a virtual reality experience. It has recently transformed into a jungle, complete with lions. This may be likened to a subconscious realm of Thanatos or death thoughts and primal, visceral forces that lie beneath daily rationality. The room is an Id of repressed fierceness.

The children are fine postwar consumers. They want their virtual reality, and they desire the convenience provided by all the new appliances and accessories in their home. They reject having their games taken away. They want to keep their "voice clocks" and "shoe tiers," their back scratchers and massagers, the devices that brush their teeth and comb their hair. (Bradbury appears to anticipate attachment to cell phones and a world of apps, Siri, and Alexa.) A child-psychologist friend is called in to intervene. However, this "Happylife" home appears to have a mind of its own. Lydia asks, "What prompted us to buy a nightmare?" George responds: "Pride, money, foolishness." The children, determined to keep their conveniences and their virtual reality, soon turn on their parents who indeed enter a nightmare.[20]

"The Fireman" was a work of inspiration. Bradbury commented that he had been seized by an idea. "The story wrote me," he wrote of "The Fireman." "The concept was so riveting I found it hard at sunset to flee the library basement and take the bus home to reality." In contrast with his spontaneous creation of the short story, Bradbury was now working on a defined project on a regular schedule. This meant that Bradbury's novel was from the first connected with books, publishing, and the literary marketplace, as Evan Brier points out. Thus, it was propelled into life not only by Bradbury's social critique and concern with books and reading but also within the publishing context. Even as *Fahrenheit 451* critiques mass culture it is part of it, observes Brier.

Throughout his youth, Ray Bradbury was a regular visitor to his local library. It was a fine place for a young man of limited means to go to read and stretch his imagination. This was his education.[21] He was attracted to Burroughs's Tarzan stories, to John Carter novels, and Walker Thompson's writing as Valentine Wood. He read Clark Ashton Smith in *Wonder Stories*, Edmond Hamilton in *Amazing Quarterly*, and Jack Williamson in *Weird Tales.* As an adult, Bradbury took a public position on books. Free reading, he concluded, can help us overcome intolerance.[22] He asserted that freedom from fear, including McCarthyist scrutiny, was necessary in a democracy. Bradbury wrote: "To put your hand freely in a library is to put out your blind hand and touch humanity."[23]

The increasing production of paperback books, growing market for books, and developing popular culture in America during the time when this novel was written is observed by Evan Brier in his work on Bradbury's fiction. Brier points out that Bradbury's novel was from the first connected with books, publishing, and the literary marketplace. Thus, it was propelled into life not only by Bradbury's social critique and concern with books and reading but also within the publishing context. Books were the foundation for Bradbury's critique of his times. Among the novels that had an impact on Bradbury's writing of *Fahrenheit 451* was Arthur Koestler's *Darkness at Noon*. Bradbury was concerned about human freedom and concerned by an increasingly dangerous nuclear world. The hydrogen bomb was tested by the United States in October 1952 and by the Soviet Union in July 1953.

Bradbury commented often on books: "First, they can help us lay away those dreams, dreams which might hurt us, they can tell us we are not so good as we think we are . . . the second thing books can give are new and better dreams to replace the bad old one."[24] He called his own work "the fiction of ideas, the fiction where philosophy can be tinkered with, torn apart, and put back together again, it is the fiction of sociology and psychology and history compounded and squared by time. . . . [F]or we all evade the world and its rushing responsibilities at times." Bradbury envisioned radio earpieces that people would wear throughout the day. "I thought I had raced ahead of science, predicting the radio induced semi-catatonic. In the long haul, science pulled abreast, tipped its hat, and fed me the dust." What if Bradbury had known the iPhone? He asked, when does the device "stop being a reasonable escape mechanism and start being a paranoiacally dangerous desire?"[25]

TOM RATH IN SLOAN WILSON'S *THE MAN IN THE GRAY FLANNEL SUIT* (1955)

Despite suburban growth in the 1950s, many of the era's fictional characters do not easily settle into the suburbs. For some of them, there seems to be something missing in life. Sloan Wilson's *The Man in the Gray Flannel Suit* provides one example. Tom Rath, a World War II veteran, works in a corporate office at Rockefeller Center in New York. Tom and his wife Betsy Rath have a home in the suburbs, and Tom takes a train from Connecticut into work in Manhattan. They married before Tom was drafted into the military, where he became a paratrooper. Can he adjust to the gray flannel world? Tom is still trying to be a postwar tough-guy, but his life seems rather empty, divided as it is between his work life and his home life. A ceiling in his home has a crack in it the shape of a question mark. His expenses remind him that he needs to remain ambitious at work, and he applies for an executive role at the United Broadcasting Corporation. He defines himself in terms of the external things that he owns: his car, his house, his GI plan insurance. He is much like poet W. H. Auden's "The Unknown Citizen": dutiful, conforming, helpful but not distinguished by any unique personal qualities or action in the world. He is the ordinary man. His life is closed in, rather than authentic and natural. He wishes upon the stars painted on the ceiling at Grand Central Station.

Tom pauses reflectively from his routine, standing there in Grand Central a bit like Robert Frost's narrator in "Stopping by Woods on a Snowy Evening." In such moments, he wonders what role defines him. Is he a father, a soldier, a hero who killed enemy soldiers in the war? Or is he this cipher riding the train, a man who loves his wife and hates opera? Maybe he should be playing the mandolin more often. Even so, Tom Rath seldom pauses to reflect upon what is shaping his worldview, or why he has corporate business aspirations. The boss asks him how to market mental health. He knows in his heart that mental health is more than a slogan, or a commodity to be marketed and sold. Life ought to be healthy and rich with meaning. Betsy, his wife, says: "We've learned to drag along from day to day without any real emotion except worry. We've learned to make love without passion." Where is passion, desire, hope in their lives? Tom has put on that gray flannel suit and has entered that "frantic parade to nowhere."

JOHN GALT IN *ATLAS SHRUGGED* (1957) BY AYN RAND

In *Atlas Shrugged*, John Galt's key speech spells out the tenets of objectivism. He speaks a rationale for the strike by creative and productive people. John Galt seeks to give values "expression in material form." In this way, an individual's existence will be connected with his or her convictions.[26] In this view, "productive work is in the process by which man's consciousness controls his existence, a consistent process of acquiring knowledge and shaping matter to fit one's purpose, of translating an idea into physical form, of remaking the earth in the image of one's values."[27] In this novel, Rand never says why one has these values or where they may derive from. Nor does she explore why humans have the drive to construct things. When John Galt tells us, "Life is a process of self-sustaining and self-generated action," it seems that we are not far from Charles Darwin's natural selection. The human's saving tool is reason, which directs action. For Galt, "reason is your means of survival" and "man is a being of volitional consciousness."[28] This is a life affirmation, "a single choice: to live."[29]

John Galt, the architect, says that the individualist will engage in "translating an idea into physical form . . . remaking the earth in the image of one's values."[30] The individual mind is not bound by the collective. The individualist is inventive, not imitative; he does not produce in "an uncritical stupor, a routine he has learned from others." Rather, he recognizes that reason and self-reliance is his means for survival. One acts and creates value.[31] Rand's antagonists are those who would curtail John Galt's freedom and would prefer mediocrity and business as usual. John Galt is Nietzsche's superman, or *Ubermensch*: the overman who rejects church and state and relies upon reason and integrity. To be heroic is to realize one's values.[32]

Ayn Rand claims rationality as a virtue. "The virtue of rationality means the recognition and acceptance of reason as one's only source of knowledge, one's only judge of values and one's only guide to action." One makes "a commitment to fullest perception of reality within one's power."[33] The goal is to use reason to avoid "evasion" or "unfocusing your mind and inducing an inner fog to escape the responsibility of judgement. Reason must achieve happiness."[34]

Atlas Shrugged was published in October 1957, within a year of similar Nietzschean emphasis on individualism in Colin Wilson's *The Outsider* and John Osborne's play *Look Back in Anger*, which was focused on the angry young man in Britain in 1956. Concurrent with these works were sociological critiques of conformity that appeared in 1956: *The Organization Man* by William Whyte and *The Power Elite* (April 1956) by C. Wright Mills. Whyte pointed out a collectivist ethic that was at work in American society. Mills shed light on the power of a government and business elite. Rand, amid concern about Soviet totalitarianism, rejected collectivism and asserted the priority of the creative individual. Whereas Rand prized the rational, Norman Mailer and Jack Kerouac wrote with romantic fervor against a limiting rationality. In 1957, Norman Mailer wrote against conformity in his controversial essay "The White Negro." *On the Road* (1957) by Jack Kerouac emphasized the quest for unfettered individuality and freedom.

Rand developed her thought through the 1950s. For a 1961 talk she formulated "The Objectivist Ethics," which is chapter 1 of her book *The Virtue of Selfishness: A New Concept of Egoism*. She wrote that morality is not "a code of behavior imposed on you by whim of a supernatural power or the whim of society."[35] The term *whim* has a certain rhetorical flavor. Faith, feeling, and intuition may be regarded as "whim" rather than the heart's perception, assent, and inner conviction. Rand rejects a God over and against mankind and any social system that presumes to be over and against the individual. The individual asserts his or her own free life. John Galt is a mouthpiece for her philosophy. His antagonists are those who would suffocate life and constrain the individual. For Rand, altruism is opposed to self-reliance. One ought not to subscribe to abstract phrases like "the public good." She declares "the morality of rational self-interest."

Ayn Rand claims that rationality is a virtue. She asserts an ethics of egoism. "The virtue of rationality means the recognition and acceptance of reason as one's only source of knowledge, one's only judge of values and one's only guide to action."[36] John Galt is rational, productive, and fiercely independent. Galt's key speech declares his objectivism, his faith in reason and action. Galt is a man of purpose and "a commitment to the fullest perception of reality within one's power."[37] Galt gives his values expression in his work, believing that "productive work is the process by which man's consciousness controls his existence."[38] Reason directs this action in the world. Galt asserts that a man must live fully by discovering this sense of purpose, a morality, "a single choice to live."[39]

Throughout her work, Ayn Rand asserted a necessary freedom from political constriction, a rejection of the claims of "the public good" as a means of circumscribing the free action of the individual. Rand asserted "the morality of rational self-interest." In her view, morality is not a code of behavior imposed "by a supernatural power or the whim of society." In her 1961 talk "The Objectivist Ethics," she insisted that altruism is opposed to self-reliant action. In *Atlas Shrugged*, we hear John Galt affirm: "no one came to say that your life belongs to you and that the good is to live it."[40] Rand claims that Immanuel Kant's view of moral reason is one that constrains self-interest. Galt stands for the claim that this morality of Kant's categorical imperative was imposed and suggests obeisance to some external authority. The intuitionist approach relies only on feeling or whim. John Galt declares: "It is only the concept of Life that makes the concept of value possible."[41] Indeed, man's mind "is not the mind of a mindless brute . . . but the life of a thinking being."[42]

Yet, one might argue against Rand that self-interest does not occur in isolation on a lonely planet without others. Humanity is interdependent. Immanuel Kant's ethics assert that reason owes recognition to the dignity of other individuals as ends in themselves. Kant believes that moral reason constrains self-interest. For John Galt, this feels imposed, and he will not submit to any categorical imperative. "It is only the concept of 'life' that makes the concept of 'value' possible."[43] The human is a "thinking being" who chooses a path and expresses vitality, for "life" "requires a specific course of action." Real morality is taking charge of one's own life, to be heroic like John Galt. Kant would view this as self-serving subjectivism. However, Rand asserts an ethic of egoism, "the achievement of one's values" expressed in material form. One's "existence is connected with one's convictions."[44]

ROY HOBBS IN *THE NATURAL* (1952) BY BERNARD MALAMUD

Bernard Malamud's baseball story brings together sports betting and the legend of Shoeless Joe Jackson and the White Sox throwing the World Series with the hotel shooting of a baseball player by a deranged fan. Roy Hobbs, his sympathetic and apparently compromised hero, is a character who takes on life through Malamud's imaginative extrapolation from an actual incident.

Eddie Waitkus, first baseman for the Phillies, was an all-star. He was known as "the natural." Ruth Ann Steinhagen was a stalker, an obsessed fan who shot him. On June 14, 1949, she followed him to the Edgewater Beach Hotel where he was staying. The nineteen-year-old insurance company typist used a high school classmate's name as an alias and asked him to visit her room. She gave a bellhop a $5 tip to deliver the fateful note. She ordered two whiskey sours and a daquiri that she drank while waiting. When Waitkus opened the door, he saw a woman with dark hair, a longish nose, and sleepy eyes. She pointed a rifle at him and told him to move toward the window. Then she shot him. Ruth Steinhagen spent three years in an asylum. She told investigators, "If I can't have him, no one will."

Waitkus survived the shooting. He had previously survived a tour of duty in the Philippines in World War II. Steinhagen fell for unattainable celebrities: Alan Ladd, Peanuts Lowery of the Chicago Cubs, and Waitkus. She had developed her obsessive crush on Waitkus when he played with the Chicago Cubs. He was of Lithuanian background and came from Boston, so she studied Lithuanian and ate Boston baked beans. The root of the word *fan* is *fanatic*.

In Malamud's novel, Roy Hobbs is seeking his way in life. Baseball is a metaphor. Roy is circling the bases, and he experiences his life as circular. Roy Hobbs tries to return to baseball for the New York Knights. Flashback: Hobbs boards a train to go to Chicago for a tryout with the Cubs. Max Mercy, a sportswriter, is also on the train. So is Walter ("Whammer") Whambold, the home run hitter who is leading the league and has been a three-time league MVP. Harriet Bird is a mystery woman. At a train stop, where there is a carnival, Hobbs strikes out Whammer. Harriet was going to shoot the best player in the league: Whammer. She now changes that and wants to take aim at Hobbs.

Upon reaching Chicago, Hobbs checks into a hotel. He goes to Harriet's room. She shoots him in the stomach.

Fifteen years after the incident, the New York Knights are on a losing streak as Hobbs joins them. Manager Pop Fisher and his assistant Red Blow are near the end of their careers. Roy Hobbs emerges from the clubhouse tunnel. He has been signed to a contract with the team. If the Knights do not do well in this season, that will be the end of Pop as the team's manager. Hobbs hits the ball into deep right field for a triple. In a game a few days later, Bump Bailey chases a fly ball and crashes into the outfield wall. Roy Hobbs will have to replace him. Sportswriter Max Mercy is back, with memories of the Chicago hotel incident. The sportswriter tries to get him to talk about it. He offers him money and introduces him to a bookie, Gus Sands. Hobbs spends time with Pop's niece, Memo Paris. Pop tells him that she brings bad luck. It appears that bad luck does await. Hobbs falls into a batting slump. Eventually, he hits a home run. He dates a fan, Iris Lemon, and then goes back to Memo Paris, but she rejects him. Hobbs then leads a seventeen-game winning streak for the team, but before the final game he collapses and ends up in the hospital. He has been approached with a bribe by "Judge" to lose the game. He does intend to win the game. But he splits his bat, hitting a ball that injures Iris. The pitcher Herman Youngberry strikes out Hobbs. Game over. Mercy learns that Hobbs was being paid to the throw the game.

"We like *The Natural* enormously and want to publish it," wrote Robert Giroux in a telegram to Malamud on January 7, 1952. Giroux went to Farrar, Straus in 1955 after Harcourt had not let him sign *The Catcher in the Rye* in 1951. Harcourt Brace rejected Malamud's novel *The Assistant*. Giroux took it at Farrar, Straus. Malamud's biographer Philip Davis affirms that Giroux saw "the real Malamud" in *The Assistant*.[45] The grocery was his father's place of business and was representative of an immigrant community. The story of Mr. Bober and his assistant is a moral tale. Critic Leslie Fiedler called *The Assistant* a belated novel of the 1930s. It reflects the time of the Great Depression recalled by Alfred Kazin in *A Walker in the City* (1951) in which immigrant Jews sought work in New York. Malamud told Michiko Kakutani in the *New York Times* (July 15, 1980) that in the Depression "everything went down to bedrock. Experience that deprives you of something can make you realize what it is that you need most, and it sends you inward, and that to a writer is important."[46]

SPARTACUS IN *SPARTACUS* (1951) BY HOWARD FAST

The Thracian gladiator and escaped slave Spartacus was the leader of an uprising during the Third Servile War. Was the rebellion one of an oppressed people fighting for freedom as the author Howard Fast portrays it? We do not know much about Spartacus. Plutarch identified him as "a Thracian of Nomadic stock." He was from the border of Macedonia in southwest Bulgaria. He may have been captured by the Roman legions. The slave became a gladiator, perhaps trained for gladiatorial combat. Around the year 73, there was a plot to escape. The Romans were fighting in Spain at this time. Spartacus led a rebellion. No historian has said that the revolt had the purpose of ending slavery. Gaius Claudius Glaber led troops against Spartacus on Mount Vesuvius. Spartacus went to the south of Italy and then led his people on a northern movement. Marcus Licinius Crassus was chosen to stop the rebellion with eight legions. The forces led by Spartacus moved to the hills west of Petelia (today's Strongoli). Pompey was sent south, and Crassus sought the honor of capturing Spartacus and ending the rebellion. Spartacus made his last stand near Senerchia by the river Sele. The novel and subsequent film conclude with greater grandeur than this abysmal ending. Those who survived the revolt were captured and were crucified along the Appian Way.

Spartacus is a hero of the slave rebellion and an enemy to the Roman Empire. His story acts as a metaphor of the heroic, transgressive rebel who stands up against the powers that would enslave and diminish humanity. The author of *Spartacus*, Howard Fast, implied the abolition of slavery and social oppression by the powers that be. No historian has interpreted the events in that way. For Plutarch, Spartacus sought to travel north to get slaves to bring them back to his homeland. However, we are left with the question of why he then went south. Was this an effort to escape the Roman forces? Did he ever seek to march on Rome and pillage the city? Fast presents Spartacus as a revolutionary. He was not alone in this. There was a Spartacus League in Germany 1915–1918.

The character of Spartacus has a long literary history. Jacob Jones's *Spartacus, or the Roman Gladiator* intended to draw sympathy for the Polish rebels against Russia in 1830. Robert Montgomery Bird's *The Gladiator* (1831) was a play in London. "If *The Gladiator* were produced in a slave state, the managers, players and perhaps myself would be rewarded with the Penitentiary," he said. Bird appeared to call for leadership, a Spartacus, to confront oppression. He then wrote *Shepherd Lee* (1836), which was about abolition. Philadelphia newspapers referred to Toussaint Louverture of Haiti and Gabriel who planned a revolt in Virginia in 1800 as the black Spartacus. By referring to Spartacus, Bird used a classical metaphor. The hero-gladiator was rebelling against the Roman Empire, and the slave was seeking liberty. Bird imagined actor Edwin Forrest in the role. Forrest became a celebrity as Spartacus at the Chestnut Theater in Philadelphia. (Blackface burlesque was played in the 1820s by Charles Matthews at the Arch Street Theater and Walnut Street Theater.) Forrest did blackface and, in 1826, played Othello at the Bowery Theater. The *New York Times* noted he was "fond of Negro minstrelsy." Bird presents Phasius and Spartacus as two gladiators who were required to fight against each other. There is a call for freedom in act 3. Bird showed Spartacus fighting for liberty, although not to end slavery. George Bancroft wrote in the *North American Review* that Spartacus was "a man of genius and courage" and that "slavery made [Rome] a wasteland."[47] In Howard Fast's novel *Spartacus*, as in *The Gladiator*, the antebellum plebeian rebels are cast as heroic and democratic. In the arena, Droba sacrifices himself by attacking Crassus instead of killing Spartacus. Those who join with Spartacus are also depicted as heroic individuals fighting to overcome oppression.

Howard Fast's fiction appeared as an extension of the proletarian novel writers of the 1930s. Fast wrote a short story that appeared in *Amazing Stories* in 1931. The 1930s brought *Two Valleys* (1933) and *Strange Yesterday* (1934). He then wrote five historical novels; extending into the 1940s, he wrote *The Unvanquished* (1942) on George Washington in the American Revolution; *Citizen Tom Paine* (1943); *Freedom Road* (1944); *The Last Frontier* (1944) on Cheyenne Indians; *Clarkton* (1947), a proletarian novel; and *My Glorious Brothers* (1948) on the Maccabean revolt versus Roman overlords. The 1950s began with his novel *Spartacus*, on a slave uprising against the Roman Empire. The revival of Howard Fast's fiction occurred through *The Immigrants*, a series of six novels primarily focused on California families. Throughout the 1940s and 1950s, Fast was seeking social justice through socialism. Gerald Sorin suggests that Fast was influenced by his impoverished childhood and the Great Depression.[48] How else could an attachment to the Soviet model be sustained through the Stalinist period? Fast persisted with his Marxism during the Cold War years, and this political orientation had some imprint on his fiction. In 1947, the House Un-American Activities Committee cited Fast for contempt of Congress when he would not name names or give them Joint Anti-Fascist Refugee Committee notebooks. The New York City public schools banned *Citizen Tom Paine* in 1947.

Fast was at the center of the Peekskill anticommunist riots in summer 1949. Actor Paul Robeson made visits to Fast's house. A concert was planned with Robeson, Pete Seeger, and other music acts, and Fast was to emcee. Robeson had been in Peekskill in 1946, 1947, and 1948. However, in 1949 Robeson's remarks were called anti-American by some people who saw them in the *Peekskill Evening Star* and in the *New York Times*. Robeson asserted: "It is unthinkable that American Negroes would go to war on behalf of those who have oppressed for generations against a country (USSR) which in one generation has raised our people to the full dignity of mankind."[49] In a 1949 opinion poll, 3 percent of Americans surveyed viewed communism as a most serious problem.[50] Did people in Peekskill feel that they were confronting communism, or were they antagonistic toward Robeson because of his race? The *Peekskill Evening Star* and the Peekskill mayor urged the protestors to move their protests elsewhere. Their parade blocked the highway and would interfere with the concert at the Lakeland Picnic Grounds. Chairs were lit on fire. Rocks were thrown.[51] There was no concert. The next day folksinger Pete Seeger sang in Harlem. Robeson vowed that he would return. The national veterans' organization criticized their members. The concert took place this time. However, September 4, 1949, was worse after the show, with a militant mob with bats and chains pounding on cars, throwing rocks, and banging at buses.

Novelist and short story writer T. C. Boyle has suggested that Howard Fast's language was inflammatory, calling protestors Fascists and exploiting the concert for political ends. (Boyle was born December 2, 1948, in Peekskill and must have drawn upon stories from family and neighbors in Peekskill.) In his novel *World's End*, his character Sasha Freeman is modeled on Howard Fast, and it is said that he wanted "to stir things up till they were good and hot." We read: "he hated Sasha Freeman and the worldwide Communist conspiracy." The father asks his son: "You tell me, Walter . . . who the bad guys were." We learn that Walter had no answer.[52] Truman had previously told Walter that his misshapen ear had resulted from a shrapnel wound in the war. However, he now admits that it occurred in the riots. "It's my Judas mark," he says. He was hit on the back roads by a maniac. When the son asks Truman why he was involved, Truman says that he did it "for a higher principle" and as a socialist he had hope in the socialist revolution.[53] This characterizes not only the incident at Peekskill but also the larger issues of the time.

In the 1950s, Fast was often critically rejected or ignored. Hedda Hopper wrote that *Spartacus* was "written by a commie."[54] *Spartacus* had to be privately printed. Fast asked friends to contribute $5 each toward this purpose. Fast began the novel in 1950 while in prison. Fast then wrote *The Passion of Sacco and Vanzetti* (1953), *Silas Timmerman* (1954), and *The Story of Lola Gregg: A Novel* (1955). These books were not widely read or accepted. *Spartacus* would later become a powerful film starring Kirk Douglas and directed by Stanley Kubrick. The National Legion of Decency picketed the film. (The legion, which began in 1933–1934, usually censored French and Italian films.) Kubrick's next film was *Lolita*. The voiceover at the beginning of the film declares that Rome is a republic "that lay fatally stricken with a disease called human slavery." Spartacus was "a proud rebellious son dreaming of the death of slavery 200 years before it would finally die."[55] In Fast's view, Spartacus was a liberator for the workers of the world, an icon for a time that needed a heroic voice for justice.

MINK SNOPES IN *THE MANSION* (1959) BY WILLIAM FAULKNER

Among William Faulkner's repeating characters in his Snopes trilogy is Mink Snopes, a relative who is down on his luck. Mink Snopes has been in jail for the murder of the farmer Houston, his neighbor. Flem Snopes realizes that Mink would kill him if he got out of jail. He tries to keep him there. Whereas Mink is a sympathetic, although flawed, character, Flem Snopes is among the detestable figures in Faulkner's mythical southern landscape.

We meet the despicable Flem Snopes in *The Hamlet*'s Book One, "Flem," in Frenchman's Bend in "rich river-bottom country."[56] Flem has a "tiny predatory nose like the beak of a small hawk."[57] *The Hamlet* connects the stories of Flem's advancement to power. Much of the region is owned by Will Varner: "he is primarily the owner of every enterprise in the village from the store to the cotton gin."[58] Flem works to rise in Varner's employment and becomes his partner, displacing Jody Varner. He schemes and manipulates. The story of his rise gives continuity to *The Hamlet*. V. K. Ratliff, a sewing machine salesman, tells stories of the Snopes family, including stories about Ab Snopes, Flem's father, who was supposedly engaged in barn burning, horse trading, and other activities. Book Two, "Eula," focuses on Eula, Varner's daughter, who is described as "honey in sunlight and bursting grapes":[59] a woman with a sensual quality that attracts the obsessive interest of a man named Labove. It is in Book Three that we learn that Mike Snopes let his cow out to graze in his neighbor's property. He tries to reclaim the cow from the neighbor, Houston, but is rebuffed. Mink loses his bid in court to reclaim the cow and has to pay the rich neighbor $3. He gets a gun in Memphis and kills the man.

In William Faulkner's prefatory note to *The Mansion*, he tells us that he began thinking of the Snopes family in 1925. At that time, he worked on his story "Father Abraham" (later a novel), which he set aside to work on *Sartoris*. *The Hamlet* appeared in 1940. The trilogy is not a continuous story, although the novels interconnect. The reader has to interpret which of the varying accounts is the accurate story of the Snopes family. By the time of *The Mansion* (1959), many characters had been introduced and several of them have been watching the Snopes family. Three narrators provide the stories that comprise *The Mansion*: V. K. Ratliff, the sewing machine agent; Chick Mallison, a Snopes nephew; and Gavin Stevens, a local lawyer who later becomes district attorney. (Chick Mallison has previously appeared with Lucas Beauchamp in *Intruder in the Dust*.) *The Town* is told by Chick, Gavin, and Ratliff, who have different perspectives.

Mink Snopes is at the center of *The Mansion*'s Book One. Mink's arrest has left his wife and children in poverty. He recognizes that he is "one cousin that's still scratching the dirt to stay alive."[60] When he was arrested he still believed that Flem Snopes would not let a relative be hauled from prison and hung. ("Even Flem Snopes ain't going to let his own blood be hung just to save money.")[61] However, Flem did not lift a finger to assist Mink. While Mink is not executed, he lives on with resentment. Flem is a man "belonging simply to money."[62] Mink seeks some justice in this world that seems to be ruled only by money, power, and force. He will look for "a fundamental justice and equality in human affairs" and seek resolution in his quest for revenge.[63]

Mink reflects the laborer of the South who is stuck. He is as much imprisoned by this cash-nexus system as he was in prison at Parchman. Flem Snopes is material success and prosperity turned upside down into love of money. He attempts to appear respectable, but at heart he is not. (Flem is indifferent to Armstid when she tries to get back $5 spent on a spotted pony.) Varner is no better: he has accumulated wealth without any aristocratic dignity. In *The Town*, we hear that Varner possessed "the strictest simple moral standards: that whatever Will Varner decided to do was right."[64] Linda Snopes Kohl is perhaps a character in which lies more hope. With Linda, Faulkner appears to critique the money-lust of postwar American capitalist enterprise. She is not a fully realized "new woman" of independence, but she has been educated by Gavin Stevens, has been radicalized in New York, and has embraced communism. She would leave the cramped, patriarchal world and find a more authentic freedom than can be found in the free market alone.[65]

Mink is a lost soul in a world of hierarchy based on property and financial means. He feels that this world has "continually harassed and harried him into the constant and unflagging necessity of defending his own simple rights." Mink is a man who insists upon "paying his own way."[66] Yet, he has little means to do so. He has rented a "paintless two-room cabin."[67] He laments that "some folks were born to be failures and get caught always," and he is "one of them."[68] His form of justice may rid the world of Flem Snopes, but it does not transform human indifference and neglect; it does not eliminate selfishness. The Faulkner critic Noel Polk writes: "[W]e are sorry indeed if only Mink can save our world from a Snopes."[69]

5

SAINTS, SINNERS, AND NOTORIOUS NARCISSISTS

GO TELL IT ON THE MOUNTAIN (1953) BY JAMES BALDWIN

John Grimes struggles with spirit and flesh, his environment and family legacy, religious faith and resistance to belief. His reference points are neighborhood, family, and church. *Go Tell It on the Mountain* offers us John's life journey in his adolescence toward manhood. His father Gabriel leads the congregation, and John must face what is expected of him by his family and the church congregation. His brother Roy's curses and his troubles in the Harlem neighborhood are an ongoing part of John's life. The story unfolds through the perspectives of John and the memories of his family members: his father Gabriel, his mother Elizabeth, and his aunt, Gabriel's sister, Florence. John appears to be attracted by an older boy, Elisha, who assists in the church.

Baldwin gradually reveals his character's life stories by intersecting the family member's memories and perspectives. We learn that Gabriel married Elizabeth after his first wife Deborah died. Deborah had been raped and outcast, and Gabriel married her. During the marriage, Gabriel had an affair with a servant girl, which brought a son into the world. Gabriel holds a great deal of pride and regret, and his sister Florence remains a concerned and critical voice in his life. The novel gradually unfolds the story of Elizabeth's tender relationship with an altogether decent young man named Richard, who is John's biological father. Years ago, Richard was mistaken in a subway incident caused by some petty criminals, wrongly accused, and fatally injured. We are also brought into Florence's story and into her essential aloneness. This family is broken, dysfunctional, yet ever experiencing twisted love. From within this cauldron John must recast himself and forge a destiny.

John's dramatic conversion on the threshing floor is at the center of his story. He is involved in the community's speech and practices while critical of them. His lyrical flights have the quality of the preacher. Yet, he is defiant. He will not be bound by this church community's ways, yet he is held by its structures and the presumed piety of his father, Gabriel. He struggles with the notion of sin. We read: "And the darkness of John's sin was like the darkness of the church on Saturday evenings."[1] John is engaged in a quest for insight, apart from his father's expectations. He does not subscribe to a pattern of dogma. Rather, he experiences the pain of conversion, an unquiet "terror." ("And he began to scream again in his great terror.") We read that this power "had cracked him open."[2] This is the apophatic way of a dark night of the soul and piercing illumination of spirit. John's emergence is self-discovery, a grasp of his existence and identity.

Baldwin unfolds the story through flashbacks, intersecting the lives of his characters. John is affected by his mother Elizabeth's past and her insecurities, as well as by his father's dominance. Gabriel's pride is seen "moving outward in fiery darkness."[3] Florence cannot forgive Gabriel his misdeeds, or forgive her mother, a former slave, who favored Gabriel and set Florence aside. She remains lonely and stuck in time. Florence forces Gabriel to look at his past mistakes, his sins and his brokenness, particularly his illegitimate son Royal, and at his infidelity to Deborah. In a sense, she speaks Deborah's case for her, asserting Deborah's right to womanhood and dignity.[4] Florence steadily encourages John: "you fight the good fight." She insists, "I know the Lord's done laid hands on you."[5]

One of the most arresting aspects of the novel are Baldwin's lyrical narrative riffs. There is musicality in Baldwin's writing: passages in which his phrasing breaks out and sings. There is a voice that has been forged, drawing attention to the rhythms and linguistic aspects of expression. John Grimes participates in this voice. This character evokes the quest for insight and re-creation of the self through language and expression. As Baldwin writes in his essay *The Devil Finds Work*: "Identity would seem to be the garment with which one covers the nakedness of the self." Baldwin encourages self-creation: "force the world to deal with you, not with its idea of you."[6]

James Baldwin is a writer who compels us to think. As critic William Giraldi discovered, to read Baldwin brings one of those "encounters when a reader understands he'll never be safe from a writer." Read Baldwin and one "has to imbibe him whole."[7] Baldwin challenges us still: the black, gay, artist outsider shines a perceptive light on the modern condition. This is a writer concerned with the struggle of souls, one who probes the interior spirit of his characters. Baldwin is lyrical, personal, semiautobiographical: an excavator through the sediment of social injustice. Baldwin's characters are reflective, pinned to a place and its material conditions, its religious faith, and its doubts. Giraldi cites Langston Hughes, who observed that in Baldwin's prose he "uses words as the sea uses waves, to flow and beat, advance and retreat, rise and take a bow in disappearing."[8] Baldwin's prose lifts the reader, with his framing of a sentence, his rhythmic sense of the line. In the first novel, somehow God is on the streets and in the difficult dance of love and conflict between a family, each member of which has a story and a perspective. The father-son tension in *Go Tell It on the Mountain* is intense, and the atmosphere is knotted with the struggle of individuals whose histories and thoughts are gradually revealed.

Baldwin appears to have always been keenly interested in aspects of "salvation," or the liberation of the voice and soul and freedom from oppression. He explores the problem of bitterness defeating racial understanding in his essay "The Harlem Ghetto." He begins by examining how the African American press addresses African American life. He comments on the voice of vocalist Lena Horne; the political action of Paul Robeson, which he considers not quite on track; and the problems created by congressional committee investigations (e.g., the House Un-American Activities Committee). Baldwin argues that for the black press to emulate the white press is to "render utterly unconvincing" the black experience. "It is a black man's newspaper straining for recognition and a foothold in a white man's world," he argues.[9] These newspapers and periodicals have to report on the violence in the black community of Harlem, not ignore it. Baldwin then examines religion and the faith expression in churches in Harlem. He proceeds to reflections on African Americans and Jews as both outsiders. "The images of the suffering Christ and the suffering Jew are wedded with the image of the suffering slave," he writes.[10] Salvation is bought with pain, and it is realized by commitment and hope.

HAZEL MOTES IN *WISE BLOOD* (1952) BY FLANNERY O'CONNOR

Wise Blood, Flannery O'Connor's first novel, is a strange and haunting book featuring a peculiar character, Hazel Motes. His internal struggle is presented through a narrative that is objective, reportorial, and visual. Violence works its way into Hazel's emotional emptiness. Hazel Motes returns from war questioning belief. As the story begins, Hazel is on a train. He wears a new blue suit and sits on a "green plush seat" across from Mrs. Hitchcock. Mrs. Wally Bee Hitchcock, a widow, is a respectable but shallow southern woman. "She was a fat woman with pink collars and cuffs and pear-shaped legs that slanted off the train set and didn't reach the floor."[11] "I guess you're going home," she says to him. Of course, home is one of the concerns in this story. For where is home anymore for this returning veteran? The train in motion is a conveyance of transition, tracing across the threshold of life. It takes him on a pilgrimage through the city of man to the city of God: into his own soul. Hazel is hazy. His surname, Motes, suggests little bits of dust that obscure clear vision. The returning veteran cannot see clearly. Nor does he want to. Looking into his eyes, Mrs. Hitchcock sees them as "passages leading somewhere." After Hazel leaves the train, a cab driver associates him with preachers and remarks: "It ain't anybody perfect on this green earth of God's, preachers nor nobody else."[12]

Hazel Motes is a bewildered man who tries to control the world. He tries to assert that he is not a preacher. Hazel is haunted by a dream of his deceased mother.[13] He squints through her glasses. In his rooms in Taulkinham, Tennessee, he practices self-mortification. He purchases lime at a store and blinds himself with it. Mrs. Flood, his landlady, does not understand this and thinks that Motes must be a madman. Her name suggests the liberating waters of baptism and the destructive water of Noah's deluge. She is a lonely woman who says, "If we don't help each other, Mr. Motes, there's nobody to help us. Nobody. The world is an empty place."[14] Yet, perhaps Motes may move toward inner vision though physically blinded. He recalls Oedipus and the blind seer Tiresias in Greek mythology. "Who better than the blind to lead the blind who know what it is like." Mrs. Flood sees him moving away into darkness like a pinpoint of light.[15]

A wild, ragged figure pursues Hazel. This is a Jesus figure whose reality Hazel denies. Hazel Motes has created a church without Christ. He asserts that he does not believe and pushes the Christ figure away. "I don't have to run away from anything because I don't believe in anything," he says.[16] "Jesus has been a long time gone," says the porter, at one point. The porter's observation of this absence is a recognition of the secularization of society.

Hazel Motes is not relational. He has no friends. The people in his life are only passing acquaintances. Some, like Mrs. Flood or Enoch, are curious. Others are despicable. Hoover Shoats founds a church for financial gain. He is a swindler, a corrupt preacher, and religious shallowness personified. Solace Layfield is a false prophet. Hazel opposes the divine. He is an anti-theist seeking to revise the gospel. However, he cannot live a secular gospel. He is tugged by a grace that he rejects. He has no community to turn to for care or guidance. Rather, in his attempt at re-vision he becomes unable to see.

Hazel blinds himself with lime. Yet, he seems to make a leap of faith. Upon his self-blinding what does Hazel see? Violence affects this fictional world. We may ask how grace interacts with this world. Hazel runs over Solace Layfield with a car. Good and evil crisscross here in a Manichaean world of good and evil. Frederick Assals writes: "*Wise Blood* is, in a precise sense, nightmarish in a way found nowhere else in her work."[17] *Wise Blood* is symbolic. Motes, like Oedipus, becomes a blind man. Is this conversion or disillusion? Mrs. Flood is fascinated by Hazel and moves to marry him. Hazel runs away. It is claimed that he did not pay his rent. The police chase him and club him down. In the end, he is still disconnected. He is an anchorite, not a person in community. The eyes of Hazel for Mrs. Flood are significant: "the deep burned eye-sockets seemed to lead into a dark tunnel where he had disappeared."[18] Critic Debra Cumberland sees no human connectedness in *Wise Blood*. There is apparently no love or compassion in the end, Cumberland observes.[19] If that is so, where is there a Christian resolution?

Perhaps we may say that Hazel Motes begins to make a gradual transition from a world in which God is absent through the apophatic darkness toward spiritual vision. Even so, the tension between faith and nihilism is never so certain. Hazel Motes begins to take walks and, eventually, falls into a drainage ditch at a construction site. A train has brought us into this story, and we follow a tunnel out of it. Flannery O'Connor gives us a broken grotesque, a troubled, disintegrating man seeking faith in the wasteland. It is unclear whether Hazel Motes can point the way to some redemption for Mrs. Hitchcock, Mrs. Flood, and the other characters: the floundering, the meek, and the lowly who seek a spiritual home.

HUMBERT HUMBERT IN *LOLITA* (1955) BY VLADIMIR NABOKOV

Vladimir Nabokov shocked some readers with his story of middle-aged Humbert Humbert's obsession with the prepubescent Dolly Haze. Humbert is a seductive narrator. He has experienced thoughts, emotions, and events surrounding the girl he calls Lolita and is now telling us his story. It appears that he has written this account while in a psychopath ward for observation. So, how reliable can his narration possibly be? His narrative is a self-conscious memoir that he creates for posterity, for some future audience. "I have only words to play with," he says.[20] And clever words they are. Will a reader approach him with sympathy or repulsion?

Lolita may be read as a self-conscious parody. *Lolita* is a memoir presumably written by Humbert Humbert, a European academic who is enamored with young girls and is obsessed with Dolores "Lolita" Haze. *Lolita* is set in the late 1940s and early 1950s. We read Humbert's point of view: clever, twisted, comic, grotesque, and self-serving. The frame is provided by a fictional editor, John Ray Jr. Dr. Ray declares: "As a case history Lolita will become . . . a classic in psychiatric circles."[21] We move to the narrative point of view of Humbert, who makes an allusion to Edgar Allan Poe's 1849 poem "Annabel Lee."[22] There is a suggestion of Poe's relationship with his young cousin. (The "lee" sound of Lolita echoes 'Leigh.') Humbert's oddly directed Eros is the issue, not Lolita's youthful capacity for seduction, as the later Stanley Kubrick film posters may have suggested. Lolita has little sex appeal, and she is no temptress or seductive nymph. She is the object of fascination in Humbert's psyche, and this account of her is a matter of his subjectivity. Humbert tends to view himself as a sufferer, a lover, and an intellectual.

Nabokov's prose is so enticing that we are made to become sympathetic with Humbert, critics like Martin Green, F. W. Dupee, and Alfred Appel Jr. have claimed. Lionel Trilling writes that Humbert's "unrelenting self-reference" and "impious greediness . . . seduce us into kinship with him." This man's sexual issues are "made funny, beautiful, pathetic, romantic, tragic." Humbert lures us into reader identification: "He is ourselves without inhibitions, acting out our tendencies," suggests Green.[23] Really? One may wonder who these people are that Green regards as "we." Humbert's self-deception, his wit, and social observation may be interesting, but something is surely wrong with this man. Activist Dorothy Day wrote in her journal on Saturday, December 31, 1959, the last day of the decade: "Last night I sat up reading *Lolita*, a truly terrible tale, a horrible picture of American life, a vicious tale."[24]

Humbert is the son of a Swiss father and an English mother. He was raised by his aunt and father after his mother died from a lightning strike. Educated in Lyon and in Paris, he has become an academic in Ramsdale, where he intends to focus on French grammar. From the residence at 342 Lawn Street, he sees Lolita sunning in the yard. He becomes acquainted with her mother, Charlotte, who casts him as her lover and quasi-husband. Charlotte, a postwar single mother from the Midwest, is more age appropriate. However, he is attracted to Dolores, who he refers to as Lolita. Lolita is sent away to summer camp, where she learns about sex. When Charlotte dies, Lolita is orphaned. Humbert imagines he will take her to a hotel and drug her. Lolita vanishes into this scenario, and she is captive. Lolita, like her mother, appears to be an image of the 1950s suburban consumer weaned on television, advertising, and popular culture. She is interested in fashion, has known no father, and now has no mother. Lolita might be placed alongside Holden Caulfield in *The Catcher in the Rye* and the youthful characters in William Golding's *Lord of the Flies*. All of these are troubled young characters.

The amoral and corrupted Clare Quilty is Humbert's nemesis. Quilty is a writer of plays like *The Little Nymph*. Given Quilty's perverse interests, conflict ensues between him and Humbert. Quilty is found dead, shattered by a bullet. Humbert is imprisoned. He admits to his murder of his rival, Quilty. And so, Humbert's writing of his memoir begins. Humbert confesses that if he was the jury in his own case, he might give himself a substantial prison sentence: "Had I come before myself, I would have given Humbert at least thirty-five years for rape."[25]

The novel was denied publication. It was regarded as pornographic and banned in France, taken at Canadian customs, and resisted in the United States. Penguin Books was prosecuted for its publication in Britain. Its publisher, Putnam, insisted upon its literary merit. So did several critics, notably Lionel Trilling. In an introduction to a casebook edition of *Lolita*, Eileen Pifer writes: "The outrage expressed by many of *Lolita*'s readers over the past fifty years may be due, in part, to the discomfort they feel at finding themselves taken in by the narrator's rhetoric, at realizing they have unwittingly accepted and even identified with Humbert's perverse desire." Philosopher Richard Rorty refers to Humbert as a "monster of incuriosity" and raises the question of whether Humbert has ever truly seen and recognized Lolita as a person.[26]

Tracing Lolita

There have been attempts to trace Lolita and Humbert to child abuser Frank La Salle and to Florence Sally Horner, a girl he abducted in New Jersey in 1948. *The Real Lolita* by Sarah Weinman provides an interesting account. Newspaper records also fill in some of the story.[27] Florence Sally Horner was kidnapped from a Woolworth's store located at the bottom of Broadway in Camden. Girls from school who had formed a club initiation rite cajoled her into shoplifting a small notebook. La Salle saw her taking the notebook and posed as an FBI agent, frightening her and threatening to tell on her. He then told her that she had to go to Atlantic City with him. When she complied, he abducted her. For two years, kidnapping victim Florence Sally Horner was taken to various locations across the country. On March 22, 1950, she made a phone call home while her captor was away. La Salle, pictured in a photo as a hat-shadowed "hawk-faced" man with an ugly mouth and angular nose, was arrested, tried, and imprisoned. The story came to a pitiful end when Sally Horner died in an accident in Woodbine, New Jersey, on her way home from a date at the New Jersey shore at Wildwood a few years later. How can anyone not feel sad about Sally Horner and disgusted by her abductor? Readers do not necessarily feel similarly about Humbert Humbert and Dolores Haze.

We read in *Lolita*: "Only the other day we read in the newspapers [. . .] about a middle-aged morals offender who pleaded guilty in violation of the Mann Act and to transporting a nine-year-old girl across state lines for immoral purposes, whatever they are!"[28] Of course, the source hardly accounts for the imaginative reach of Nabokov's novel. Humbert, who is haunted by this story, is in prison for the murder of Clare Quilty. The self-delusion and narrative masks with which his story of obsession is articulated are decidedly more artful than newspaper reports of a young girl's abduction by a perverse pedophile. Humbert is a complex character with a striking story and a compelling voice. To know the story behind Nabokov's tale does not give us Nabokov's creative fiction. It is what he did with this case, what it may have suggested to his creative mind, that is most fascinating.

CATHY AMES IN *EAST OF EDEN* (1952) BY JOHN STEINBECK

Cathy Ames is a troubling character at the center of John Steinbeck's *East of Eden*. Some critics have described her as evil incarnate. Steinbeck's novel is a panoramic investigation of good and evil, a parable expressed within family histories. Cathy (Kate) Trask is portrayed as an evil monster. This may raise the question of whether this is physiological and arises from a genetic defect, or whether this is a spiritual defect. Steinbeck would title his later 1961 novel *The Winter of Our Discontent*: a title that evokes memories of Shakespeare's character Richard III. Whereas *The Winter of Our Discontent* probes moral issues in contemporary society and in the mind of the protagonist and his family, *East of Eden* shows us Cathy's evil. From a feminist viewpoint, however, she may also be like the madwoman in the attic of Sandra Gilbert and Susan Gubar: a woman whose vital life is trapped by patriarchal codes who insists upon breaking out, however violently. One may ask how assumptions revolving around gender affect Cathy Ames and contribute to her resistance and her morally problematic actions. Freudian psychoanalytical approaches may also be applied to reading Cathy/Kate within the family romance. Indeed, the sibling rivalry between Adam and Charles and Adam's attraction to his stepmother can all be read through this lens.[29]

Cathy is said to have a "malformed soul." She is a moral conundrum in a story in which characters represent opposing moral views. Cathy is perverse, and she uses people. Samuel Hamilton, in contrast, reflects virtue ethics and classical elements of character, or arête, and moral self-improvement. He is a modern romantic and idealist with an aesthetic and moral sensibility. Hamilton, however, is more utilitarian and pragmatic in his work of selling Ford motor cars to consumers. Part Two begins to bring the families together as Samuel Hamilton begins to become familiar with the Trasks. Cathy has arrived at Charles and Adam's doorstep. Samuel is taken aback by Cathy's evil. He compels Adam Trask to take more responsibility.

Despite her attempt at an abortion, Cathy gives birth to twins. Cathy abandons the children and becomes a madam at a brothel. There she plans to manipulate the madam and to then murder her and seize control of the business. Samuel and Lee meet with Adam to name the boys, Caleb and Aron. The Cain and Abel motif will repeat in them, and the discussion of this at the center of the novel makes this clear. The Hamilton family appears to decline in the next section of the novel, and the story of the Trasks again moves to the foreground. Samuel and Lee, who express the good, engage in discussions with Adam that probe the problem of good and evil. In the final section, the Trasks leave their farm and go to the town. Lee assists in raising the boys and offers moral advice. Cal will reject his brother Aron, who is representative of goodness and will die. Adam, affected by the loss, has to find within himself the ability to forgive Caleb. Kate experiences transformations in conscience, although her end is tragic.

East of Eden is like a quilt of intertextual shapes and patterns. Steinbeck incorporated allegorical materials that reflect Genesis in the Bible, the myths of King Arthur and his Knights, and his own earlier California stories that are set in the Salinas Valley. He drew upon experience, imagination, family history, and newspaper accounts from Salinas. He contemplated his fiction set in Salinas for a long time and spent five years working on it. He makes use of lengthy expository passages and interjects a first-person narrative in which he appears to offer some of his own recollections. Three parts of *East of Eden* begin in the first-person narrative point of view. These are imaginative and self-reflexive passages, which may be viewed as features of romance, rather than intrusive narrative error as some critics have claimed.

HOLLY GOLIGHTLY IN *BREAKFAST AT TIFFANY'S* (1958) BY TRUMAN CAPOTE

The narrator of *Breakfast at Tiffany's* first becomes aware of Holly Golightly, his neighbor downstairs, when he sees a mailbox with her name and Apartment 2 written on it. Holly Golightly becomes the center of his story. She is around eighteen or so and plays her sexuality and charms to wealthy men, hoping to marry one someday. Meanwhile, playing with romance and trying to be a dream girl, she is sure to be taken care of. As the novella begins, the narrator, who lives in the East 70s in New York City, is reminded of her by Joe Bell, who runs the bar nearby on Lexington Avenue. The narrator, a writer, recalls that he and Holly Golightly often went to Joe's bar to use the telephone. "For all her chic thinness, she had an almost breakfast-cereal air of health," the narrator recalls. She wore a black dress. She had a large mouth, "nose upturned," and dark glasses that hid her eyes. Holly Golightly had "a face beyond childhood, yet this side of belonging to a woman."[30]

Holly Golightly sustains her life through her charm and her affairs. She clings to wealthy men who take her out to clubs. Returning late at night from her escapades, she comes in through the bedroom window. The narrator recalls that she once was homeless, an orphan. She was married as a teenager to a man to whom she never would return. Her teen life appears to have been problematic. From a rural home she arrived in the city, attempting sophistication, drawing attention. She visits racketeer Salvatore (Sally) Tomato in prison. Rusty Trawler, a would-be suitor, has been often divorced. O. J. Berman, an agent, claims that she can be an actress. If so, she is already onstage in her daily life. Meg Wildwood, her friend, has been her roommate. And what is her relationship with women? The story offers suggestions that she may be bisexual. The narrator, a projection of Capote himself, is gay. Capote challenges the heterosexual norm. The film adaptation downplays this. One sees New York City, and Audrey Hepburn in her black dress. In his novelette, Capote presents relationships in which desire, sex, and power are at play. In an interview with Eric Norden in

1968, Capote referred to Holly Golightly as a "geisha." She was, he said, like those girls who arrive in New York, spin in the sun, and then disappear.[31]

In popular terms, the film projects romantic fantasy, and Tiffany's represents glamour. However, this does not capture Capote's sly commentary on the 1950s. Capote's novelette explores a complex sexuality. Holly is a young woman exercising her sexual freedom. Yet, she is also a morally bereft problem child, a party girl who is viewed through the eyes of a nostalgic, dreamy narrator. Holly receives $100 a week for visiting Sally in prison. She brings his "weather" to his "lawyer," unaware that this is information that helps him sustain his drug trade. Holly has a romance with Jose Yabara-Jaeger, a South American politician, and becomes pregnant. Can she now play the role of a 1950s housewife? News of her brother's death in the war upsets her. She is then connected with Sally Tomato and arrested. Jose, fearing a shadow will fall on his political ambitions, does not want to be associated with her. He returns to Brazil. A riding accident in Central Park ends her pregnancy. Holly Golightly decides that she cannot inform on Sally Tomato. She will leave town.

TOM RIPLEY IN *THE TALENTED MR. RIPLEY* (1955) BY PATRICIA HIGHSMITH

Novelists of suspense like Patricia Highsmith certainly knew well their fictional saints and sinners. Tom Ripley is a sinner: he is a devious manipulator, a liar, a forger, and an impersonator. He gets the affluent Herbert Greenleaf to believe that he was a Princeton classmate of his son, Dickie. Ripley is hired by Greenleaf to find his son in Italy and bring him home. Upon completing his voyage to Europe, Ripley meets Meredith Logue and impersonates Dickie Greenleaf. He locates Dickie at a seaside resort in Italy and is soon entangled in his affairs. Dickie has a romance, gets the young woman pregnant, and then casts her off. She commits suicide by drowning, and Tom Ripley, who knows this, is supposed to keep that a secret. However, it seems that Ripley wants to be Dickie Greenleaf. He becomes increasingly entangled with him, to the point that he will attempt to take his identity . . . but first, Dickie will have to die. (Oh, there's more—but why give it away?)

There is a curious variation on the double, or doppelgänger, here. The duplicitous Tom Ripley is arguably similar enough to Dickie to impersonate him. This cunning and brutal identity theft is anticipated from the start. The suspense relies upon our acquaintance with Tom Ripley's "talent" and our curiosity about whether his clever manipulations and masquerading will succeed. We are engaged by a criminal antihero, one who is getting away with murder.

Tom Ripley is jauntily confident, superior, and inventive. He is daring, amoral, and cunning. He achieves what is possible and expedient as if it is all a clever game. Tom is a solitary, disturbing figure who lacks conscience. He gets away with his schemes and rationalizes away his deeds. His journey to Europe is that of an expatriate who will create a new identity abroad. Dickie Greenleaf, who had gone to Europe to try to become a painter, is of a different class. Tom Ripley is intrigued and moved by material desire. Yet, he is cold. We read: "You were supposed to see soul through the eyes." However, looking "in Dickie's eye Tom saw nothing more than he would have seen if he had looked at the hard, bloodless surface of a mirror."[32] Tom never sees Dickie Greenleaf. He sees himself and his possibilities.

MAURICE BENDRIX IN *THE END OF THE AFFAIR* (1951) BY GRAHAM GREENE

In *The End of the Affair*, British novelist Graham Greene retreats from melodrama to meditations on faith and fidelity and infidelity. This is the story of the affair and conversion of Sarah Miles, who has an affair with Maurice Bendrix while living with her husband Henry in Clapham Common. (This is a location whose name recalls a nineteenth-century evangelical religious sect that advocated missionary work and opposed slavery.) The narrator is Maurice Bendrix, a writer, and we see this world largely from his point of view. Attention is given to the inner life, or psychology, of Bendrix and of Sarah. Bendrix is an unreliable narrator, caught within his issues and perspective. However, Greene also brings to this narrative a discovered diary by Sarah and letters that Bendrix writes to Sarah.

Sarah is having an affair with Maurice. Henry Mills, a civil servant, is upset about his wife's apparent adultery. We see him in the first pages of the story walking through the rain. The affair casts a lingering doubt over Bendrix's relationship with Sarah. Bendrix is a writer. He insists upon writing five hundred words a day. Of Sarah, he writes: "I liked her at once, because she said she had read my books and left the subject there. I found myself treated at once as a human being rather than as an author."[33] Bendrix recognizes when "the bitterness leaks again" from his pen and his spirit. He writes: "Sometimes I see myself reflected too closely in other men for comfort, and then I have an enormous wish to believe in the saints, in heroic virtue."[34] Yet, he rejects the notion of a God. Meanwhile, Sarah is sympathy and goodness, realizing grace. Bendrix reflects that it sometimes seems to him that "her abandonment touched that strange mathematical point of endlessness, a point with no width, occupying no space."[35] This is, in other words, a more mystical point not easily defined by reason: perhaps that still point of the turning world suggested by T. S. Eliot in his poem "Burnt Norton" in *Four Quartets*.

Sarah's adultery and sexual relationship with Bendrix leads to her spiritual awakening. While in Bendrix's apartment, they face an air raid. A bomb explodes, and Bendrix, who has gone downstairs, gets trapped under the rubble. Sarah prays for Bendrix's safety and makes a bargain that she will detach from the relationship if God will spare Bendrix's life. When Bendrix survives the incident and returns upstairs, she insists that his survival was miraculous. Sarah seeks religious instruction from a priest, Father Crampton. Bendrix, an atheist, does not understand her turn toward God or from her relationship with him. He discovers entries in her diary in which she speaks of her love for him.

Bendrix writes: "The words of human love have been used by the saints to describe their vision of God, and so, I suppose, we might use the terms of prayer, meditation, contemplation to explain the intensity of the love we feel for a woman."[36] An affair has led Sarah through a *via negativa*, or dark night of the soul, toward intimacy and a sense of transcendent experience. Bendrix does not have a path through the dark other than his recognition of Sarah's passion and love for him. Bendrix is unable to accept God as a possibility.

The End of the Affair has been sometimes viewed as the end of Greene's "Catholic phase," which included *The Power and the Glory*. Greene meditated on approaches to Christian faith. For Greene, the convert, faith was intuitive, a gift of God. Belief was factual, based upon reason. Similar approaches to faith may be found in the rational approach of Scholasticism, or St. Thomas Aquinas, or in the volitional approach of St. Augustine and the path of the mystics. Greene appears to have reflected on the apophatic approach of mystics.

The Quiet American, which followed, is a political book in which news reporter Thomas Fowler tells us about life in Vietnam. The story emerged from Greene's four winter visits to Indochina. He watched the failing battle of the French to hold their colonial possession against the communist nationalists. Greene appears to have had some sympathy for the effort. However, he later continued to be critical of the American presence in Vietnam. In *The Quiet American*, Alden Pyle is a sympathetic character, an innocent man who believes in the mission. Pyle is confident but not sophisticated, sincere and well-intentioned but ill informed. He possesses courage, and he saves Fowler in a communist guerilla region. When Fowler is wounded, Pyle carries him to safety across a swamp. Fowler, in contrast, is more cynical. He is a man who is displaced and alienated. As a reporter, he must remain objective in his work as he observes and inquires. He is a witness to the failure of the French to maintain their colony ("let them fight, I would not be involved").[37] Thomas Fowler is anti-American. He is also a doubting Thomas: a man separated from both God and society, an observer.

Several critics have observed in *The Quiet American* Greene writing a political novel and getting away from his previous focus on religious themes. However, religious elements are present. Caodaism among the Vietnamese is a syncretic cultural religious practice that combines elements of Buddhism, Christianity, Taoism, and folk religion. In it "all truths are reconciled, and truth is love."[38] Fowler remains agnostic. For Fowler, God is absent. People have needed "a being capable of understanding."[39] So, they have developed "a fable of the changeless and permanent."[40] We hear that God is "so vast." God must "look different to everyone."[41] Fowler's cynicism and rationality limit his ability to have faith. He concludes that death is certain; God is not. Greene remains interested in the apophatic way: the passage through the dark night. Toward the end of the novel, we meet Granger and hear the statement: "I was praying. I thought if maybe God wanted a life, he could take mine."[42]

Fowler's Vietnamese mistress Phuong will eventually be lost to Pyle, the quiet American who represents American culture. Pyle's naïveté gets him into trouble. He believes that Vietnam can achieve the ideal of a noncommunist and nonimperialist state. He arms a local warlord who then detonates a bomb in a crowded market area, killing civilians. Fowler wants to avoid future calamity. Yet, choices lead to Pyle's death. Fowler wonders: Why didn't Pyle stay home with his family photographs? He belonged in "the skyscraper and the express lift," not in Vietnam.

The situation that America was in during the 1960s would generate new readings of *The Quiet American*. One might consider Pyle's idealism, or his naïveté and inexperience in the Far East. Or one might question the French colonial enterprise and see America's involvement in Indochina as a continuation of it. Greene's anti-American attitudes appear to have been directed at the trivialities and vacuous aspects of popular culture rather than at U.S. overseas political involvements.

The novels of Graham Greene in the 1950s intrigued readers on both sides of the Atlantic. Preceding the 1950s was his novel *The Heart of the Matter* (1948), which is set in Sierra Leone during the Second World War. Greene served there in the British Secret Service. Scobie is a worn-out man facing a moral crisis. He feels like he is caught in a dull and tedious marriage. (We only see Louise from his point of view: a limitation of perspective Greene later regretted.) He has been passed up for the commissioner's position. Scobie finds his colonial life similarly unstimulating. Yet, he will not retire. He wishes for peace.

Following *The End of the Affair*, Greene wrote *Loser Takes All* (1955), a novella that involved another couple's romance, marriage, and separation. An accountant, Bertram, is going to be married to Cary. The company boss, Dreuther, reframes their wedding plans and pushes them to marry in Monte Carlo aboard his yacht. Once they arrive in Monte Carlo, they look for Dreuther, but he never arrives. Bertram gets involved with gambling and suddenly becomes very successful, winning a lot of money. Mr. Bowles, an enemy and rival of Dreuther, wants access to Bertram's money and to steal Dreuther's business. Cary does not like seeing Bertram caught up in his gambling system. She meets an eligible individual and thinks of leaving Bertram. Then, finally, Dreuther arrives.

With *Our Man in Havana* (1959), Greene takes a comic turn and plays upon absurdities of the Cold War. His spy story is set in Cuba, where Warmold, a vacuum salesman, is recruited by the British MI6.

Warmold needs money, so he takes the job. Warmold's wife has left him with his sixteen-year-old daughter Milly. He begins to make up stories about spies lurking in the vicinity. The British spy agency believes the reports he sends to London. They are concerned about the secret installation he says that he has seen in the hills: one he fabricates with used vacuum cleaner parts. They send a secretary, Beatrice Severn, and a radio assistant, code-named "C." Soon Warmold draws the attention of the Soviets and potential danger.

SERGIUS O'SHAUGHNESSY IN *THE DEER PARK* (1955) BY NORMAN MAILER

Sergius O'Shaughnessy has escaped to Desert D'Or, which appears to be a cross between Palm Springs–Palm Desert and Las Vegas. The environment is sunlit, surrounded by desert, golf courses, the natural and the unnatural, and the artful and the artificial. It is through the consciousness of Sergius O'Shaughnessy that we look at this scene. He casts a moral gaze over Desert D'Or: a seedy bar, and the image of "a fat old man in a Palm Beach leisure suit talking to a young girl with orange lipstick." It is a world of gangsters, actors, showgirls, the "theatrical darkness of afternoon" fading into "illuminated night."[43]

Shaughnessy grew up in an orphanage. Sergius tells us that he got his "princely name" from his father.[44] After his mother died, his father raised him until he was five. Then he was placed in the orphanage. He ran away five times from the home that was run by the religious sisters. He read a lot, especially adventure stories about brave men like Robin Hood. ("I read constantly when I was a boy.") He declines to tell us much about it. "It's a trap to spend time writing too much about it," he says. "Self-pity comes into the voice."[45] He tells us about his time in the air force, his surrogate family, and where he saved pilots and they saved him. He recalls his time at an airfield near Tokyo in postwar Japan.[46] Sergius recalls war: "I realized that I had been busy setting fire to a dozen people or two dozen, or had it been a hundred?" He says that he did not like bombing villages but focused on technique: "from the air a city in flames is not a bad sight."[47] Yet, he suffered a "small breakdown," spent time in a hospital, and gave up flying. He tells us that, while in the orphanage and in the air force, he "had such a desire to be like everyone else, at least like everyone else that had made it."[48] To escape it all, he went to Desert D'Or.

Sergius is living on gambling winnings and overcoming his breakdown. Seeking freedom, he makes a journey through memories, temptation, shadows, and bright lights. "I was understood to be an Air Force pilot whose family was wealthy and lived in the East."[49] We meet Dorothea O'Faye, a former actress and nightclub singer, who is at the center of a club called the Hangover where hangers-on gather. When drunk, she becomes violent and throws things.[50] She dislikes film director Charles Francis Eitel, who is befriended by O'Shaughnessy.[51] Dorothea hooks up with Martin Pelley, an oil-rich man with "a pear-shaped head, a dark jowl, and sad eyes."[52] Her son has "an arrogance which was made up of staring at you."[53] We meet Marion Faye, who is doing dope deals. Charles Eitel has an affair with Elena Esposito that is falling apart, like his film career.

Sergius O'Shaughnessy wonders why he ever became friends with Charles Eitel in Desert D'Or. "But then who can explain friendship?"[54] Eitel's film career is fading, and he still feels a deep need to be successful. Herman Teppis is the studio boss who has some afternoon delight with his secretary, a bit actress named Bobby. Teppis says, "There's a monster in the human heart." We are given excerpts from a twenty-page report of Eitel's testimony to the congressional investigating committee.[55] When asked if he has ever been a Communist Party member, Eitel replies that he had never been a member of any political party. "Do you love your country?" he is asked. "I've always thought of love in connection with women," he says. O'Shaughnessy tells us Eitel's story: his films, his first wife, his involvement with the Spanish Civil War, his army commission and training films, his fancy house, and the results of his promiscuity—his second divorce and his third divorce from Lulu Meyers. O'Shaughnessy falls for her, but she cares little for him. We hear toward the end of his adventures in this toxic environment of hope in "the fires of his imagination." When all is lost "there still remains that world we may create."[56]

MISS AMELIA EVANS IN *THE BALLAD OF THE SAD CAFÉ* (1951) BY CARSON MCCULLERS

Miss Amelia Evans is the protagonist of Carson Mc Cullers's *The Ballad of the Sad Café*. The neighbors pass rumors about Miss Amelia Evans and a man who arrived in town one day carrying a suitcase. She must be a sinner, or else this stranger must be up to something. The man tells Amelia that he is a relative, and Miss Amelia brings him home. People wonder if she wants whatever the man has in that suitcase. She has not harmed the man. He is in her store. She takes out some liquor and crackers and thus offers the first gesture of southern hospitality that results in this space becoming the café. Cousin Lyman, the hunchback with the suitcase, thus creates the café where they will all meet on Sunday evenings. Has she fallen for Lyman? She has been married to Marvin Macy—for ten days anyway. He was nice for a while, but now he's bad again. Macy and Amelia have a fight, and Lyman intervenes. The café is wrecked. Then Marvin and Lyman take the money and leave Miss Amelia alone. The story is presented alongside the short stories "The Twelve Moral Men," about a chain gang; "Wonderkind"; "The Jockey"; "Madame Zelinsky and the King of Finland"; "The Sojourner"; "A Domestic Dilemma"; and "A Tree, a Rock, a Cloud."

ARTHUR WINNER IN *BY LOVE POSSESSED* (1957) BY JAMES GOULD COZZENS

This is James Gould Cozzens's Pulitzer Prize–winning novel, published in August 1957. Arthur Winner, an attorney, tells his wife Clarissa that he simply does not know how to love. He has an affair with his legal business partner's wife, an act that calls the meaning of his life into question. Meanwhile, he insists that his son Warren become a lawyer. *By Love Possessed* takes place across two days, with flashbacks into the past to fill in information for us about the protagonist and his relationships with the other characters. Arthur Winner married the daughter of his father's legal partner. Hope died giving birth to their child. Arthur is currently married to Clarissa, his daughter's tennis coach, but his attention wanders. Arthur works with Julius Penrose. He is at work on the probate of the estate of Michael McCarthy and a case in the arrest of

Ralph Detweiler for rape. McCarthy's investment in the trolley went bankrupt because of the wide availability of cars. Detweiler is in trouble. The pastor of an Episcopalian church has asked Arthur to help supervise the church.

Arthur Winner is a man of reputation, a man of ideas. Yet, he seems to lack self-awareness. He functions outwardly in his role as a lawyer like a true man about town. He thinks about the town, its people, and his experiences. He practices law, reads and quotes Shakespeare, and believes he has a set of values. He believes that he has integrity. After all, his father was a man of reason. Yet, now he reflects upon his doubt. He realizes that his code of reason has broken down. At the start of the novel, Arthur is confident. Arthur has played his social role well. He appears to be sure of his moral code. He is able to resolve problems for others but not the problems he has created for himself. His past affair with Julius Penrose's wife still haunts him. He is then troubled by Helen Detweiler's suicide. Her brother Ralph got into trouble and was charged with rape. Arthur never told Helen, the secretary, that the charges against Ralph were dropped. Recalling this, Arthur rationalizes that he was shielding Helen by hiding the truth from her. In his life, Arthur assumed that he was a principled man. However, he has been pragmatic and is caught between principle and pragmatism. He is rattled by his sense of guilt.

Winner's father and Julius Penrose started the firm. Julius has known about the affair Winner had with his wife. Yet, he has remained supportive of Arthur. The firm is affected when it becomes clear that Noah Tuttle has embezzled money. Arthur recognizes the fraud of Noah Tuttle and must confront him and report the misdeed. Julius counsels to not make this public. The novel explores professionalism and morality. Perhaps "suburbanization and consumerism threatened masculinity," as Joan Shelley Rubin suggests. Rubin sees that Arthur "evinced the postwar anxiety surrounding the survival of those ideals in mass society."[57]

Dwight Macdonald was critical of the novel, casting it as middlebrow and its characters as artificial. In his essay "By Cozzens Possessed" in *Commentary* (January 1958), he asked why any man of decency would ever have an affair like Arthur Winner had. Macdonald was particularly critical of Cozzens's prose style. Strunk and White this was not. (Cozzens favored inverted sentences.) Macdonald found Cozzens's inversions pointless and "as bad as prose can get." He asserted that the critics who approved of the novel were lowering literary standards.[58]

Joan Shelley Rubin points out that *By Love Possessed* contributed to the idea of the "big novel" or "magnum opus": the book of heft that appears stately on the bookshelf. She points to James Jones's *From Here to Eternity*, Herman Wouk's *The Caine Mutiny*, and MacKinlay Kantor's *Andersonville*—books of similar physical dimensions. Perhaps one cannot judge a book by its cover, but if it is bulky maybe it is also good. Rubin conjectures that perhaps such big books corresponded to readers' "aspirations to certify themselves as beneficiaries of the ample leisure and educational advantages that middle-class affluence had made possible."[59] Rubin also recognizes that Cozzens was well placed in the publishing industry, with his Harvard connections and the agenting of Carl Brandt. Cozzens was secular and stoic, finding religion sentimental. A *Time* magazine cover story depicted him as "classical, dry, cerebral, and unsentimental."[60] In *By Love Possessed*, his sentence structures are more complex than in his World War II novel *Guard of Honor*. However, it was *By Love Possessed* that won the Pulitzer Prize. As Frederick Bracher recognized in his 1957 study of Cozzens's novels, "The traditional social novel, with its high seriousness and moral urgency, is still viable in a period of experiment and disorder."[61]

6

THE HAUNTED AND THE TERRIFIED

In the first pages of John Knowles's *A Separate Peace* (1959), the narrator, Gene, recalls a sense of fear that hovered around the Devon School when he attended there. He describes it as something felt but unseen, "like stale air." Now there is only "fear's echo" and the "unhinged, uncontrollable joy" of other, better memories.[1] Gene's visit to the past is a recollection of halcyon days swallowed up in disturbances at a prep school during the war years. However, that vague, pervading anxiety he felt then characterizes some of the tone of the time when the novel was written. A New England boarding school may seem an idyllic and protected place apart from the world. Yet, it is embedded in its time, and its "glossy surface" holds ghosts and glimmers of memory.

When Dwight Eisenhower took the oath of the presidency on January 20, 1953, America held a hope for stability and security. Eisenhower offered a theme of unity and asserted the ideal of a common purpose, mutual respect, and equality for all. However, this veteran of forty years in the military was clear about the dangers of the modern world. "Science seems ready to confer upon us, as its final gift, the power to erase human life from this planet," he said.[2] Yet, there was his smile, his earnestness, and the assurance that this commander would usher in an era of calm.

The war was now a memory. The dream of an era of normalcy, one of postwar hopes lifted by an expanding economy, lingered across America. Yet, while America, like Gene in *A Separate Peace*, now "had more money and success and 'security,'" a "little fog hung over the river."[3] The 1950s had come with the threat of nuclear destruction, shadows of the Cold War, a tension about communist infiltration, and war in Korea. This time of newfound hope launched a quest for security: for a secure job and a paycheck, family dinners in the kitchen, television and schoolwork, baseball, children in the yard playing jump rope, Mom ironing clothes, and the sound of the commuter train passing through the suburbs. From the train, one saw the new design of suburban hope: broad lawns and neighborhoods, homes and stores, and Memorial Day flags flying proudly their red, white, and blue.

Yet, underneath the surfaces of American life were veterans' efforts at readjustment, housewives' desire for a vital life, and tensions of the Cold War. The public remained at least dimly aware of a fear of things that seemed to lie beyond America's shores but might break in through complacency and security at any time. "The oldest and strongest emotion of mankind is fear," H. P. Lovecraft once said.[4] Nuclear arms provided a reason for fear in the 1950s. In *The Bad Seed* (1954), the narrator, Christine Penmark, overhears two men in a park: "I was reading the other day," said the taller of the two, "that the age we live in is an age of anxiety."[5] The story raises that specter of fear. W. H. Auden had coined the term in his poem in 1947. William Faulkner in his Nobel Prize acceptance speech referred to the threat of nuclear arms: "Our tragedy today is a general and universal fear." In 1957, Norman Mailer would write, "The stench of fear has come out of every pore." However, the philosopher Søren Kierkegaard had, more than one hundred years earlier, looked at anxiety in a way that was more rigorous and challenging. Anxiety, he wrote, is "the dizziness of freedom."[6]

ELEANOR VANCE IN *THE HAUNTING OF HILL HOUSE* (1959) BY SHIRLEY JACKSON

One must pass through Hillsdale to get to Hill House and its iron gate. Dr. Montague's letter to Eleanor says: "The people there are rude to strangers and openly hostile to anyone inquiring about Hill House."[7] Any sense of domesticity and suburban order has declined in Hillsdale. The town of Hillsdale is described as "a tangled, disorderly mess of dirty houses and crooked streets."[8] The local diner is "unattractive." The curbs are "broken." Eleanor sits in the diner drinking coffee that looks cloudy. The conventional world lapses into creepiness and shadows.

Eleanor is strangely gifted. When she was twelve, shortly after her father died, stones "rained" on her house across three days, perhaps manifesting poltergeist activity and extrasensory perception.[9] For eleven years, she cared for her mother who was an invalid. She is now thirty-two years old and lives with her sister. Her sister and brother-in-law do not like her. In Eleanor's journey to Hill House, some critics say, she may be searching for the perfect home that her culture has suggested is an ideal. The search reflects Eleanor's alienation, loneliness, and dream of fulfillment. "I'm sure I've been here before, in a book or a fairy tale perhaps," she says.[10] Hill House seems to take on a life of its own. It becomes a maze, an alternative to her lonely reality. Is it a conscious, demonic force to which Eleanor ought to surrender herself and her dreams? Do Eleanor's psychic powers prompt Hill House to manifest emotion or un-repress some ancient curse? Hill House itself becomes a central dark figure in this story.

Dr. John Montague makes inquiries into the supernatural. He always appears like a rational father figure. Luke Sanderson has been sent by his aunt who owns Hill House. Theo has escaped her lover's tryst and has been recruited by Dr. Montague, along with Eleanor. He recognizes that both of them have supernatural talents. Can Eleanor and Theo create supernatural phenomena?

Eleanor is conventional, while Theo is a rebel. Theo reflects Eleanor as a double, a mirror self, or a divided self. She also reflects, perhaps, some elements of Eleanor's potential. Theo is self-determining and willful and has a spirit of independence that flies in the face of conventional reason. Eleanor subscribes to a wishful escapism while Theo argues for a fierce break from any repression. Luke is cast by Eleanor as her hope, her prince, but Luke flirts with Theo. Words appear over a wall: "Help, Eleanor. Come home, Eleanor."[11] "It was my fault my mother died," Eleanor confesses to Theo. "I ought to have brought her the medicine."[12] Perhaps absorbed by the house, she climbs to the tower.[13]

The house—a mirror for the self—appears to consume Eleanor. Hugh Crain's 1880s house destroyed his family. His wife was killed in a carriage accident. His second wife died in a fall. His daughters' claim to their inheritance resulted in estrangement. The elder daughter moved into the house and also died there, hanging from Crain's tower.[14] Some feminists have interpreted Hill House as a patriarchal ancestral structure that is destructive of women. They have viewed Hugh Crain's insistence that his wife maintain "humility" as restrictive. "The haunted house comes to represent the vast web of expectations and obligations, of female duties that enmesh the central character, Eleanor Vance," writes Dale Bailey. Behind this story, Bailey sees the "faint outlines of another and more terrible personality, the madwoman in the attic": Charlotte Bronte's character Bertha Mason in *Jane Eyre*, who is the central figure of Sandra Gilbert and Susan Gubar's notable feminist work *The Madwoman in the Attic*. One may also parallel the anonymous woman in *The Yellow Wallpaper* by Charlotte Perkins Gilman.[15]

Shirley Jackson may have not been seriously regarded because she wrote twisted domestic novels in the horror genre. She wrote at a time when realism was usually expected and when New Criticism was ascendant and did not embrace genre fiction. Critics have attempted to reconcile Shirley Jackson's domestic comedy and satire with her disturbing horror tales where the breaks in domestic life become dark. She wrote *Life among the Savages* (1954), her comic treatment of home, family, and children, partly based upon her married life with literary critic Stanley Hyman and their children.[16] Then she went to the dark side with stories like *The Haunting of Hill House*. "Miss Jackson is not, however, a major writer," wrote her biographer Lenemaja Friedman, "and the reason she will not be considered that is that she saw herself primarily as an entertainer, an expert storyteller and craftsman."[17] Jackson's use of the Gothic, mystery, and plot twists, however, draws a reader into stories that may reflect 1950s issues and anxieties. Shirley Jackson's horror is psychological. Ruth Franklin believes that Shirley Jackson's life "embodies the dilemmas faced by so many women in the twentieth century." "Jackson had a palpable design on her readers," observed Harold Bloom, "her efforts are as calculated as Poe's."[18]

Jackson takes a psychological approach to the human condition and explores fears and anxieties, hopes and terror, loneliness and daydreams. "The typical Jackson protagonist is a social misfit," writes Lynnette Carpenter. She is not beautiful, charming, or idyllic.[19] Shirley Jackson's fiction suggests that women in America in the 1950s experienced the pressures of domesticity in an age of anxiety. Certainly, postwar America showed potential for "the American century" but was also searching for security and home, to resettle and resume after the Second World War. America was a place of new suburbs, consumer products, and men returning to work and a thriving economy. Yet, there was lingering Cold War anxiety, concern about Soviet spies or hidden communists, the 1954 desegregation of schools and racial prejudice, new technologies, and the tensions of daily life.

Shirley Jackson wrote six novels between 1948 and 1962—Gothic-tinged family stories that transposed contemporary anxieties into stories. An entertainer in the line of Nathaniel Hawthorne with *House of the Seven Gables*, Edgar Allan Poe with "The Fall of the House of Usher," and Henry James with "The Turn of the Screw," she wrote the haunted family story to disturbing effect. As Edmund Fuller wrote in a 1959 review essay, Shirley Jackson in the 1950s was "the finest master currently practicing in the genre of the cryptic, haunted tale."[20] It is appropriate that she has been receiving increased critical attention in recent years.

MARY (MARION) CRANE AND NORMAN BATES IN *PSYCHO* (1959) BY ROBERT BLOCH

Fear in the 1950s came with monsters. Norman Bates, at first, appears ordinary, innocent, and fragile. However, it eventually becomes clear that he has psychoanalytic issues, murderous intent, and dissociative identity disorder. For Norman eliminates people and casts them into the swamp. Sherriff Chambers is fooled: "I know this fellow Bates. He's no murderer."[21] In Robert Bloch's novel, the Bates Motel is a ghostly place. Motels in the 1950s were fashionable stopovers for family trips. From the Thunderbird Lodge in Redding to the 1958 Stardust Lounge at Lake Tahoe, they featured neon signs, broad parking lots, and welcoming rooms. The Bates Motel, off the road in northern California, seemed innocent enough to Mary Crane. (Mary Crane in Bloch's story becomes "Marion" in Hitchcock's film.) Mary Crane in Robert Bloch's *Psycho* (1959) drives from Phoenix to a secluded motel. Norman Bates is fixated on holding onto his mother forever. Joseph Stefano rewrote the story for Universal Studios. Hitchcock's infamous shower scene, twice postponed by actress Janet Leigh, was filmed between December

17 and December 23 in 1959 using seventy-seven camera angles, with close-ups.

As the novel *Psycho* begins, Norman Bates is reading. His mother dislikes his reading material. Norman has a fight with his mother, who berates and challenges him. He imagines killing her, but the doorbell rings, interrupting him. Mary Crane is at the door. She has taken $40,000 from a client of her real estate business employer and intends to use it to support a marriage to her boyfriend Sam Loomis. Mary has stopped at the Bates Motel along the way. Norman Bates gives her a dinner invitation. Mary thinks she hears Norman and his mother arguing. He claims that his mother keeps him from life and freedom. Mary suggests that if she is insane, perhaps she should be institutionalized. Norman, upset by this, yells, "she's not crazy!" Mary decides that she will return to Phoenix and return the money. However, an old woman attacks and kills Mary. (The shower scene is the famous invention of the Hitchcock film.) Norman wakes and suspects that "Mother" killed Mary, and he must hide the body. Mary's body is dumped in the swamp behind the motel. Mr. Lowery has hired a private detective, Arbogast, to find Mary and the $40,000. Lila, Mary's sister, now fears that something has happened and seeks her. She is joined by Sam Loomis, and they trace Mary's path to the Bates Motel. Arbogast, who has also traced Mary to the motel, encounters Norman. As he climbs the stairs to investigate, he is killed. His body is dumped in the swamp. Lila investigates in the house, as Sam diverts Norman's attention. Sam is hit over the head with a wine bottle by Norman. Lila discovers the corpse of Mrs. Bates. Norman stands threateningly behind her in a dress. He has taken on the identity of his mother, Norma. Sam regains consciousness just in time to save Lila from Norma/Norman's grasp. The history of Norman Bates, a dual personality, is uncovered.

Psycho extends Bloch's previous psychological horror fiction into further explorations of split personality. Critics point to themes in his short stories: double personality in "Enoch" (1946) and "Lucy Comes to Stay" (1950), as well as mirrors in "Hungry House" (1951).[22] Bloch did not regard himself as a stylist.[23] In his film, Alfred Hitchcock achieved emotional impact. Norman Bates cuts back the curtain on normalcy and reveals naked fear with the phallic violence of a knife. Cameras record the act from multiple angles as violins shriek.

Bloch completed three novels in 1954: *Spiderweb*, *The Kidnapper*, and *The Will to Kill*. He wrote these suspense potboilers primarily to support his family. *Psycho* was preceded by *Shooting Star* (1958), a mainstream novel, and *This Crowded Earth* (1958), a science fiction novel. Bloch brought psychology to the horror story and was known for his use of interiority. The anxious and disturbed minds of his characters lived amid various settings of urban horror.

POPULAR CULTURE

Postwar anxiety was mitigated by television entertainment. The television networks (CBS, NBC, ABC) reigned over television broadcasting. Marshall McLuhan told everyone that "the medium is the message" and that television created a change in perception. In the mid-1950s, 66 percent of American homes had televisions.[24] On TV's *The Honeymooners*, Brooklyn bus driver Ralph Kramden and his sewer worker pal Ed Norton squabble over the use of a television set. Norton wants to put on his space helmet and watch *Captain Video and His Video Rangers*. In another comical episode, they participate in a live television commercial to sell a new kitchen product. The 1950s game show trend is featured when Ralph is a guest on a television game show, on which he has to name that tune. While television brought entertainment and laughter, it also brought the news and serious commentary. Edward R. Murrow criticized Senator McCarthy on national television, saying: "He didn't create this situation of fear; he merely exploited it."[25]

The world of innocence pervaded much of American film, television, and popular fiction. However, some serious novels like *Invisible Man* and *The Adventures of Augie March* probed identity and the struggle of individualism against systems and structures that bound the individual. Historian William H. Chafe concludes that the decade was a transitional time. However, "the 1950s seemed as much a time of complexity and contradiction as of blissful complacency."[26] One ballast against this silent anxiety was the reawakening of religion. The growth in organized religion was likely related to the search for normalcy, security, and meaning following the Second World War. Church membership increased to 110 million.[27] This was reflected in book publishing with best sellers like Norman Vincent Peale's *The Power of Positive Thinking* and

Catherine Marshall's *A Man Called Peter* and on television with the talks by Fulton Sheen. Parish life intersected with family life and community participation in potluck dinners, bowling leagues, and other group activities that created community.[28]

The dissolving of these social bonds reported by sociologists like Robert Putnam (*Bowling Alone*) and Robert Bellah (*Habits of the Heart*) may be a feature of our time. As millennials who are often attached to their phones and social media accounts communicate less person to person, skills for interpersonal connection and civic development appear to be breaking down. The recent attraction to supernatural horror in film and television may be, in part, a displacement of religious impulses. It carries a belief in vampires, werewolves, ghosts—or at least a suspension of disbelief about them. In the early 1950s, a concern with UFOs connected "wonders" and "the deep anxieties and dreams of the day," observes Robert Ellwood.[29]

Recognizing the fears that nuclear arms fomented in the world, Albert Einstein argued that the postwar connection of militarism with nationalism was problematic. In 1947, he affirmed his pacifism and expressed his concern with what he called "the military mentality."[30] Fourth of July parades ought to celebrate democracy and freedom, not planes, trains, and automobiles stacked with armaments. Einstein expressed deep concern about the means of destruction that were being "perfected behind walls of secrecy." He asked: "Is there any way out of this impasse created by man himself?"[31] He recognized that the nuclear arms race that had arisen between the United States and the Soviet Union was "initiated originally as a preventive measure [but now] assumes hysterical proportions."[32] In a radio interview on June 16, 1954, Einstein was asked if it was an exaggeration to say that "the fate of the world is hanging in the balance." It was not any exaggeration, he said. "The fate of humanity is always in the balance . . . but more truly now than at any known time."[33]

World government was the answer, Einstein said. His hope for a world federation was perhaps quixotic and naive with respect to realpolitik and the global situation in the 1950s, but he earnestly held a consistent position in this regard. In 1951, Einstein had voiced his support for the United Nations and the Universal Declaration of Human Rights that had been issued in 1948. He affirmed that the United Nations represented "a modest beginning of international order" and that

UNESCO was a hopeful agency to "pursue cultural tasks." However, he recognized that to attain global understanding "presupposes a new kind of loyalty on the part of man" and a need for "reciprocal confidence" between nations.[34] By now Einstein had begun to appear as that iconic image, with bushy waves of white hair. On February 20, 1954, he received an award for his support of human rights. He commented that he was not worthy of such an award and that human history has been "replete with the struggle for those human rights." Einstein affirmed the need for intellectual freedom. "The existence and validity of human rights are not written in the stars," he said.[35]

HORROR FICTION AND INVASION SCARES

Film adaptations and 1950s television brought fictional characters whose lives were imperiled by aliens, monster figures, and invaders. The invasion story appeared in science fiction and horror fiction. The invasion scare novel was a regular feature of the fiction of H. G. Wells. Behind his alien invasions and extinctions lay a concern with eugenics to limit population and the Fabian ideal of a technical elite to guide the masses. As John Carey wrote in 1922, figures like Wells and Wyndham Lewis disparaged the masses, whereas the author Arnold Bennett, whose realist fiction was so sharply criticized by Virginia Woolf in her essay "Mr. Bennett and Mrs. Brown," embraced new popular forms and continental literature.[36] Critics have associated the invasion theme in the 1950s with fears about communist infiltration in Western society. More recently, one might connect such anxieties with concern about refugees on the U.S. southern border and the fomenting of fear about crime and illegal "others."

In the 1950s, a democratic impulse lay behind the social criticism of writers like Rod Serling, Richard Matheson, and Jack Finney. Serling's scripts underscored the need for compassion and community in a Hobbesian world where the gentle and good could be alienated or marginalized and life could devolve into a Hobbesian war of all against all. Matheson, who adapted his short stories for Serling's *Twilight Zone* series, expressed a similar concern in stories of science fiction and horror. Perhaps influenced by the climate of their time, Matheson and Jack Finney wrote horrific tales of alien invasion.

Miles Bennell, a doctor, returns to his hometown in California in Jack Finney's *Invasion of the Body Snatchers*. He discovers that aliens have replaced the people there. Miles believes that modern technology has alienated people. He lives a life of quiet desperation in a small town where humanity has begun to collapse. The town is as stifling as Sinclair Lewis's Main Street or Sherwood Anderson's Winesberg, Ohio, and soon there is a diminishment of identity. People assent to give way to the invasion, and soon the town is filled with grotesques. The town is a nightmare. Finney's story probes human psychology and paranoia. The surface of Santa Mira, its daily mediocrity, dissolves in dehumanization. This invasion is deeper than fears of communist intrusion or foreign invasion. It is an instability that arises when vitality is suppressed, where not only bodies but also souls are "snatched" by insidious forces and fears.[37]

Robert Neville in *I Am Legend* (1954) is faced with a city that has collapsed into hostility. His neighborhood has been claimed by monstrosity and vampirism. Ruth speaks for the vampires when she warns him that he will inevitably be captured. This apocalyptic scenario, like much of Richard Matheson's fiction, has an ethical dimension. It reflects a surface life that has given way to darker impulses. Matheson reveals human failings. The universe is cold and indifferent, and men and women are in a fight for their lives.

Richard Matheson wrote dozens of stories, fourteen *Twilight Zone* television scripts, and screenplays for films. His screenplays for "Nightmare at 20,000 Feet" and "Nick of Time" became *Twilight Zone* episodes with William Shatner in the lead role. He later created an episode for the popular *Star Trek* series in which Captain Kirk, played by Shatner, is a divided self, both good and evil. Matheson's experience of the Second World War, which permitted the power of the gun, fed his vision of civilization collapsing and his sense of the shadow in humanity. Perhaps in a time of the loss of masculine power men wished to vicariously reclaim that power through westerns, detective stories, and film noir. Matheson critiqued society with cautionary tales. His stories "The Third from the Sun" (1950), "Advance Notice" (1952), and "The Last Day" (1953) preceded *I Am Legend* with apocalyptic themes. Matheson wrote "Born of Man and Woman," in which a monstrous child is in a couple's basement, and "Disappearing Act," in which people around the narrator begin to disappear and the narrator is also sure to vanish as well. In *I Am Legend*, the Gothic reveals fissures in the American dream. Matheson observed that his story reflects a central theme in many of his stories: "The isolated individual in a threatening world, attempting to survive."[38]

That isolated individual in a threatening world was considered by psychologist Rollo May in *The Meaning of Anxiety* (1950). "Anxiety is inescapable," he said. It ought not to be confused with stress. Anxiety is "a subjective reaction," he later commented in an interview that was recorded on tape in 1978. As Søren Kierkegaard observed in *The Concept of Dread*, it is part of the human condition. It may be correlated with the awareness that someday we will die. Anxiety ought to be treated if it becomes disabling. However, a little anxiety may be beneficial: stirring awareness and action. May also concluded that anxiety had a cultural aspect. Rationalism and individualism don't always work so well in our society, he said. "It is a sign that we are in a transition."[39]

CHARACTERS WHO ENTER *THE TWILIGHT ZONE*

The fictional characters created by Rod Serling exemplify his concern with social problems, the individual and society, social order, technology, and time. Serling's teleplays, which extended into the first years of the 1960s, employ 1950s fiction themes. In *The Twilight Zone*, which first aired in October 1959, one enters an imaginative realm where common reality is transformed. Individuality either prevails or is sacrificed to conformity. *The Twilight Zone* stories oppose fascism, discrimination, racism, and all forms of authoritarian tyranny. They explore space and time and counsel that the way to oppose fear is to believe in people. This includes an appeal to viewer sympathy for the apparently inept, outcast, or weak, who are surprisingly resilient. Characters like Mr. Bevis, or the librarian who asserts he is not obsolete, exercise a personal quality of sensitivity, courage, or intelligence not quite understood by the society around them. The humanistic is set against the mechanistic. The nanny in "I Sing the Body Electric" (from a Ray Bradbury story) is more humane than some humans. In "From Agnes with Love," a bumbling scientist seeks an attractive female coworker. When he turns to his computer for assistance, the computer falls in love with him. In "Kick the Can," an elderly nursing home community is transformed and regains their playful youth. In "The Changing of the Guard," a disillusioned teacher who has been forced to resign is visited by the ghosts of students who tell him how deeply he affected their lives. There are time-bends, spaceships, and a journey in "Back There" to try to prevent the Lincoln assassination. In "Willoughby," a businessman named Gart, whose wife Janie is all about materialism and things, escapes on a train to a slower-paced, more idyllic time in the past—although his escape culminates in the grisly end of his jumping from the train. Earl Hamner Jr.'s "The Bewitchin' Pool" introduces us to two children playing at poolside who hear their parents argue as their mother prods their father toward more affluence. They escape the shallow pool of 1950s suburban life by diving into the water, which opens into a magical world. These protagonists show that materialism does not itself make a better society, but care does.

In her book *Spaceships and Politics: The Political Theory of Rod Serling*, Leslie Dale Feldman refers to *The Twilight Zone* as a world that is much like the world portrayed by the philosopher Thomas Hobbes in the 1600s. In *Leviathan*, Hobbes asserted that a social contract that included a strong monarch was needed because this "nasty, brutish, and short" life was essentially an atomistic war of all against all. For example, in "The Monsters Are Due on Maple Street" and "The Shelter," neighbors turn on each other in paranoia and mutual accusation when terrified. Feldman points to the concept of fear and how it is used in the television series.[40] The actor Telly Savalas is threatened by a doll. Child actor Bill Mumy is the boy who must be placated because he transforms things into monsters. ("You're a bad man. You're a very bad man," he says and turns a disillusioned man into a jack-in-the-box.) Even so, despite this harshness, all is not forsaken. There are signs of hope in characters that are loving and compassionate. In one of the earliest episodes, in 1959, a street salesman played by Ed Wynn saves the life of a dear little girl from the neighborhood by addressing Mr. Death with the greatest sales pitch of his life.

Rod Serling in 1950 received a degree in literature from Antioch College. He had been involved with radio in Binghamton, New York, while in his teens. He had served with distinction during the Second World War and was wounded in battle and was awarded the Purple Heart. Working for WLW in Cincinnati, he earned around $75 per week writing radio scripts. His 1949 radio script "To Live a Dream" won a contest prize. Serling went on to work at the Crosley Broadcasting Corporation and with WKRC-Cincinnati, where he rewrote his radio scripts for television. For Kraft Television Theatre, he scripted the Emmy Award–winning "Patterns" (January 12, 1955). In 1956, he wrote the award-winning "Requiem for a Heavyweight" for Playhouse 90. (Serling was also a boxer who fought in the Golden Gloves.) *The Twilight Zone*, beginning on October 2, 1959, aired fifty-six episodes on CBS. Following the opening segment of each show, Serling appeared on camera, within the setting, and commented that the characters were entering the Twilight Zone. Serling's later series *Night Gallery* appeared on NBC. He appeared on camera and wrote several scripts for the series across four years. However, he was not writing scripts toward the end of the series. *The Zero Hour*, a radio drama series, was aired in 1973–1974.

SCIENCE FICTION TAKES OFF

Fiction was adapted and became a source for 1950s film, television, and fiction. Many fictional characters and their stories reached audiences through adaptation, blending into the cultural imaginary with television and film. Alongside situation comedies like *I Love Lucy* and *The Honeymooners* that provoked laughter at the dreams, schemes, and mishaps of Lucy Ricardo and Ralph Kramden, there were puzzling crimes, lustful liaisons, and unexpected visitations from outer space. Wartime masculine camaraderie was transposed to the western frontier. Scandal and sensationalism, fear and peril, and daydream desire sold books and kept the public entertained. On television, *Leave It to Beaver* and *Father Knows Best* portrayed an image of American family life, while *Gunsmoke* brought viewers to the wild west. Fiction like *Peyton Place* titillated readers, and science fiction films like *The Day the Earth Stood Still* (1951) and *When Worlds Collide* (1951) prompted shivers and wonder.

The paperback revolution brought pulp fiction into paperback books. The paperback broadened the reading experience of Americans, and modernist fiction mixed with the popular catalog of Pocket Books, New American Library, and other paperback publishers. Armed services editions encouraged reading during the Second World War and created a habit that lasted long after it. Popular 1950s fiction "lured readers with provocative covers" and affordable prices and created what Paula Rabinowitz has called "demotic reading."[41] Science fiction, romances, westerns, and detective fiction appeared both in magazines and in books as objects available at drug stores and train stations. In those pages, "the mundane became fantastic," as Ray B. Browne and Gary Hoppenstand pointed out in one of their anthologies.[42]

Small publishers promoted the growth of science fiction. The transition from pulp fiction in magazines to mass market books was assisted by publishers like Gnome Press, Prime Press, Shasta, Fantasy Press, Hadley Publications, and New Collections Press. Gnome Press printed and circulated Isaac Asimov's *I, Robot* with its laws of robot conduct, his *Pebble in the Sky*, and *The Foundation* trilogy. They published L. Sprague de Camp and Fletcher Pratt's *The Carnelian Cube*, Arthur C. Clarke's *Against the Fall of Night*, and Robert A. Heinlein's *Sixth Column* and *Sands of Mars*. Soon publishers like Doubleday started science fiction lines, catching onto the wave of commercial success these books were having in the market. Unable to compete, the small companies faded away. Even so, while the 1953 Doubleday science fiction book club prospered, the company's science fiction lines' editors in Garden City could not forecast the future. The Doubleday complex Franklin Avenue would one day become the Doubleday Court Condominiums.

Science fiction visions of the future sought to entertain and to speculate, not to be literary. From this imaginative energy emerged reflections on society, science, and the future. Philip K. Dick's *Second Variety* addresses a nuclear war between the United States and the Soviet Union and people in a wasteland. In Heinlein's *Tunnel in the Sky*, Rod Walker takes a survival test from Deacon Matson's class. He cannot return to Terra but is stuck on a troubled planet and cannot return to Terra. The decade brought dozens of science fiction stories, from Frederik Pohl's *The Space Merchants* (1953) and Heinlein's *Double Star* (1956) to James Blish's *A Case of Conscience* (1958). Arthur Bester's *The Stars, My Destination* (1956) is set in the twenty-fourth century. Golly Foyle is lost in space and feels rejected when he is not rescued. He seeks revenge. In *A Canticle for Leibowitz* (1959), William M. Miller Jr. tells the tale of life in a postapocalyptic world in a monastery. In the southwest United States after nuclear war, society must be reconstructed.

Of course, science fiction revealed that there was much concern about a nuclear world. The 1950s brought a new horizon for the modern world. Hope for health and prosperity and economic growth existed alongside a guarded awareness about the potential for nuclear war. Novels like Nevil Shute's *On the Beach* (1957) and Pat Frank's *Alas, Babylon* (1959) expressed this concern.

PETER HOLMES IN *ON THE BEACH* (1957) BY NEVIL SHUTE

Peter Holmes in *On the Beach* (1957) is married to Mary, the daughter of a naval officer, and they have a baby named Jennifer. His story opens with a sense of normalcy in their home near Melbourne after Christmas. He has recently been promoted in rank in the Royal Australian Navy. Peter learns that he will be assigned to a new posting. On his way, he meets Mr. Paul, a farmer who walks with a limp from an injury in the war. He is going to Melbourne to the Navy Department. "I think they've got a job for me at last."[43] He meets with the admiral who tells him that he will be posted on a U.S. naval vessel. It is an atomic-powered submarine guided by Commander Travers, an experienced Word War II veteran. "She was the biggest submarine Peter Holmes had ever seen."[44] We are drawn into the mystery of where the USS *Scorpion* will go and what the mission ahead will be. Radiation is the issue. A nuclear conflict has released a deadly, invisible drift that cannot be contained and begins to spread across the earth.

Peter Holmes's challenge is to face humanity's ultimate demise. In an analysis of postapocalyptic fiction, Claire P. Curtis points out that *On the Beach* and Cormac McCarthy's *The Road* are novels that "defy expectations about the genre."[45] The postapocalyptic novel appears in the context of other novels that present "plausible ends" and are didactic. They provide what Curtis calls "caution zones." They contend that "this is what we need to be careful of." However, *On the Beach* and *The Road* both suggest that there is no point in banding together in a social contract.[46] As Peter Holmes goes to the West Coast of the United States to observe the destruction there, people in Australia know that the radiation is approaching. Other postapocalyptic novels may provide "some thought that life can go on."[47] This one does not. A submarine may cross the world to look for places that are less affected. However, the end is inevitable.

On the Beach is a cautionary tale, but it does not tell us much about how to avoid a nuclear apocalypse. Indeed, it suggests that radiation drift across distances can present a horrible health risk to humanity and all living beings. Today seismic monitoring enables scientists to determine whether nuclear testing has occurred. Such monitoring can recognize North Korea nuclear testing, for example. Countries that have signed on to the 1996 Nuclear Test Ban Treaty have set up seismic stations. Above-ground testing could send radiation into the atmosphere. International agreements prohibit such testing. However, testing has been conducted underground, where impact of a detonation may register much like the shaking caused by an earthquake.

RANDY BRAGG IN *ALAS, BABYLON* (1959) BY PAT FRANK

Randy Bragg is following the path of a bird, a small creature in a world poised on the brink of disaster, as *Alas, Babylon* (1959) by Pat Frank begins. His neighbor, Florence, a pleasant busybody, assumes that he is a voyeur peering into her windows. News of Mideast conflict and of Russia and Sputnik crackles over Florence's radio from Orlando, Florida. Randy's brother Mark, an officer in military intelligence, sends the signal—"Alas Babylon": their code to signal that nuclear war is imminent. Mark is stationed at the nuclear command post in Omaha, Nebraska. Randy is urged by his brother to meet his family at the airport and to keep them safe at his home in Fort Repose, Florida. Randy has served in the military also and recognizes the severity of the issue. He is a resilient individual who appears to care deeply about family, neighborhood, and nation. He hurries to the airport to meet Helen and her children, a boy named Benjamin Franklin and a girl, Peyton, who have arrived in Florida. Randy is jolted from sleep. The bombing has begun.[48] Hearing jets, Benjamin Franklin realizes what is going on. Before long they are surprised by flashes of light, distant explosions, and reports of devastation. Peyton is blinded by the light. Randy goes into action to provide supplies and security. Locating his friend Dan, a physician, he requests his help for Peyton. Dan, who is now increasingly involved in assisting people, arrives at Randy's house with his medical bag. The admiral, Randy's esteemed relative, has a typewriter and a short-wave radio: their only source of news. He has tuned in his radio to get the world news, and the news is not good.

Blame it on a pilot who follows a surveillance plane and unleashes firepower that falls on the Syrian port city of Latakia. Broadcasts report a bombing attack, civilian casualties, and physical destruction. While the United States contends that this was inadvertent, it sets off a chain of events that result in nuclear war. The scarcity of supplies—food, gas, tools, medical supplies—is emphasized in page after page as Randy attempts to secure the family's material needs. There is no word from Omaha, and Helen worries about Mark. The executive leadership of the United States and much of the Congress has been obliterated. A woman, who is described as a minor cabinet official, has taken the reins of the government and issued executive orders and mobilized the National Guard, to which Randy belongs. While she is highly competent, the fact that she is a relatively minor cabinet member may be a sign of women's professional limitations during the 1950s.

Randy assumes a leadership role, and Dan takes on a mission of mercy as the world collapses around them. This is a different sort of war. We read that "nobody in the Western Hemisphere ever saw the face of a human enemy." A few people saw radar screens, and fewer people saw airplanes or submarines. "Most of those who died in North America saw nothing at all, since they died in bed, in a millisecond slipping from sleep into deeper darkness."[49] Fort Repose has been spared the ferocity of bombing. However, the area is deeply disrupted and experiences supply shortages and medical issues. Dan attempts to treat people in need, but while driving down the road, he encounters rioters, escaped prisoners, and addicts who seek to rob him of drugs he needs to assist people. Thugs beat him up and take his medical bag. Randy, who has been protecting the public, seeks justice and goes to Marine Park: a place where people, including the homeless, assemble. It is a place where "Man absorbed strength from the touch of his neighbor's elbow."[50] With the admiral, Randy has set out orders from the government to maintain peace, health, and order. Randy and his neighbors seek out the "highwaymen" with cunning plans for their capture. Off Randy goes "to face the thousand-year night."[51]

The appearance of nuclear arms had "changed objective reality for the present," wrote Robert Heilbroner in *The Future as History* (1959). "If any single happening of our age has made its impact felt upon this nation, it is the prospect of mass destruction to which we are now exposed."[52] Heilbroner, an economist and public intellectual who taught at the New School in New York, observed that it was "rather paradoxical" that technological advancement in weaponry has caused a "diminution of the traditional power of military force on history." The potency of this technology of war made "coexistence with Russia and with communism" a necessity.[53] It required continual preparedness and "a condition of readiness." The new technology increased the "magnitude of organization" of the military. It generated "a larger number of workers to tend it." For "[n]uclear capabilities cannot wait on a leisurely industrialization if they are to serve as a valid psychological or physical threat."[54] Heilbroner thus spelled out some of the dimensions of what Dwight D. Eisenhower would later call "the military-industrial complex." Meanwhile, it was clear to the security establishment that the extension of nuclear arms to "secondary powers in the near future" would "add uncertainty and risk to the prospects for international history."[55]

The impact of technology on contemporary life was more broadly considered as Heilbroner considered "the ubiquitous presence of our machines." Technology brought new powers and benefits for humanity but also created a new, demanding environment. Along with increasing complexity were "the size and impersonality of the offices and factories in which we work" and what he regarded as a sense of impotence that was related to this depersonalizing scale of life that could be "traced in large part to the environment which science and technics create in our midst."[56] He cites philosopher Susanne Langer, who said: "Technical progress is putting man's freedom of mind into jeopardy." Humanity was becoming increasingly "at the mercy of his artifacts" and was now experiencing "a higher order of social control."[57]

The discovery of nuclear energy was momentous. Jonathan Schell in *The Fate of the Earth* wrote: "When men split the nucleus of the atom, they unleashed into terrestrial nature a basic energy of the cosmos—the energy latent in mass—which had never before been active in any major way on earth."[58] The reality of the bomb became one of the great problems of the 1950s era. During the Second World War and after,

Klaus Fuchs passed nuclear secrets on to American industrial chemist Harry Gold, who was an intelligence operative for the Soviet Union. The information was given to Lavrenty Beria, director of the Soviet bomb program. The Soviet Union was able to produce a nuclear weapon. The prospect of nuclear war permeated the Cold War. Eisenhower in 1956 wrote a letter in which he asserted that one day both the United States and the Soviet Union must "meet at the conference table with the understanding that the era of armaments has ended."[59]

PIGGY IN *LORD OF THE FLIES* (1954) BY WILLIAM GOLDING

Piggy is a sympathetic and rather contradictory character at the center of British novelist William Golding's *Lord of the Flies*. He and Ralph first see the wonder of the island upon which they are stranded. They use a conch shell to signal to the other boys who may have survived and may be somewhere not far away. When the boys at last gather, Ralph becomes their leader. However, Jack, in charge of the choirboys, soon claims his own command, and the group splits into factions. Jack becomes increasingly sadistic and has his group paint their faces with ritual warpaint, suggesting the call to a barbaric, primitive hunt. "Kill the pig," he calls. "Cut her throat. Spill her blood."[60]

Piggy is an intelligent boy, and he later becomes the scapegoat. He is a chubby, eyeglasses-wearing boy, a little Prometheus whose eyeglasses can start a fire. His aunt did not let him play outside with other children because of his asthma. So Piggy is socially awkward. Even so, Piggy is inclined toward rules and social order. Jack Biles, who interviewed Golding in 1968, called Piggy "a multi-faceted figure . . . a study in contrasts." Biles was surprised when Golding referred to Piggy as "the scientist" who might end up someday at Los Alamos. On this island, Piggy is in danger.[61]

Lord of the Flies frighteningly depicts the problem of tribalism. Golding appears to totally reject Jean-Jacques Rousseau's vision of the potential of the primitive. Rather, sin and aggression and divisive darkness lie in the human breast. The boys' society splinters and devolves into something fascist and tribal. Jack's version of survival is tooth-and-nail violence without law, social contract, or order. In contrast, Simon is sensitive and picked on. He is something like a Christ figure.

With *Lord of the Flies*, William Golding wrote a moral tale for the age. Rather than Daniel Defoe's presentation of building civilization on a deserted island, in William Golding's *Lord of the Flies* we have British boys unable to establish social order and the group devolving into violence. Did this novel reflect an anxiety about society stranded on an island of postwar uncertainty? Was there a sense of impending loss of faith or youthful innocence? If England was forming a postwar civilization, what hope was there if life on this fantastic new island collapsed into barbarism? These boys had apparently become like the Hitler Youth of Nazi Germany. Was nightmare aggression irrevocably rooted in adolescent egomania? Might the destruction of the Western world happen from most anywhere?

Golding, who taught at an all-boys school, created a dystopian fiction that has, across the years, become a staple of junior high and high school English classes. *Lord of the Flies*, however, is a rather depressing story to require young people to read. Is the purpose to introduce them to a difficult world, or to remind these bright young spirits that they, too, can degrade into the nasty? Golding appears to underscore the doctrine of original sin. Or else, even though he claimed to have not read Freud, the psychoanalyst's characterization of humanity as naturally aggressive is everywhere present in this novel. The Darwinian struggle outlined in *Origin of Species* (1859) also appears to lie beneath this novel. There is a ruthless, competitive spirit among the boys, rather than the more cooperative dimension of animal life that Darwin recognized in *The Descent of Man* (1871).

While it was published in 1954, *Lord of the Flies* was launched into popularity and into the public schools following the appearance of a 1959 paperback edition. It was a boys' adventure story with a macabre twist, a suspense story filled with that great question of suspense: "what will happen next?" Then would arise another question: "Why do they behave this way?" The boys lapse into savage behavior. Clearly, Eden is lost. Humanity has fallen into evil.

William Golding once commented that *Lord of the Flies* was an act of self-knowledge. The novel included self-observation as well as observation of schoolboys. He acknowledged that he could see in himself the potentiality to succumb to violence as had the Nazis. "I am of that sort of nature," he admitted. War brought "a religious convulsion" and "a kind of framework of principles" into Golding's life, says his biographer.[62]

Peter Green commented in the *New Republic* that he saw a "spiritual cosmology" in Golding's fiction. For Green, who knew Golding, the author of *Lord of the Flies* was a man wrestling with his father's scientific worldview. In 1963, Green saw Golding as a writer creating fiction from a religious perspective. More recently, Green has reaffirmed that insight into Golding's work. In *Lord of the Flies*, Green says, Golding inverts cheerful colonialism into a nightmare, countering H. G. Wells's "evolutionary rationalism."[63] Green points out that Golding lived in Salisbury where the cathedral spire rises, reaching up into changing hues of the sky, extending as if to heaven and beyond rational explanation. Golding sees beauty in human potential; yet, he also asks: what of the monsters within? *Lord of the Flies* is one of Golding's isolated settings where he attempts to work out his understanding of this light and shadow in humanity. What may be humanity's future? *Lord of the Flies* has a mythical quality, as many critics have recognized.

The paperback of *Lord of the Flies* sold roughly forty-three hundred copies in 1959 and fifteen thousand in 1960. Sales jumped to seventy-five thousand in 1961 and 1.2 million in 1962. Peter Brooks filmed an adaptation, which was presented at Cannes in 1963. It is Golding's best-known work, although not his most carefully or painstakingly crafted. (That might be *The Inheritors* or *Spire*.) When William Golding was awarded the Nobel Prize in 1983, the Swedish king Carl XVI, who presented the award to him, told him that he recalled reading *Lord of the Flies* in school. It seems fitting that the schoolteacher's most memorable work would first be encountered by most readers in one of their classes in school. Yet, one may wonder what sort of lesson might be learned through this gripping study of a descent into hell.

7

DEMOCRACY'S DEFENDERS

In the 1950s, there were some significant differences of opinion about how to defend democracy. Some saw spies everywhere. They believed that the United States had to head off a communist threat before it infiltrated the federal government and major institutions of the country. Others sought stability and order, and genre fiction echoed these cultural anxieties and the need to set the world right again. Characters like James Bond, the lawyer Perry Mason, and the detectives of crime fiction were popular figures. Fictional politicians emerged from Allen Drury's *Advise and Consent* (1959) and Edwin O'Connor's *The Last Hurrah* (1956). The Truman and Eisenhower administrations each had a variety of domestic and international issues that required attention. The first years of the 1950s were characterized by concern with the Korean War and congressional investigations of suspected communist influence. Visible figures on the national stage included Dwight Eisenhower, John Foster Dulles, General Douglas MacArthur, and a variety of U.S. politicians, including the notorious Senator Joseph McCarthy.

Cold War tensions lingered throughout the 1950s. In the first years of the decade, concern about communist infiltration in American government and institutions was fostered by Senator Joseph McCarthy of Wisconsin. In 1950, for Lincoln Day celebrations, McCarthy visited Wheeling, West Virginia, where he would begin to shake the nation with claims that communist sympathizers were working in the State Department and were serious security risks.

In the *Wheeling Intelligencer*, Rebecca West had recently reported on Klaus Fuchs's trial for betrayal of secrets of the atomic program. Alger Hiss was accused by Whittaker Chambers of being an agent for the Soviet Union. Hiss was found guilty of perjury by a jury. President Truman announced that the Soviet Union was developing a hydrogen bomb. News like this set the tone for Senator Joseph McCarthy's charges of communist influence in the State Department. On February 9, 1950, in Wheeling, West Virginia, McCarthy claimed to have a list of 205 State Department employees who he said were communists. At the McClure Hotel, he raised papers in his hand: "I have here in my hand a list."

Frank Desmond's articles appeared the next day. Across the center of the *Wheeling Intelligencer* was the headline: "M'Carthy Charges Reds Hold U.S. Jobs." In the column to the left, the headline read: "Truman Blasted for Reluctance to Press Probe." Desmond wrote that McCarthy "was given a rousing ovation last night." He reported that McCarthy said, "There the bright young men who are born with silver spoons in their mouths are the ones who have been the worst." Desmond wrote: "I have in my hand 57 cases of individuals who would appear to be either card carrying members or certainly loyal to the communist party."[1] Frank Desmond never saw that list. He had only heard McCarthy's allegations. His story was picked up by the Associated Press and became national news.

In William F. Buckley's novel *Redhunter* (1999), we follow Harry Bentecou of the U.S. Army on a journey through the story of Senator Joe McCarthy. Buckley writes of McCarthy's speech in West Virginia: "There would be very long and heated debates over exactly what he said that night." He repeats, "I have here in my hand a list."[2] McCarthy cited security risks. Haynes Johnson writes that McCarthy was "aided by powerful factors [that] combined to make Americans feel threatened."[3] These included the possibility of nuclear war and the fact that spies and traitors did exist. Berlin was "a tinderbox"; Mao, in China, had signed a pact with Russia; war in Korea was impending. Perhaps most of all, Americans had trust in government. The U.S. public then had confidence that anyone holding such a high public office would never declare a deliberate falsehood. The Tydings-McMahon investigation of McCarthy's claims began in March. In June 1950, Margaret Chase Smith of Maine and six other Republicans set forth a Declaration of

Conscience against McCarthy. They stated their belief that he had undermined the dignity of the office of the Senate, reducing it to "hate and character assassination."[4] The Internal Security Committee was established in December to locate and expose communists.

A sampling of McCarthy speeches suggests an increasing demagoguery in his tone. On February 9, 1954, upon returning to Wheeling, West Virginia, McCarthy asserted that homosexuals should be removed from federal positions because they were susceptible to being blackmailed. "There's another group about which I hesitate to talk," he began. In his next breath, he disparaged both Dean Acheson and homosexual Americans, remarking that Acheson had stated that the State Department had hired "good, loyal, clean living Americans." While McCarthy said that he did not regard homosexuals as communists and affirmed that they could be good government workers, he referred to homosexual individuals as "morally weak" and cited a document that claimed: "the pervert is easy prey to the blackmailer."[5]

On March 15, 1954, in Manitowoc, Wisconsin, he defended himself against accusations by radio and television broadcaster Edwin R. Murrow with ad hominem attacks on Murrow. McCarthy alleged that Murrow had participated in a summer program in Moscow in 1934–1935. Therefore, he and all the participants presumably had been passive recipients of communist dogma and indoctrination. This man Murrow, he said, is "a man who thinks it is his duty to attack anyone who attacks communism." He received a laugh when he commented on an article in the *New York Times* and called the *Times* "not my favorite paper."[6]

On April 21, 1954, at a speech in Houston, McCarthy declaimed that "for a number of years" they had been "looking into" communist sympathizers infiltrating into the atomic and hydrogen bomb installations. "There is no such thing as a secret from the Communists," he said. "We are in the Model T era of the nuclear bomb," he added. "It is time to close the gates—against treason." He insisted that it was time to "get the names and have Americans see the faces."[7]

In Wausau, Wisconsin, on May 8, 1954, he spoke on the goal "to expose the few rotten apples in the Pentagon." It was the start of his attack on the U.S. Army that would before long result in his demise. He received some laughter from the partisan crowd during a flippant "shine shoes" remark and mention of G. David Schine.[8]

Joseph N. Welch, special counsel for the U.S. Army, defended the U.S. Army against McCarthy's claims. On June 9, 1954, Welch's interrogation cut into McCarthy's pose. When McCarthy targeted a member of Welch's legal staff, insinuating that he was a communist, Welch was taken aback. "Until this moment, Senator, I think I never really gauged your cruelty or your recklessness," Welch said. "Have you no sense of decency, at long last?"[9] The U.S. Army hearings concluded. In December, McCarthy was held in contempt by his Senate colleagues.

On the capitol steps in Madison, Wisconsin, in 1952, Henry S. Reuss opposed Joseph McCarthy's approach to extirpating communist influence. In his memoir, written when he was in his eighties, he recalled: "I laid into McCarthy and challenged him to sue me for libel if I, lacking his senatorial immunity, had spoken anything but the truth."[10] Reuss entered Congress as representative for Wisconsin's Fifth District. He was the likely Democratic candidate to run against McCarthy until Tom Fairchild entered the race and won the Democratic nomination for the U.S. Senate. Fairchild lost in the Wisconsin election to McCarthy. In Congress, Reuss promoted legislation that led to the formation of the Peace Corps in 1961. According to Reuss, "government was good" from 1948 to 1968. He wrote in his memoir that during that time he observed "presidents willing to assume the responsibilities of leadership; Congresses that were generally civil, unbought, and constructive; a Supreme Court ready to interpret the Constitution for modern times." Writing during the Clinton administration, he added, "Today I am saddened by our retreat from the golden age."[11]

Across the Atlantic, the golden age of Britain appeared to be fading from imperial power into steady efforts toward sustenance. In Britain after the Second World War, the Atlee government developed a welfare state in which national health care was provided. Britain opposed the Soviet Union and strongly supported NATO. The Conservatives came to power in 1951 and the Tory government retained most of the state provisions, although the steel industry did not remain nationalized. There was economic investment in maintaining world status. Britain needed a new hero, and James Bond emerged from Ian Fleming's stories as the archetypal world traveler maintaining honor and security.

JAMES BOND: IAN FLEMING'S CRUSADER

James Bond is dynamic, mobile, and daring. The Bond one sees depends upon where one stands in time and culture and which media one sees him through. For James Bond has been 007, with license to kill; a virile playboy, a misogynist, the spy with technical gadgets, the man with a classy and well-equipped sportscar, a pop star, a British postwar nationalist, and a recognizable global figure appearing in print, television, film, comics, action figure merchandise, and video games. He has been an archetypal image for dozens of secret agent characters. James Bond was widely read by American readers, and he became an iconic archetype worldwide.

As British power declined after the Second World War, Bond appeared as a suave and canny hero. Bond enters the scene undercover, stepping beyond the ordinary, investigating the twisted shadow world of his enemy. Fleming casts his character within a conservative realm that must be preserved against the intrusions of modernity. That is, for all the cutting-edge technology, Bond's world is, as Kingsley Amis recognized, "substantially right of centre."[12] Bond on the printed page is essentially conservative. He reads the London *Times* and drives a Bentley, circa 1930s. In *Dr. No*, we read that he prefers "a world of tennis courts and lily ponds and kings and queens."[13] He is not a club gentleman, and he is not easily defined by class. He seems to be a rising professional, committed to secrecy and following the lead of M., a father figure.

Kingsley Amis applauded the Bond books as entertainment. The books, he said, are "more than simple cloak and dagger stories with a bit of the fashionable affluence and sex thrown in." Rather, they held "a sense of our time."[14] However, in 1958, critic Bernard Bergonzi complained of the violence in *Dr. No*. Ethics simply did not enter Fleming's fiction, he said. Bergonzi saw "a strongly marked streak of voyeurism and sadomasochism in his books."[15]

Women are the target of romantic escapades and phallic adventures for Bond: they are sex objects to be saved and taken care of. *Casino Royale*, the first Ian Fleming novel, gives us a picture of Bond's noncommittal, adolescent relation to women: "Bond sighed. Women were for recreation. On the job, they got in the way." We read that women have "emotional baggage" and "one had to look out for them and take care of them."[16] A feminist might argue that Bond appealed to a postwar male culture of patriarchal machismo and behavior that has increasingly come under attack from the Me Too movement. Michael Denning has suggested that the Bond approach to women was "an early form of the men's pornography that characterizes the consumer society, the society of spectacle."[17] *Playboy* magazine appeared in the same year as Fleming's first Bond novel.

The Bond woman is "erotic spectacle," says critic James Chapman. She is tall and athletic and has firm breasts that are beautifully displayed yet slightly concealed in bathing suits or lingerie. Sometimes she too is adventurous, and sometimes she is villainous. She falls into Bond's arms, and she falls into peril. She is characterized as beauty to be looked at: a subject of the male gaze.[18] Chapman has suggested that the representation of women in print is more "progressive" than it is in the films in which Sean Connery or Roger Moore play the character of James Bond. He writes that "the Bond novels are paradoxically more sexist in their attitudes yet at the same time allow greater narrative agency to the female characters than most of the films that have been spun from them."[19] The popular reputation of James Bond increased with paperback sales and films. The paperbacks sold forty-one thousand copies in 1955 and fifty-eight thousand in 1956. Sales steadily increased to seventy thousand in 1957 and then jumped to 105,000 in 1958.[20]

FRANK SKEFFINGTON IN *THE LAST HURRAH* (1956) BY EDWIN O'CONNOR

Frank Skeffington, a career politician, and his nephew Adam Caulfield are the central characters of *The Last Hurrah* (1956) by Edwin O'Connor. Frank Skeffington, seventy-two, mayor and former governor, is going to make another run for office. Times are changing, and current politics may be leaving him behind. Yet, he insists that machine politics and political contacts will continue to influence elections. He is a speechmaker who likes to mix among the constituents, shaking hands. Skeffington's nephew Adam Caulfield is a cartoonist for a local newspaper. Maeve Caulfield is his wife. Maeve's father, Roger, is critical of Skeffington. As Adam gets involved with the campaign, he learns more about politics in Boston. There is a widespread view that Skeffington's cronies are corrupt. (They include Ditto Boland and John Gorman.) Skeffington will not admit that his style is of an old school of politics or that he is less than vital. He asks his nephew Adam to do historical research. For this election will be his last hurrah.

The Last Hurrah focuses on city politics and political campaign strategy in the 1950s: a kind of politics and contact with the electorate that has changed since that time. While Skeffington has been politically successful in the past, some members of the party wonder if he should run for reelection. Charlie Hennessey, a candidate, is supported by the banker Norman Cass Jr. and newspaper editor Amos Force. Kevin McCluskey is a new political candidate, and he will be Skeffington's opponent in the election. McCluskey is inexperienced in politics. He is a handsome World War II veteran without much of a political strategy.

A friend of Adam's says that the election is going to be "the last hurrah" for the style of politics that Skeffington represents. U.S. public life has changed, and now television ads have become important. So is media presence: something Skeffington lacks. Amos Force, a Protestant city newspaper owner, opposes Skeffington. So does the highest-ranking Catholic Church official, the Cardinal. Sam Weinberg, an aide to Skeffington, worries that the former governor may lose this election. Ditto Boland, a political hanger-on and lackey, imitates everything that Skeffington does, including his voice and his manner.

One may ask if Skeffington is heroic or too jaded and compromised to be a hero. He blackmails a banker for refusing to fund public housing in one of the Irish wards. He practices populism, meeting constituents and shaking hands. Skeffington remains a power broker in the city. He has been the city boss and has encountered the city's evils.

Skeffington reminded some readers of Mayor James Curley of Boston. Thomas H. Eliot, in his 1956 article in the *New Republic* titled "Robin Hood in Boston," begins by recalling a *Saturday Review* report that a Boston newspaper sent *The Last Hurrah* to Boston mayor James M. Curley, who referred the novel to his lawyers. Legal action was not pursued. Eliot writes that the novel is a good book that "does not portray evil and brutality in all their darkness."[21] John Ford's film adaptation condenses the story. "Politics is the greatest spectator sport in the country," proclaims Skeffington, who is played by Spencer Tracy.

Surely, times have changed. In the 2020 campaign, Joe Biden and Bernie Sanders, both in their seventies, circled the country, appearing vital and vigorous on television and in town halls, local establishments, and rallies. Donald Trump, in his early seventies, matches them in energy. Like McCluskey, a young man with military background, Senator Tom Cotton (R-Arkansas), Mayor Pete Buttigieg (D-South Bend, Indiana), and others are quite media savvy. The Democratic field was enriched by the presence of highly capable women like Senator Kamala Harris (D-California), Senator Elizabeth Warren (D-Massachusetts), Senator Amy Klobuchar (D-Minnesota), Congresswoman Tulsi Gabbard (D-Hawaii), and Senator Kirsten Gillibrand (D-New York).

ROBERT MUNSON IN *ADVISE AND CONSENT* (1959) BY ALLEN DRURY

Senate Majority Leader Robert Munson is the first character we see in Allen Drury's *Advise and Consent* (1959). The Michigan senator is deliberating the appointment of Leffingwell to the post of secretary of state and anticipating the Senate confirmation hearings. Munson, at fifty-seven, is a widower, now engaged to Dolly Harrison. He is conservative on foreign policy and tends to be a little more liberal on domestic issues. Upon receiving a phone call from the president, he tells him that he supports the nomination. "That's a hell of an appointment," he says. The president is a voice on the phone. He vouches for the "brains, character, ability of Leffingwell." Munson agrees but says that moving the appointment through to confirmation "is going to take a little doing."[22]

Advise and Consent is a Washington story, a novelization of politics and a Senate confirmation hearing. Drury created a compelling plot and brought to his fiction a journalistic style and a sure knowledge of Senate procedures. The relationship of the executive to the Congress is highlighted in this novel. Drury features the Senate, and his political perspective tends to be conservative. John J. Miller in his 2015 article in the *National Review* pointed out that Washington is more journalistic than literary. As Drury writes, Washington is "a city of temporaries, a city of just arriveds and only visitings, built on the shifting sands of politics, filled with people passing through."[23]

The president seeks confirmation of Leffingwell. Ought the Senate to deny Leffingwell the position of secretary of state? The confirmation process has brought backroom conversations and rumors. This is set within international concerns, particularly with regard to the Soviet Union. The imperial presidency is one that assumes powers beyond those that have been granted by the U.S. Constitution. The imperial presidency had arisen increasingly with Roosevelt, and Arthur Schlesinger examined this development. The president could be held accountable by Congress, by the courts, and by the press. When Schlesinger addressed the issue, he wrote with concern about whether these resources were being eroded and the executive branch was going beyond its prescribed role and limitations.[24]

Plausible is the term used by Thomas Mallon to describe Drury's characters. In 2009, Mallon, who has written novels set in Washington, DC, wrote that "Drury's Senate is such a passionate, full-throttle place" where printed newspapers "drive the action." He recognized that some of these Senators are concerned with Russia, and many of them "hope to do good." Drury's characters are better at making speeches than at conversation, he concluded. He added: "His mid-20th Century Senators certainly speak better than those serving today." Journalists might consider studies that indicate that the intellectual level of presidential rhetoric has declined since the 1950s, even as far more broadcast media has devoted attention to American politics.[25] Long before the rise of Fox News, CNN, and MSNBC, sociologist David Reisman, in 1950, focused his concern on politics, the media, and the American public. Of politics, he wrote, "with the mass media behind it, it invades the privacy of citizens [and] plunges the individual directly into the complexities of politics, without any clear notion of where his interests lie." He asserted that there was "a drop in the general level of skills relevant to understanding what goes on in politics."[26]

The reissue of Drury's novel was the occasion for other reviews. In 2009, Scott Simon in the *Wall Street Journal* called the novel "the definitive Washington tale." Ten years later it may have become an interesting mirror for Washington politics. A contest between the Congress and the Executive was waged in 2019 over issues of transparency in the Mueller Report. In *Advise and Consent*, the constitutional system of checks and balances is put to the test. Roger Kaplan, in 1999, wrote that when Allen Drury created his novel in the 1950s the Senate's "grand traditions" were such that they "protected the states and the republic against the excesses of the executive's grasp for power." In

May 2019, the *New Yorker* magazine placed on its cover caricatures of Senator Mitch McConnell, Senator Lindsey Graham, and Attorney General William Barr as obsequious lackeys: shoe-shine boys for President Trump. In contrast with today's political polarization, the goal of Drury's Senate is reasonable compromise.[27]

Even so, an underhanded dirty politics is at work. Utah senator Brigham Anderson has pointed at the nominee's apparent communist sympathies. He is sent threats to blackmail him about a past homosexual affair. Interestingly, Drury's most McCarthy-like character in his novel is a liberal. This seems to suggest that intolerance and political chicanery can be initiated and propagated both on the political left and on the political right. Senator Cooley tried to stop the nominee by any means.

CROSS DAMON IN *THE OUTSIDER* (1953) BY RICHARD WRIGHT

Cross Damon is a troubled character: a man desperately seeking freedom who is cast aside by society and turns to ideology and to violence. When we meet Cross Damon, he is drinking heavily to numb the pain and his sense of alienation. He feels pain because he is constantly thinking about things and finds the world alienating and troubling. Cross Damon has long tried to escape his identity. He is a Chicago African American who is in debt and is in a troubled marriage. He has a mistress who is pregnant. When it is assumed that he may be dead in an accident, he seizes the opportunity to change his identity. He fakes his death and takes the identity of another man who has been killed. He rejects religious answers, joins a communist group, and acts out a path of violence and murder.

Critics have suggested that the character of Cross Damon is a product of Richard Wright's interest in existentialism. Richard Wright's existentialist concerns appear in his autobiography, *Black Boy*, and in his story "The Underground Man" (1942). Wright's time in Paris contributed to his novel *The Outsider*. However, there is in this character's world more the hopelessness of *Huis Clos* (*No Exit*) by Jean-Paul Sartre than the determination and humanism that may be found in the novels and essays of Albert Camus. Cross Damon seems more a nihilist than an existentialist. (And certainly, this is not the perspective of a religious existentialist like Søren Kierkegaard or Gabriel Marcel.)

Cross Damon is a modern man who breaks from his roots. He has to reinvent his life. He has become no one: an individual in the modern dilemma. Wright's outsider is no-man, an individual of no race or tradition, of no faith and no culture. Bereft of any depth, dimension of spirit, or any sustaining myth or sense of purpose, he tries to make a getaway from responsibility and from identity. Yet, to Damon Cross we must say, with the existentialists, that an individual who is thrown here into life on earth must choose and act. Running away is not really an option.

CIVIL RIGHTS

The presence of African American voices in American literature extends from *Invisible Man* (1952) by Ralph Ellison and James Baldwin's *Go Tell It on the Mountain* (1951) and *Notes of a Native Son* (1955) through Gwendolyn Brooks's poetry and *Maud Martha* (1953), her only novel, and Lorraine Hansberry's *A Raisin in the Sun* (1959).

The challenge of the civil rights movement echoed across America.[28] Martin Luther King Jr. moved to Montgomery, Alabama, on Sunday, October 10, 1954, and became the minister at the Dexter Avenue Memorial Baptist Church. King saw the movement toward a therapeutic culture and asserted the critical importance of Christian ethics. In his sermon "A Knock at Midnight," King referred to a parable from Luke 11:5–6 (Revised Standard Version). He said, "it is also midnight in our world, and the darkness is so deep that we can hardly see which ways to turn."[29] He recognized the psychological orientation of the time and suggested that it advocated something that fell short of conversion and transformation: "Go ye into the world, keep your blood pressure down and lo, it will make you a well-adjusted personality."[30] He observed that "bestsellers in psychology are books such as *The Modern Man against Himself*, *The Neurotic Personality of Our Times*, and *The Modern Man in Search of a Soul*." King asked: [Is this] "midnight within the inner lives of men and women?" In the moral realm, he said, "We have unconsciously applied Einstein's theory of relativity which properly described the physical universe, to the moral and ethical realm."[31] "We have turned to science for help and it has helped often. But alas, science cannot now rescue us, for even the scientist is lost in the terrible midnight of our age."[32]

Rosa Parks's refusal to move from her seat on Thursday, December 1, 1955, led to her arrest and to the Montgomery bus boycott announced on December 3. Back in 1943, she entered a bus and paid her fare. The bus driver, James F. Blake, told her she had to get out of the bus and enter by the back door. When she complied and stepped out to do so, he sped off, leaving her standing at the curb. On December 1, 1955, Rosa Parks entered a bus driven by the same man. She took a seat behind the first ten rows reserved for white passengers. At a bus stop in front of the Empire Theater, several white passengers stepped onto the bus and sought seats. Blake moved his "colored only sign" behind Rosa Parks and other African American passengers sitting nearby her. Rosa Parks slid over toward the window but did not move from her seat. Blake told her that he had to call the police. Parks was arrested and charged with a violation of City Code Chapter 6, Section 11, even though she had been in the designated section for black passengers. She was fined $10 plus court costs. She then chose to challenge racial segregation. The Montgomery bus boycott emphasized the point.

On December 5, 1955, in response to Rosa Parks's action, Martin Luther King Jr., at the Holt Street Baptist Church, addressed "the disinherited of this land" and told them: "We are here because of our love of democracy. . . . We reserve the right to protest." A powerful moment came as he used parallel structure to make his point: "If we are wrong, then the Supreme Court of this nation is wrong. If we are wrong, the Constitution of the United States is wrong. If we are wrong, God almighty is wrong."[33]

THE INVESTIGATORS

Detective fiction in 1950s America may be seen as a moral fiction that addresses the insecurities of a democratic postwar society. The detective's inquiry into trouble sets the world right again. Back in the 1930s, the Black Mask group, including Dashiell Hammett and Raymond Chandler, connected hard-boiled pulp fiction with times of socioeconomic distress and anxieties. Their stories generated a sense of fear, as Chandler observed. Their characters existed in a world gone wrong that needed to be investigated by a moral force. Although compromised personally by vulnerabilities, the detective represents this moral energy and quest. The patterns of life have been disrupted. Trauma creates an existential dilemma, a tone of disillusion that raises questions that beg for solutions.

Popular detective genre fiction was frequently dark and shadowy. In America, the detective spoke in familiar earthy vernacular. He was a diligent individualist who appeared in the hard-boiled detective novels of writers like Dashiell Hammett, James M. Cain, Cornell Woolrich, Raymond Chandler, and Ross Macdonald. In Mickey Spillane's *I, the Jury* and *Kiss Me Deadly*, the Mike Hammer persona embraces hard living, disposable relationships, hot cars, and a lot of smoke. The detective stories of Chester Himes featured Harlem detectives Coffin Ed Johnson and Grave Digger Jones. Himes, during his own incarceration for a robbery, turned to writing about black experience in America in *If He Hollers* (1945) and *The Lonely Crusade* (1947) and crime fiction in *Cast the First Stone* (1952) and *The Real Cool Killers* (1959). In *The Real Cool Killers*, Ulysses Galen, a white man, is attacked in a bar in Harlem. He escapes outside, where a drunken man named Pickens chases him with a gun. Galen is killed. When the detectives arrive and locate Pickens, they discover that his gun is a stage prop. So, who shot Ulysses Galen?[34]

The tough and detached American detective of the 1950s may owe something to Hemingway's laconic style. These 1950s fictional detectives encounter cynical characters, adventurers, convicts, men with amnesia, and traumatized people with anxiety. Their investigations act out the concerns of a society in transition. Following a disruptive war, Americans are starting over. Masculine images and types are experiencing redefinition. There is a search for authenticity, and there are issues of duplicity, forgery, and the inauthentic. There is a desire for security and for justice.

The detective stories of the 1950s scan the beat of American cities like Los Angeles, New York, and Chicago. They connect with postwar feelings of alienation. American individualism focuses upon self-creation and a happiness that is attained by striving and ambition. However, the crime films of the 1940s and early to mid-1950s have "characters whose defeat or death seems fated."[35] There are barriers to class mobility and obstacles to racial equality and gender equality in postwar America. In this critic's view, film noir questions the American dream of self-invention and rejects the notion that consumerist product acquisition or a therapeutic ethos can be liberating. For there are forces beyond the individual's control that overshadow these dreams. "The war has sliced a gap in citizen's lives," says Osteen. "The war and its aftermath were by far the most significant cultural influence on noir."[36] Thus, we have characters who are beset by problems and anxieties, characters who are trapped. Criminality and violence are seen as a displacement of the violence of war. In Frank Krutnik's view, there was a "breakdown of confidence in the defining and sustaining cultural regimentation of identity and authority."[37] Other Hollywood films seek restoration, nostalgia, and sentimentalism, or to reinvigorate hopes and dreams.

"Genre fiction articulates cultural conflicts," observes Leonard Cassuto.[38] He connects hard-boiled detective fiction with earlier sentimental narratives, which he demonstrates prepared the way for the modern crime novel. The sentimental novel, as Jane Tompkins has pointed out in *Sensational Designs* (1985), is family oriented and focuses on human feeling and extensions of sympathy. The values and stability of a community are at stake in the detective crime novel. The pulp detective novel drew upon naturalism. It gave attention to plot and to suspense. It responded to the impact of modernization and represented the home-work divide.[39] Willard Huntington Wright (S. S. Van Dine) likened the detective story to a crossword puzzle, a fitting together of parts. He insisted that in a detective mystery "the culprit must turn out to be a person who has played a more or less prominent part in the story." Dorothy Sayers said that the story of detection necessitates a method of "fair play" by the author with the reader.[40]

PHILIP MARLOWE IN *THE LONG GOODBYE* (1953) BY RAYMOND CHANDLER

Philip Marlowe emerged from the pulps into a well-rounded character in Raymond Chandler's fiction. He is a man directed toward conscience, while driven to find solutions to crimes. Moving through an everyday world of mishaps, human error, and evil, Marlowe is a loner, a plain-spoken man confronting danger. He drinks whiskey and brandy and smokes cigarettes and sometimes a pipe. With his first-person narration comes Chandler's keen eye for social critique. He is witty and sometimes satirical, and he makes wisecracks to cover his more aesthetic side. Marlowe plays chess. He is thoughtful and persistent. He is ever a bachelor, until he decides to marry Linda Loring in Chandler's final unfinished manuscript of *Poodle Springs*. He works out of an office in the Cahuenga building on Hollywood Boulevard, and in *The Long Goodbye*, he lives in a house on Yucca Avenue. Through Marlowe's reportorial voice, we enter a Southern California world of the criminal and the rich runaway. It is the rhythm of that voice and Chandler's sentences that lift these novels to a realm of quality.

The Long Goodbye, at around 120,000 words, is one of Chandler's longest novels and among his best. Chandler critiques the contemporary world in this adventurous mystery. Set in Southern California amid a set of wealthy characters, the story features Philip Marlowe's encounters with Terry Lennox and Sylvia Lennox and with Eileen and Roger Wade. Sylvia Lennox dies early in the novel, apparently the victim of a homicide. Philip Marlowe befriends Terry Lennox, an alcoholic veteran suffering from post-traumatic stress disorder. The Eileen Wade and Roger Wade story overlaps and intersects with this. Roger Wade, an alcoholic writer, is in a sanitarium, a clinic where he is supposedly drying out. The strength of this story lies in the rhythm of Chandler's prose and the interweaving of these plots.

It is autumn and we are outside "Dancers." Marlowe encounters the alcoholic and scarred Terry Lennox. The next summer, Lennox appears at Marlowe's residence in trouble and on the run. He urges Marlowe to take him over the border to Tijuana. Sylvia Lennox, Terry's wife, is dead, and he is being sought for the murder. Now, with Terry Lennox gone, the investigators arrest Marlowe. They attempt to get him to admit that he helped Lennox get away. Before long, they find Lennox dead, and he has left a suicide note with an apparent confession. However, there is more to it than this. Lennox has left a "portrait of Madison" (a $5,000 bill) for Marlowe to investigate the case.

Meanwhile, Marlowe is called by a New York publisher, Howard Spencer, to investigate the disappearance of one of his finest writers. Roger Wade has been missing. Eileen Wade also asks Marlowe for his assistance in finding Roger. He is found in a sanitarium detox clinic. However, something about the Wades' story does not add up. Marlowe's further investigation could be tripped up by Mendy Menendez, Lennox's father-in-law, the Wades' servant Candy, or by Eileen Wade.

By the 1950s, Raymond Chandler was tiring of writing for films. His first novel, *The Big Sleep* (1939), famously became a film starring Humphrey Bogart as the detective Philip Marlowe. That detective novel was developed from his short stories "Killer in the Rain" and "The Curtain." By working from other stories, he later created *Farewell, My Lovely*, *The Lady in the Lake*, and *The Long Goodbye*. Chandler always had the hope that he would write a literary novel. However, he was most successful with his hard-boiled detective fiction. *The Long Goodbye* has been considered by several critics to be some of his best writing.

In 1940, Chandler resided in a cabin by Big Bear Lake when he wrote most of *The Lady in the Lake* (1943). He also continued work on *Farewell, My Lovely* (1940). The war was on his mind. However, he was denied entry into officer's training in the Canadian military because of his age. In 1941, the film rights for *Farewell, My Lovely* were bought by RKO. Soon afterward, *The High Window* (1942) was published. In 1943, the James M. Cain novel *Double Indemnity* was given to him for film adaptation by Paramount studios and director Billy Wilder. He received an Academy Award for his screenplay. When *The Lady in the Lake* was purchased by Paramount, Chandler returned to Hollywood. Chandler was busily at work on *The Blue Dahlia*. The story was targeted as a star vehicle for Alan Ladd, who had been drafted into the army. Chandler had not finished his story and was not sure how it would end. He decided to get drunk so that he could finish it. The decision did not come easily. Chandler recognized his past history of inebriation, and he had stayed away from liquor for a decade. He enlisted medical care, a driver, and secretarial assistance and then, primed by his genie in the bottle, wrote an Oscar-winning script. Whereas Hemingway drank heavily in the 1940s *after* writing, Chandler drank during the writing. He risked his health in the process.

Despite a lucrative movie deal, Raymond Chandler began to lose his interest in writing for Hollywood studios. He reluctantly took on a contract to adapt Patricia Highsmith's *Strangers on a Train* for a film by Alfred Hitchcock. He did not get along well with the British director. The medium of film challenged the suspension of disbelief that was necessary for Chandler's story. There was too much realism, too little left to the imagination of the viewer, Chandler recognized. A reader of fiction accepts the "implausibility" of characters and their actions within the imaginative world of the story. The audience for Hitchcock's film was going to see a more objective presentation. Chandler argued with Hitchcock: If you are going to just do the film your own way what do you need me for?[41] Chandler had had enough of studio restrictions and strong-willed directors. He was going to write whatever he felt like writing. *The Little Sister* (1949) followed. He visited England with his wife Cissy, conscious of her health issues. He began writing *The Long Goodbye* (1953).

Raymond Chandler's *Playback* was written from a screenplay into a novel. He wrote the first part in 1953 and resumed writing in 1957. Chandler wrote his film script *The Blue Dahlia* and wrote film scripts for James M. Cain's *Double Indemnity* and Patricia Highsmith's *Strangers on a Train.* In his novelization of *Playback*, Chandler designed a first-person narrative. Philip Marlowe replaced Jeff Millane, who was the protagonist in the screenplay. Betty Maysfield escapes a murder charge that she killed her husband and travels under an assumed name to Southern California. Unfortunately, she is charged with Larry Mitchell's death. Philip Marlowe will attempt to show that she is innocent of the crime.

PERRY MASON IN THE NOVELS OF ERLE STANLEY GARDNER

Perry Mason, one of the most popular fictional characters of the twentieth century, was the legal brainchild of Erle Stanley Gardner, a California attorney and writer of formula fiction. Grappling with criminal cases and overcoming obstacles, Perry Mason provided Americans with images of the practice of law. In print, the Perry Mason books regularly rose to top positions on the nation's best-seller lists. There were twenty-five Perry Mason novels during the 1950s. The *Perry Mason* television series, beginning in 1957, ran for nine seasons.

Perry Mason is a man of action, not a contemplative character. He is an archetypal attorney figure; intelligent, resourceful, and crafty, he is always a sharp interrogator in the courtroom. However, he does not have much of an inner life. Erle Stanley Gardner's creation works primarily in Los Angeles; he is a moral figure who stands for the law and justice. From 1933 through the 1950s, there were eighty-two Perry Mason novels. They were plot-driven popular fictions that were readily adaptable to television. The early Perry Mason was part hard-boiled detective and part lawyer. Like other figures in the detective genre of the 1930s, he was tough, determined, and not above using devious tactics. For the audience since 1957, Perry Mason is associated with the voice and face of actor Raymond Burr, who Gardner called an ideal fit for his fictional character.

The iconic attorney explores cases with his associates Della Street and detective Paul Drake. An innocent person is accused of a crime and enlists the assistance of Perry Mason. Frequently, the case revolves around a family business, and the innocent individual has made mistakes and has been implicated in a murder. Mason and his team seek evidence to explain the case and attempt to exonerate his client. As he pursues his investigations, he regularly encounters Lieutenant Arthur Tragg. Inevitably the case ends up on trial in the courtroom, where Perry Mason, as defense attorney, faces off against Los Angeles prosecutor Hamilton Burger. In the syndicated television series, the courtroom drama typically ends in a confession from a witness on the stand or the perpetrator passionately declaring his or her guilt from the gallery. The tight format of the television series reflects the formula fiction from which these cases are derived.

The detective fiction sets the world right again by confronting mystery, violence, death, and crime. Duplicity is overcome by justice. The detective's inquiry derives from Edgar Allan Poe's Auguste Dupin and his emphasis on ratiocination and from Arthur Conan Doyle's perspicacious Sherlock Holmes. They are extended by writers like Agatha Christie, Dorothy Sayers, and John Dickson Carr. Erle Stanley Gardner was writing pulp fiction in the 1920s with a variety of protagonists. (He also wrote under the pseudonym A. A. Fair.) Perry Mason appeared in 1933 in *The Case of the Velvet Claws*.

In contrast with the adventurous and lusty James Bond, Perry Mason is a thinker and a gatherer of information. He explores crime methodically. Mason is compassionate, tough, and thoughtful. In Gardner's fiction, he is the hard-boiled detective who was popular in 1930s and 1940s detective stories. As the series proceeds, Della Street and Paul Drake become like family members. Perry Mason appears like a clear-eyed moral father to his younger clients, solicitous and sympathetic when called to care for them, and stern and straightforward when bringing their mistakes to light. At home in his office, he is a tactical strategist, a seeker of truth, and a defender of law and justice. The law becomes a sturdy resource in Perry Mason stories. Perry Mason eventually evolves into a fearless moral figure.[42]

MIKE HAMMER IN *ONE LONELY NIGHT* (1951) AND *KISS ME DEADLY* (1952) BY MICKEY SPILLANE

Mike Hammer in *Kiss Me Deadly* (1952) by Mickey Spillane is a comic book figure: tough, conservative, cynical, and suspicious of people, including his secretary Velda. The female hitchhiker he picks up is nude under her trench coat. At a police barricade, a policeman asks Hammer if he saw a hitchhiker. Hammer tells him that he and his "wife" saw no one. He is told that a patient has escaped from a sanitarium. (Hammer's encounter with the female escapee, in this respect, is a bit like Walter Hartright's encounter in Wilkie Collins's *The Woman in White*.) Hammer heads back on the road with the woman, Berga Torn, beside him, and they are followed. There is a fight with a gunman, and Mike Hammer is knocked unconscious. He awakens as Berga Torn is being tortured for information and then murdered. Hammer and the dead woman are placed back in Hammer's car, which is sent over an embankment. Hammer is thrown from the car and survives. When Hammer investigates, he discovers that Berga Torn was the ex-mistress of crime syndicate boss Carl Evello. She was scheduled to testify against him. Velda assists Hammer with his inquiry into records on the activities of the Mafia. Hammer goes to Berga Torn's Brooklyn address to look for clues.

One may ask if Mike Hammer revels in killing as he exhibits a sense of duty to rid the world of criminal evil. His almost comic-book-hero violence sold thousands of books in the 1950s. In *One Lonely Night* (1951), Mike Hammer is criticized by a judge who casts him as a lawless murderer. The shadow of this judge, the voice of law and order, lingers throughout the story. Mike Hammer believes he must go beyond the letter of the law to rid society of evil. The judge has referred to the war and the power of the gun "sanctified" by it. Mike Hammer will use violence, if necessary, to deal with the local situation. As for the world picture, he recognizes that he does not comprehend it all. In the news, he sees "[m]ore about the trials and the Cold War. Politics. I felt like an ignorant bastard for not knowing what it was all about."[43]

Mike Hammer's aim is to uphold law in spirit, even by lawless violence. Democracy and rule of law is insufficient and must be transcended with holy righteousness and concerted action. Hammer is on a mission to preserve society. He is violent to maintain order. Philip Wylie wrote of the violence in Spillane's fiction: "If Spillane's millions of readers suddenly began acting like Spillane's detective, Mike Hammer, the Soviets could take us over without dropping a bomb because the United States would be in chaos."[44]

In his essay "Simenon and Spillane," Charles J. Rolo pointed out that the righteous fervor displayed by Mike Hammer is moralistic. There is "religious content to this violence," he wrote.[45] If law has failed, then Hammer, acting on a higher law of justice, must be the avenger. Might this suggest that a "religious" violence was also transposed into anticommunism by Joseph McCarthy? From this perspective, it may appear that McCarthy's crusading was a form of violence for God and country, as well as self-serving enjoyment such as Hammer appears to get from the violence he justifies as his mission. Is Hammer like Sophocles's Antigone proudly fighting for justice, or is he a latter-day Raskolnikov, believing he is above the law? Hammer is convinced that rule of law may sometimes be weak and that it is his responsibility to seek justice and dare to fight the good fight.

NANCY DREW IN THE NOVELS OF MILDRED WIRT BENSON, HARRIET STRATEMEYER ADAMS, AND OTHERS (CAROLYN KEENE)

The most famous of female teen investigators, Nancy Drew, was the creation of Mildred Wirt Benson and Harriet Stratemeyer Adams, who took over the series from her father, Edward Stratemeyer. The Nancy Drew character has changed across the years, adapting across time to culture, while ever displaying independence, sureness, morality, and good manners. Does it matter that Nancy Drew was written by a collective of ghost writers? Is she now an artifact, fondly remembered by generations of readers? Or, does the revamped Nancy Drew still have something to say about energetic and resourceful young women in America?

Nancy Drew, in her original incarnation, spoke well. She was smart, active, adventurous, determined, and skillful. She acted older than her years, and she was heroic. That may be, in part, because Mildred Wirt Benson was a feminist and Harriet Stratemeyer Adams and her sister Edna supported female independence and voice. Even so, as Amy Benfer argued in the *New York Times* in 2004, "She came off like a prissy automaton of perfection." At last, she is now "more human and self-effacing."[46]

Of course, one might expect a Nancy Drew of yesteryear to be different from her post-1980s image. In 1929–1930, Edward Stratemeyer, creator of the Hardy Boys series, marked her as a Victorian girl of the period. His daughter, who submitted Mildred Wirt Benson's feisty young protagonist to editing and packaging under the pseudonym Carolyn Keene, gave Nancy Drew greater freedom and daring. Nancy Drew was blonde, blue eyed, and perpetually about sixteen or seventeen years old. She lived in the fictional River Heights, Illinois, without a mother to love, coach, or control her. Her father, the lawyer Carson Drew, supported her and was proud of his daughter. Nancy Drew emerged as daring but well mannered, a girl in a blue roadster who appeared completely unaffected by either the Great Depression of the 1930s or the shortages of the Second World War.

Nancy Drew in the 1950s became less rural and more oriented toward Chicago and New York. One might call her preppie. She is now illustrated again, in 1954. Her companions Bess Marvin and Georgia (George) Fayne are an interesting gender study. Bess is softer, "feminine," and "look" oriented, while George is a tomboy, logical, with short dark hair and brown eyes. In 1959, Nancy gets a convertible and becomes eighteen, after miraculously remaining sixteen or seventeen for more than two decades. She takes on a sporty image. Harriet Stratemeyer Adams and her ghost writers rewrite the series to get rid of now awkward ethnic and racial stereotypes.

More recently, in the 1980s, Nancy Drew received a makeover, courtesy of Nancy Axelrod and Simon & Schuster. *Ms. Magazine* called her a "Barbie Doll detective." In "Girl Revised," Amy Benfer suggests that all the looks into the mirror at her own hair "runs the risk of turning Nancy into a totem of our self-referential age." What a pity it would be if taking selfies, excessive texting, and Facebook, Instagram, and Twitter time were to take Nancy Drew away from solving crimes![47]

LEW ARCHER IN THE NOVELS OF ROSS MACDONALD

Lew Archer is the detective at the center of Ross Macdonald's novels. Archer is cynical and suspicious about people's motivations. He follows a value system, his code, which he may have to violate in self-defense at times. Archer is a bit more sensitive and attuned to people than his predecessors in the stories by Dashiell Hammett and Raymond Chandler. Yet, he knows the human capacity for evil. He makes use of forensics and developments in criminology. Lew Archer tends to investigate family crime cases, much like Perry Mason does. The narrative voice of Archer and the suspense of the plot are the elements that keep a reader intrigued.

Moving Target (1949) was the first of Ross Macdonald's Lew Archer novels. It was being read by mystery enthusiasts as 1950 began. The detective must find millionaire Ralph Sampson. He meets Sampson's daughter, Miranda. A gang may have Sampson. They send a ransom note. The family will pay. Archer follows the mail carrier, a member of the gang. The letter carrier is killed by the gang. He follows a pilot and his lover and accomplice Betty. He seeks where Sampson is hidden. Betty and the pilot have committed the crime to obtain money for their escape as lovers to a new life beyond California. As Lew Archer pursues the case, he comments on his dreams. He tells us that he works on cases in a "steel and concrete jungle."[48]

Lew Archer appeared in several more novels in the 1950s: *The Way Some People Die*, *The Barbarous Coast*, *The Doomsters*, and *The Galton Case*. In *The Way Some People Die*, Lew Archer is on the case when Mrs. Lawrence gives him money to find her missing daughter Galatea (Galley). His discovery that she was married to a mobster takes him to the criminal underground and its seedy characters. He follows the case from Los Angeles out to Palm Springs and up the coast to the fictional Pacific Point and San Francisco. True to the title, the story has a lot of characters dying in mysterious circumstances. In *The Barbarous Coast*, Hester Wall has disappeared somewhere along the coast of California, and Lew Archer has to trace and find her. In *The Doomsters*, Lew

Archer is hired by a mental patient, Carl Hallman, who has escaped the asylum to investigate the suspicious deaths of his parents. His mother drowned in a pool and his father, a senator, has recently died. He claims that he was sent away by his brother to guard family secrets and because of his claims about the deaths. Then Carl's brother dies, and Carl is blamed for his death. However, Lew Archer begins to uncover clues that lead him to several possible suspects. The secret history of a family comes back as a theme in *The Galton Case*.[49]

Other suspense novels of the period were written by Graham Greene, such as *Heart of the Matter* (1948), set in Sierra Leone, and *Our Man in Havana* (1958). Paul Dixeburger wrote *Atomsk* (1949). China specialists for the CIA Edward Aarons and Sam Durrell wrote the "Assignment" series. British author Desmond Cory wrote *Secret Ministry* (1951) with his character Johnny Fedora as a secret agent–assassin. Donald Hamilton wrote *Death of a Citizen* and *The Wrecking Crew*, both published in 1960. E. Howard Hunt was both a spy and a writer in the 1950s. He wrote *East of Farewell* (1943) and joined the newly formed CIA in 1949. *The Violent Ones* (1950) was followed by a series of spy novels and hard-boiled detective stories. Meanwhile Hunt worked on "political action and influence" in the "Special Activities" Division. In 1950, he recruited William F. Buckley, who would later be a godfather to three of Hunt's children. William Buckley wrote in the *Los Angeles Times* that he met E. Howard Hunt upon arriving in Mexico City in 1951 as a deep cover agent. Presumably Buckley left that post in 1952. In the article, he called Hunt's Watergate misdeed a "fateful wrong turn."[50]

8

ADVENTURERS

The discovery of the double helix, the twisting structure of DNA, by James Watson and Francis Crick in 1953 ushered in a biological age. The detonation of the hydrogen bomb prompted further calls for peace from nuclear scientists. The 1950s was an era of technical innovation: jet aircraft, the UNIVAC computer, transatlantic cable, a vaccine for polio. Thor Heyerdahl sailed on his Kon-Tiki expedition. Edmund Hillary climbed Mount Everest. The Sputnik launched into space. But many adventures in 1950s fiction lay closer to home.

Saul Bellow brought readers into Augie March's adventures in Chicago. Philip Roth brought them down the road with Neil Klugman from Newark to Short Hills. Intellectual adventures and issues came from fictional colleges. Scandal came from New England suburbs. The sexual adventures of *Peyton Place* and the homosexual awakening of David in *Giovanni's Room* broke apparent taboos. Sal Paradise took to the open highway. These were characters seeking freedom but were somehow also bound.

James Michener's *Hawaii* provided an adventure for readers to a place that was exotic and new to most. His novel, well timed for the admission of the fiftieth state, was one of the most popular books of 1959 and 1960. Michener was proudly middlebrow and wrote expansive historical novels, covering wide stretches of geography, culture, and human time. *Hawaii* was a further development of his stories in *Tales of the South Pacific*, which were drawn imaginatively from his experience in the navy. In 1951, Michener, witnessing America's postwar role in the world, contrasted the popular novel with the modernist novel and asserted the value of moral fiction. In "The Conscience of the Contemporary Novel," Michener wrote: "We present the anomaly of a nation seeking world leadership before it even knows itself."[1] American literature needed to speak to the world and participate in world literature, he declared. For America to be a leader in the world, its literature ought to become more of a world literature. Consequently, Michener, in an apologetics for his own work, supported the popular novel. He wrote in *The Voice of Asia* (1951) that "the novelist is essentially a popular artist, and as such his responsibility is very great."[2] He claimed that knowledge about America was important, rather than aesthetic and formal innovation or experiment. Literature can be an effective medium for moral values, he wrote. For many "of the humane and liberal ideas which circulate to keep the conscience of the world are customarily circulated by novels."[3]

AUGIE MARCH IN *THE ADVENTURES OF AUGIE MARCH* (1953) BY SAUL BELLOW

The Adventures of Augie March is a novel of poetic fluency and imagination. The novel is a work of narrative freedom, crisp vernacular, and picaresque adventure through which Saul Bellow gives us a vibrant Chicago world. Augie's narration of his life story begins: "I am an American, Chicago born."[4] The novel takes the form of a retrospective autobiography. ("I was eternally looking for a way . . . but the question was whether I was a man of hope or foolishness.")[5] Bellow seeks an insight of the heart, rather than a rationalized society. A heteroglossic interplay of voices emerges from within Augie's first-person narrative, which expands across many characters and the Chicago area landscape. With this novel, Saul Bellow further distinguished himself as a storyteller and craftsman of imaginative scope, moral concern, and philosophical depth.

Augie March's story begins with his family: his mother and father, his brother Simon, his mentally challenged brother Georgie, and the inimitable boarder, Grandma Lausch, who is "not a relation" but is clearly an important presence in Augie's life.[6] Mama is described as simple, "meek and long, round-eyed," with green eyes that look gently through round glasses. She is a hard-working woman with reddened hands, big feet, and missing teeth. She wears a "ravelly coat-sweater."[7] Her husband has left them, and he is described as a memory of one who liked certain meals and read the Chicago newspapers. The boys vaguely recall that he may have worn a uniform: maybe as a driver for Hall Brothers laundry. Grandma Lausch is a Polish-Russian Jew from Odessa, who reads *Anna Karenina* and *Eugene Onegin* every year and makes sure that Augie and Simon read entries from the *Encyclopedia Britannica*. Grandma remembers Mr. Lausch with a candle and cooking—her "kitchen religion." Grandma Lausch is a plotter, a "Machiavelli of small street" who boils chicken, has a poodle named Winnie, and is fluent in Russian, Polish, and Yiddish.

Among the neighbors is Mr. Kreindl, a former Austro-Hungarian military man with a big belly, a "masterly look of independence" despite a reddened face and "a drill-sergeant's bark." Kreindl slaps the table with his big hands. He has a wife with whom he quarrels and a son, Kotzie, who works in a drugstore and is studying to be a dentist. Mama calls Kotzie "that trashy Hungarian" and calls Mrs. Kreindl "the secret goose."[8] Living among Polish children, Augie and Simon see in neighborhood kitchens the images of saints, "baskets of death flowers," and "communions."[9] They are confronted by their Polish Catholic neighbors with anti-Semitism, with the claim that because a few Jewish religious authorities referred Jesus to the Romans for execution all Jews are to be blamed. Even so, Augie makes friends easily. He recalls being "pals . . . with Stashu Kopecs," who is remembered as a little thief who stole "coal off cars, clothes from the lines, rubber balls from the dime store, and pennies off the newsstands."[10]

Augie has left home at twelve on his first peripatetic adventure. He goes to the North side of Chicago for a job delivering newspapers. There the day begins before dawn, and the half-hour ride on the trolley from home is too much to do at that early hour. So, he lives with his mother's cousin Anna Coblin and her husband, Hyman Coblin. He has been "farmed out . . . to get a taste of life and the rudiments of earning."[11] The Coblins' son Howard ran away with the undertaker's son and ended up in the Marines on a mission in Nicaragua. Anna is distraught about that. She is caught up in her memories, sustained by her religious imagination, and inclined to cast her enemies as "hell's angels and deputies" because Howard is gone. The Coblins are trying to set up

Augie with Freidl, a girl of about ten, for a future marriage. Grandma Lausch encourages Augie and Simon to someday attend college. Simon becomes class valedictorian and gives his class commencement address, and Augie skips a grade. Grandma Lausch tells them that if Kreindl's son can be a dentist, either of them can become the governor of Illinois.

Augie March characterizes mid-century mobility. He drifts along, rather unheroically, with no set plans, trying to understand his place in the world. We see how he is affected by the disabled real estate tycoon Einhorn. We watch him dealing with a lifeboat issue during wartime. Augie passes through a series of affairs.

Saul Bellow places his story in a material world of specific objects and images, a family story, and an array of characters who affect Augie's life. Augie responds to the world around him. He seldom plans action. Rather, he reacts to people and to experiences. "All the influences were lined up and waiting for me," he tells us.[12] He embraces work, faces necessity, and responds to the assertions of Grandma Lausch or the suggestions of his brother Simon. From the news route, Augie moves through a series of jobs. There is a failed job with Borg and a department store job from which he is fired because of his alliance with the mischievous Jimmy Klein. He describes his first day with Borg: "It was stiff cold weather, the ground hard, the weeds standing broken in the frost, the river giving off vapor and the trains leghorn shots of steam into the broad blue Wisconsin-humored sky."[13] He tells us about how Grandma Lausch warned him about Jimmy Klein. The Klein family admired her "for the task she undertook" with Augie and Simon. However, they could not control Jimmy, who "pocketed every tenth quarter" at the department store. Shortly after Christmas, they are caught and have to pay back the money.[14] He begins to deliver flowers for a flower shop operated by a man with gangster connections, and he rides on streetcars to make deliveries to funeral homes. Meanwhile, Augie has become infatuated with Hilda Novinson and experiences what he calls "an idiot desire to follow her." Hilda is the daughter of a tailor who has a shop in the neighborhood. She is tall, "light-voiced, hasty spoken and shy" and has a "Russian facial angle" always "denying you a direct glance."[15]

One day Grandma Lausch decides that Georgie is getting older and may become unmanageable for the family. She declares that he ought to be placed in an institution, so he will stay out of trouble. The family is heartbroken about this, but they agree.[16] When Grandma Lausch gets a letter in Russian and begins to pack up her belongings, Simon and Augie are concerned for their mother. Mama relies upon Grandma Lausch's company and she has poor eyesight. Grandma Lausch is at the family's center, even if she is domineering and has sent Georgie away.

One of the chief characters of Augie's teenage years soon appears. William Einhorn is a well-connected businessman who is confined to a wheelchair. Augie goes to work for him. "William Einhorn was the first superior man I knew," Augie tells us. From Einhorn came "the lessons and theories of power."[17] Einhorn is "very pale, a little flabby in the face; considerable curvature of the nose, small lips and graying hair." He has a dutiful, attractive wife who is a bit heavy and who always likes "things to be ready."[18] Mrs. Einhorn, he says, is kindly but selfish. Mr. William Einhorn is "engaged in small swindles," carries on with women, and is engaged as a real estate broker with properties, lawsuits, and a club where he meets his cronies. Einhorn is not religious but goes to the synagogue for appearances and "form."[19] He is "[s]elfish, jealous, autocratic, carp-mouthed."[20] Yet, Einhorn encourages Augie. He gives him a set of the Harvard classics. Augie attempts to read Plutarch, Martin Luther, and Charles Darwin, but he acknowledges that he has little "studious peace" at night.

Einhorn has two sons. One is studying at the University of Illinois. The other son, who is nicknamed Dingbat, is more conspicuous. Dingbat likes to party. He plays the ukulele with friends on the beach at Lake Michigan. He provides "recitations and hoarse parodies . . . turkey grindings and obscene cackles that make the girls scream." He is protective of Augie: "This kid is a buddy of mine."[21] As a member of the National Guard, Dingbat is temporarily diverted to respond to a prison break at Joliet. Dingbat swears that he has the ability to make a fortune and what he wants is to be a boxing promoter. He sets up a fight between his star boxer, Nails, and a hulking drill operator named Prince Jaworski. Before Dingbat's short-lived career as a boxing promoter, Dingbat and Augie and other associates were assisting Einhorn, taking him to the beach. At home, Einhorn still drinks Coca-Cola, spits on the floor, and often breaks into monologue about his life: "Augie, you know a man in my position might be out of life for good," he says.[22] If somebody had any sense, they'd euthanize him.[23] He passes along his notes of wisdom. There are advantages to the roughness of Chicago. In this world, "marvelous" and "savage" things do not only happen in the past; they are all around us. Augie wonders, "What did I, out of all of this, want for myself?"[24] His life appears securely anchored to Chicago, although later in the story, Augie's affair with Thea Fenschl moves him from Chicago to a sojourn in Mexico.

In Robert Penn Warren's 1953 review, Augie is "The Man with No Commitments." He is "the antithesis of . . . the Hemingway hero." By this, Warren appears to have meant an active character who subscribes to code and makes decisions. Steven M. Gerson concluded that Augie prefers to live in dreams, rather than in reality.[25] Bellow's narrative moves inward and is well attuned to the feelings and life rhythms of his character. The novel is a bildungsroman, a character study. Delmore Schwartz called Bellow's novel "a new kind of book." He commented on Augie's "satirical acceptance, ironic affirmation, the comic transcendence of affirmation and rejection." Leonard Kriegel pointed out that Bellow's bildungsroman "has no real plot."[26]

Saul Bellow's Augie is a character of optimism. Augie tries professions. He seeks nobility. He is a voice, a language. He seeks to create a life in self-discovery, gathering up experiences and venturing into the world with independence and ambition. Augie March on Chicago's lakeshore in the 1930s is like Sal Paradise at the end of *On the Road*, or Nick Carraway gazing from the shore of Long Island. They look for America—its rich past and its uncertain yet still promising future.

SAL PARADISE IN *ON THE ROAD* (1957) BY JACK KEROUAC

The 1950s brought an age of mobility, and readers stretched out their sense of imagined community across the miles of a growing highway system. The road was wide and open for them to experience new locales and to set forth new dreams. In Jack Kerouac's *On the Road*, they followed the traveler who lives in restless motion across those spaces "only because he had no place he could stay in without getting tired of it and because there was nowhere to go but everywhere."[27]

Sal Paradise is a wanderer, a participant observer. He flees from stasis. He seeks freedom and to be unregulated. Dean Moriarty is his companion on the journey. Together they are representative of the Beats, who expressed individuality and rejected conformity. The individual self ought to be free to be mobile and not absorbed into the masses. Sal Paradise reflects Kerouac but is not Kerouac. His voice is linked with Kerouac's development of his spontaneous prose, which one critic has described as like music unfolding in time. Kerouac's search for a new writing method has as its goal to connect life and art, with the writing "as life itself."[28] Sal wants to connect with life itself, within his own rhythm.

With *On the Road*, Jack Kerouac began to develop his rhythm as a writer. Kerouac started his story in 1948. In 1951, at 454 West Twentieth Street, Jack Kerouac again wrote a version of *On the Road* on a 120-foot scroll. The scroll of *On the Road* was retyped in 1951 and 1952. He developed his manuscript with "insets" and "sketching." He practiced "jazz writing" with a tape recorder. After a divorce, he moved in with Lucien Carr and Allen Ginsberg. In 1955, he met poets Lawrence Ferlinghetti, Gary Snyder, Kenneth Rexroth, Michael McClure, and Philip Whalen. On September 5, 1957, *On the Road* was published. There are five versions of *On the Road*. The fourth is the Viking published edition. Finally, there was *Visions of Cody* (1972).

In *On the Road*, Sal Paradise, arriving in San Francisco, realizes that he is three thousand miles away from his aunt's house in Paterson, New Jersey. "I wandered out like a haggard ghost, and there she was, Frisco—long, bleak streets with trolley wires all shrouded in fog."[29] We meet Dean Moriarty and hear that "[h]e was Beat—the root, the soul of Beatific."[30] When Sal is in San Francisco, we read: "I looked out the window at the buzzing night street of Mission; I wanted to get going and hear the great jazz of Frisco—and remember, this was only my second night in town."[31] Sal Paradise's San Francisco experience is filled with a jazz aesthetic in which words unfold like music, seemingly improvised, swinging and rolling, popping and hissing, and buzzing with intensity.

Leaving town, Sal meets a Mexican girl on the bus. He persists to make contact, and she becomes his fellow traveler. So begins a journey that zigzags across geography. There is much restless movement. There are bus trips and drives that criss-cross the nation. Dean says, "I'm cutting along in my life as it leads me."[32] In the Third Part, they wander in the rain in the Hudson Valley north to Poughkeepsie. They watch a baseball game and then they play ball by the railroad tracks. A bus trip takes Sal from Washington, DC, across Virginia to West Virginia, and from there on to Kentucky, the Ohio River, and Cincinnati. After this is the "endless poem." There is the long road to Kansas, a fellow passenger Henry Glass, and on to Denver where Sal meets Stan with his "con-man smile and slow, easy-going Gary Cooper movements."[33] He reconnects with Dean, who has plans to go to Mexico. In May, they head south from Colorado through Texas. There are stretches of land between the cities, from "the burning sidewalks of Abilene" and Laredo ("a sinister town in the morning") to San Antonio. They pass through the heart of Texas, "wildernesses of brush," and cross the border into Mexico. Sal tells us: "The old car bopped and struggled on."[34] Dean reads Marcel Proust's novel, which suggests memory and an interior journey, as they go on to Mexico City.

The narrative is episodic. On Sal's bus ride, he is among schoolteachers. There are no books, only the open road and a new education awaits. Sal has "split up" from a wife, and it is time for him to reshape his life and his identity. He is learning the region of the West: broad landscapes, boxcars, hitchhikers, and hobos.[35] There are no binding societal ties. There is little clear direction, and there is more surface than depth. There is always the horizon. Sal Paradise has epiphanies, or visionary moments: "And for just a moment I had reached the point of ecstasy that I always wanted to reach, which was the complete step across chronological time into timeless shadows."[36]

Where would Sal Paradise be if he were alive today? Would he be a wistful baby boomer settled into the suburbs at long last, as *New York Times* columnist David Brooks imagines he might be?[37] Would he be "a graduate student with an interest in power yoga on the road to the MLA convention," driving a Prius and staying at Comfort Inns? Are Kerouac's original readers—who are still blessed with life nostalgic—less exuberant, less cheerful? Have any of them found "the Intrinsic Mind," the center that Sal Paradise sought? Have they been only on the road to the shopping mall, or on "the road to character" that Brooks has spoken of? Nowadays many people live in a less localized environment than people did in the 1950s. There is mobility. There is a near immediacy in communications. Thoughts move across geographies, and people are linked electronically and via the internet, Skype, cell phones, and other technologies. They are on the information highway.

Sal Paradise's peripatetic world is characterized by restlessness. Dean Moriarty seeks experience. The road itself is a setting or fluid series of locations. It is Twain's Mississippi, and they are like Huck Finn and Jim on the mighty river of life. To pause may bring Sal some disorientation: "I didn't know who I was—I was far away from home, haunted and tired with travel, in a cheap hotel room I'd never seen."[38] The restless movement of Sal Paradise and Dean Moriarty opposes provincialism. The security of a stationary community is experienced as conformity. The Beat contrasts with the organization man. He is the migrant of Steinbeck's *The Grapes of Wrath*, the marginal immigrant seeking new life. He has the independence of Natty Bumppo and the frontier spirit of Daniel Boone. He is Ishmael bound for adventure, and he resists the machine like a mythical John Henry. Yet, he does join with others in bohemian community. Sal continually links with Dean Moriarty, although their paths sometimes diverge. Most of their social affiliations are transitory. Their world is not particularly multicultural, although they pass through black communities and encounter Mexicans. They express instinctive energy. Yet, one may wonder if any civilization can be built upon ephemeral relationships and spontaneous journeys alone.

Eventually, the journey of Sal Paradise and Dean Moriarty concludes in New York City. Sal, who has to go to a concert, leaves Dean at the Port Authority bus terminal. *On the Road* concludes with Sal sitting on a river pier looking out at the sky over New Jersey, thinking out to America. He looks toward the setting sun, toward "all that road going, all the people dreaming in the immensity of it."[39]

BILL LEE IN *NAKED LUNCH* (1959) BY WILLIAM S. BURROUGHS

Bill Lee in William S. Burroughs's *Naked Lunch* is an addict who seeks freedom. He runs from the police, wanders away from Washington Square in Greenwich Village, and crosses America. He goes to Mexico. He later is in Tangier and in the fantasy world of Interzone. His life is a restless adventure.

Naked Lunch strings together a series of vignettes. Its characters drift and move, as does the language and the novel's images, in a modernist exploration of an underworld of drug use and drug trafficking, wandering and escaping. We begin in the subway at Washington Square

Station. A door is held open by a man in a white coat, and the narrator is followed by a narcotics detective. A young man with a Florida tan, "crew cut, Ivy league" appears as an advertising executive type in a Brooks Brothers shirt. Lee describes his own fingers as "dirty, junky" and gives us the image of heroin-needle-in-the-arm deaths and streets where the ash men congregate. To the Automat he goes, where Bill Gaines, in an overcoat, looks "like a 1910 banker with paresis," and we see Old Bart, "shabby" and "drinking" pound cake. We see "spectral janitors," "old relics," "phantom porters," and "a toothless old woman with canceled eyes."[40] A wino is pissing, and a radical Jew is handing out leaflets. Amid the run of language, the narrator is thinking of Chicago, "panhandler of dreams," and of escaping to Mexico. So, he goes to America's heartland, where the interior is "a vast subdivision of antennae of television" and people "in life-proof houses." For him, this is a land "always with cops" and "car trouble." This character finds America to be a place of oppression, a policed mechanism. Junkies are subversive and must find freedom. So, then south he travels to New Orleans, to then "backtrack for Mexico," crossing the border.[41] He tells us: "Something falls off you when you cross the border into Mexico, and suddenly the landscape hits you straight with nothing between you and it, desert and mountains and vultures." He wonders at "the shattering bloody blue sky of Mexico."[42]

You may dive in anywhere along the journey, Burroughs once said. Readers enter language and hear a voice, and they encounter a point of view, images and free associations, section cuts, and disruptions. The story is not linear. It is held together by the narrative voice, pulling one into his subjectivity. In Bill Lee, there is little stability of character: only change, fluency, curious characters, and narrative movement.

DAVID IN *GIOVANNI'S ROOM* (1956) BY JAMES BALDWIN

David is attracted to Giovanni, an Italian waiter in a gay bar. David's hesitation to love, his awareness of his vulnerability, and his difficulty with his homoerotic feelings result in a failure of relationship. *Giovanni's Room* has often been categorized as a gay novel. However, the novel more broadly considers human connection, identity, and how Eros may move among people. Baldwin said of the novel, "It's about what happens to you if you're afraid to love anybody."[43] David sees "beneath these faces. These clothes . . . the sorrow of the disconnected." David seeks to find "something to be moored to."[44]

David is in Paris, looking back at America. He considers which of these is home. David says, "perhaps home is not a place but simply an irrevocable condition."[45] In *Notes of a Native Son*, Baldwin affirms his love for America. He digs in to reveal its flaws and limitations, what he refers to as its "depthless alienation." David is a complex individual who struggles with his homoerotic desire. He says that being "entangled with a boy" was for him "but one tiny aspect of the dreadful human tangle occurring everywhere, without end forever."[46] Jacques tells him "not many people have ever died of love." That has come from lacking love, and for this lack, love may "perish . . . in the oddest places."[47] He declares: "Love him. Let him love you. Do you think anything else under heaven really matters?"[48] Love is between persons, not ideas or constructions.

We hear David's attempt to tell us his story, but he seems to hide aspects of it, even from himself. David discloses but also withholds. He has ambivalent feelings about Giovanni. He struggles with his sexuality in this Parisian context and with his American identity. He must acknowledge his difference from the norms or conventions of 1950s America. He is transatlantic but is not quite able to transcend being a 1950s American.

Baldwin tries to name a place for being a black, gay, transatlantic artist. To be gay is to be in a position that reflects that of the African American as minority or outsider. In this sense, race is part of this novel, where the affirmation of identity and the vulnerability of difference is deflected onto homosexuality. David experiences a kind of alienation, a dislocation in modernity and from himself. Paris seems to be more open than America to David as he works through constructions of masculinity and his attraction to Giovanni.

THE WOMEN OF *PEYTON PLACE* (1956) BY GRACE METALIOUS

Adventure and ambition, transgression and freedom, energy and will are marked out in the popular novel. *Peyton Place*, the racy best-selling potboiler, is a cultural marker of the 1950s. That hundreds of readers overtly or surreptitiously read the controversial novel surely affected public awareness. Who did female readers see in the characters of *Peyton Place*? How did they relate to them? With Constance MacKenzie and her daughter Allison, Selena Cross, and Betty Anderson in this fictional landscape, Grace Metalious portrayed unfaithful wives, burdened souls, and strong and ambitious women who break from respectability and convention. In the context of postwar America, this novel entered the psyche of women who sought a voice, passion, freedom, and self-worth. *Peyton Place* reflects the expansion of suburban life where rumored affairs emerge under the ordinariness of daily life. It is a story of dreams and ambitions, marital infidelity, and unwanted pregnancy. The novel evidently corresponded with emotional needs and fantasy. It provided a release from the prosaic life, conformity, and domestic roles.

Constance is ambitious. Bored by suburban life and "the limitations of Peyton Place," she goes to New York City and becomes a wealthy man's mistress.[49] At home, her mother, Elizabeth Standish, is burdened by criticisms of her daughter who her neighbors call a whore.[50] Constance's relationship with Allison MacKenzie "up in Scarsdale" in Westchester results in a pregnancy and the birth of a daughter who is also named Allison. Eventually, Constance returns home to Peyton Place with her girl. The neighbors acknowledge that it is hard for a woman to raise a child alone. Constance reflects, "Soon I will have to tell Allison how dangerous it is to be a girl."[51]

Allison MacKenzie has "a head full of silly dreams" and spirit for adventure. She will dream of freedom and of being a writer. Her friend Selena Cross, a young woman described as having a dark complexion and "gypsyish beauty," has been abused by her stepfather and ends up pregnant. Lucas is anathema and is forced from town. Doc Swain will perform an abortion: a procedure that, pre–*Roe v. Wade*, could result in prison for him. Selena is a young woman who seeks to transcend her victimization and to tell her story. She recovers, but Lucas returns on a snowy day before Christmas. Selena reacts to his aggressive advances and hits him with fireplace tongs, killing him. She and her brother bury the body.

Norms of sexual propriety are broken. Betty Anderson's sexual desire wanders outside of marriage, as have Constance's impulses. Betty is the "bad girl" of Peyton Place who, while in high school, flirts and flaunts her sexuality. She pursues Rodney Harrington, son of a mill owner, gets pregnant, and is ostracized. Whereas Betty is forced from town in disgrace, Rodney gets on with his life.

Women's reading had long been a concern in the nineteenth century. Enlightenment reason favored the rational over the passionate. Novels of sensation, the Gothic, and other romantic fiction stirred imagination. Presumably these novels upset one's rationality. Men were presumably more rational, and females, supposedly, were less able to guard against fancy. Daydreaming would disrupt industrious work. Those attitudes lingered in industrial America.

LEWIS ELIOT IN C. P. SNOW'S *THE MASTERS* (1950) AND *THE NEW MEN* (1954)

Adventures of the mind are encouraged in science and the arts through a liberal education. This was among the concerns of British novelist and scientist C. P. Snow. C. P. Snow's *Time of Hope* (1959) and *The Masters* (1950) feature the lawyer Lewis Eliot, who is a witness to scientific development and bureaucratic decision making in academia. Snow's slow-paced fictions portray Lewis Eliot's coming of age: his professional and intellectual adventure. They also reveal the professional ambitions and human foibles of individuals at work within academia and scientific and technological research.

In *The Masters*, Eliot observes conflict as individuals vie for an administrative promotion in an academic setting. A humanist and a scientist appear in competition for the coveted role. (Snow drew upon the experience of medieval historian Anthony Steel. Denied election as master, Steel went on to be the principal at Cardiff's University College.) At the college, the headmaster is dying. The fellows have to elect a new master and prepare for a transition in management of the school. Lewis Eliot, a lawyer, is our narrator. Paul Jago, who is a historian, is nominated and is favored by Eliot. Thomas Crawford, a scientist, is also nominated and becomes Jago's rival for the position. The fellows realize that the nomination will likely have implications for the college's management style and its curriculum. The college could receive a bequest for science studies if Crawford is elected. (This would be an endowment, or it would be comparable to a large STEM grant.) On the surface, these men are quite mannerly, but violence lies beneath. Lewis Eliot is our viewpoint character through which we see this society, its institutions, and its social perspectives. He is a man who attempts to tamp down his emotions. However, the loss of people who are significant in his life makes this difficult. His first wife committed suicide. His mentor, Roy Calvert, is bipolar and dies in an RAF bombing mission over Germany. Eliot becomes a lawyer and enters a world of politics and policy: a world of decision makers. Eliot is always a man closely connected with the events of his time. Despite his losses in life, he is usually optimistic. He is an observer of the work and action of leaders in government, science, and education. The critic Malcolm Bradbury has called Eliot "a wide ghost" and has viewed him as "a Victorian who drifts by observing other people's lives."[52]

The New Men (1954) addresses the atomic bomb. Readers meet Lewis Eliot's brother Martin who, with Walter Luke, is attempting to perfect the nuclear bomb. They are what sociologist David Reisman called "other-directed" men, and they are tragically alone. "To Martin it was jet-clear that, despite its joys, individual life was tragic: a man was ineluctably alone, and it was a short way to the grave. . . . Martin saw no reason why social life should also be tragic: social life lay within one's power as loneliness and death did not."[53] Martin's private concerns are linked with public issues, politics, and the science of nuclear fission.

Science had considerable social and political impact in the 1950s. C. P. Snow's concern went beyond academics to the identity and future of Britain and the nation's competitiveness in the world. Snow was concerned with what the "two cultures" meant for policy in Britain. Snow recognized that Britain's leaders and elites were educated in a tradition that emphasized classics. Snow believed that science could drive development and thus saw a clear need to continue to advance scientific-technological learning. It is, of course, not clear that an education in physics is any better preparation for world leadership than an education in history, philosophy, or English, observes historian Stefan Collini.[54] One ought to consider how we treat our natural world, our manner of business, and our extensions of scientific control, he points out. There is an "unease, lest science be overvalued."[55]

Snow's associate, J. H. Plumb, likewise affirmed that the traditional liberal arts education was designed for "gentlemen" who would become the "governing class."[56] The humanities now needed to "adapt themselves to the needs of a society dominated by science and technology." Plumb and Snow both connected this necessary move with democracy and modernity. As Collini points out, Snow's "Two Cultures" thesis and the responses to it "belonged to a particular period of British political and cultural history." These were "the Sputnik years, in which military and economic anxieties were displaced onto the issue of technological competitiveness."[57]

Snow knew well that the "new physics" had shifted perspective, and quantum theory had broken mechanistic models and the Newtonian worldview. Molecular biology and biochemistry were also making strides, and the 1953 discovery of the double helix and DNA by Crick and Watson was a scientific milestone. However, the paradigm shifts emphasized by Thomas Kuhn's *The Structure of Scientific Revolutions* (1962)—those discontinuous leaps by which science progresses—were only dimly recognized. Modern society was only gradually absorbing the impact of these sweeping shifts in worldview.[58]

It appears that Snow intended to advance a conversation concerning the cultural role of science. He surely elicited responses. F. R. Leavis's rejoinder included a harsh, snooty ad hominem directed at Snow's fiction: "as a novelist he doesn't begin to exist."[59] He claimed that the Rede Lecture itself showed no evidence of scientific training. However, it is unclear what Leavis's own training provided as a basis for this judgment. Evidently, Leavis regarded Snow's prose to be as lumbering and jowly as Snow: an earnest and kindly man who had spent years in laboratories. When it came to fiction, Snow was a realist. Unlike the modernists, he was not a stylist, an artist crafting literary sentences. Snow was a writer of didactic tales, concerned with society and power in science and politics.

Intellectual historian Stefan Collini traces concern about this divide to the nineteenth century. He observes that there have always been "distinct domains of human knowledge" and "different reflective minds."[60] He points out questions that remain relevant for us: How to "feed the world"? How to help the poor? What hope is there for humanity? To what extent ought these questions be part of the professional activity of scientists? C. P. Snow suggests social hope and a road of progress. Television did not figure in Snow's cultural calculations, Collini points out.[61] Television disseminates scientific-ecological thinking quickly. Our micro-electronic world and the internet were unknown to C. P. Snow. There has been a significant expansion of the social-institutional impact of universities since Snow's time.

In the United States, emphasis on technical education was associated with the development of postwar prosperity. In 1954, theologian Reinhold Niebuhr pointed out that extending "the margins of physical security" and comfort did not "guarantee the further development of cultural values" and could lead to "obsession with creature comforts."[62] He reflected upon an American tendency to seek solutions "for practically every problem of life in quantitative terms" while not being "fully aware of the limits of this approach." Niebuhr added that "the constant multiplication of high school and college enrollments has not made us the most intelligent nation whether we measure intelligence in terms of social wisdom, aesthetic discrimination, spiritual serenity, or any other basic human achievement."[63] American education may have made some individuals more technically proficient. However, this may only prove that this "technical efficiency is more easily achieved in purely quantitative terms than any other values of culture."[64]

With his scientific and technical training, C. P. Snow was aware of the need for scientific literacy. When he was a doctoral student, Charles Percy Snow studied infrared spectroscopy at the Cavendish laboratory that was supervised by Lord Ernest Rutherford. It appeared that he was destined for a career as a research scientist. Experiments conducted along with his colleague Philip Bowden resulted in their apparent discovery of the production of Vitamin A. Their research was published in *Nature*. However, upon further research it was determined that the vitamin could not be produced by this method. Snow retreated from that research career.

In 1932, Snow wrote "Death under Sail," and soon he was plotting a series of stories about a young scientist. This led to further fiction writing. The Strangers and Brothers series that he began in the 1940s provides us with an overview of British history in the twentieth century. As we have seen, *The Masters* is concerned with higher education and educational administration. *The New Men* concerns the atomic bomb. *Corridors of Power* (1964) focuses on the Suez Canal. Lewis Eliot ascends through the social hierarchy.[65]

JIM DIXON IN *LUCKY JIM* BY KINGSLEY AMIS

The novel set in academia in the 1950s is often satirical. Kingsley Amis's *Lucky Jim* (1954) and Mary McCarthy's *Groves of Academe* (1952) observe college academic life serio-comically. In each case, the university is subject to critique and is featured as a stage for a theater of the absurd. Amis explores relationships with a light-hearted touch. McCarthy's theme is academic freedom and the right to speak one's mind. The adventures of the mind seem to be of less concern than the adventures, ambitions, and mishaps of the characters. Even so, there were serious concerns about university education in the 1950s. In Britain, the red brick universities developed, and Oxford and Cambridge continued to provide a common background for much of the British leadership. C. P. Snow's concern with scientific education remained relevant for a nation that wished to keep pace with an increasingly technological-scientific age. The weight of the classics, the humanities, and the literary "science" of the New Critics lingered. Still in the air was the declaration of F. R. Leavis that the true university was "a centre of consciousness and human responsibility for the civilized world."[66]

Jim Dixon, in *Lucky Jim* (1954) by Kingsley Amis, is a lecturer at a red brick university in the Midlands. His sometime girlfriend Margaret Peel fakes a suicide, claiming to be shattered by a broken relationship. She tries to get Jim back into her romantic life. Jim submits an article that he hopes will pass through peer review and be published so that he can establish himself as a working scholar. However, the editor steals the manuscript and translates it into Italian for publication. Margaret sets up a weekend activity for Jim's supervisor, Professor Welch. Although he hopes to ingratiate himself with the administration, Jim makes a series of mistakes. He gets drunk and drops a cigarette onto a bed, burning a hole through the sheets. Meanwhile, Professor Welch's son Bertrand, a painter, is using his girlfriend Christine to gain contact with her uncle in Scotland so he can move up in the world. Jim Dixon is attracted to Christine. When Professor Welch informs Jim that his contract with the university will not be renewed, he and Christine head off together for London.

HENRY MULCAHY IN *THE GROVES OF ACADEME* (1952) BY MARY MCCARTHY

Henry Mulcahy is at the center of Mary McCarthy's probing of the issue of academic freedom. A literature instructor at Jocelyne College, he is an outspoken critic in a conservative institution. Henry is just past forty, with rimless glasses and thinning red hair. His "long, pear shaped body" is stuffed into "drooping trousers." He is described as quite clever, although he is contentious, "soft-bellied, nearsighted, lisping."[67] Henry is interested in the symbolists, as well as in James Joyce and in modern literature. He has published in the *Kenyon Review* and in the *Nation*. He is intelligent, liberal minded, and evidently academically keen. However, as a James Joyce scholar, he is, like Joyce, an iconoclast. Henry questions policies and allocations for buildings and grounds, and he criticizes "mismanagement."[68] He calls for a lighter teaching load and for faculty salary increases. He also critiques Maynard Hoar, the college president. (Curiously, Maynard Hoar has written an essay titled "The Witch Hunt in Our Universities.") Mulcahy has taught for fifteen years, but in his self-pity and pride he has begun to regard himself as "a prophet of modern literature" and a martyr like the self-exiled Joyce, or a man in a puzzle like a character in a Kafka novel.

Henry holds in his hands his letter of termination: "Your appointment will not be continued beyond the current academic year." He rather expected it. Yet, he feels betrayed and wounded.[69] In Henry's view, he has been targeted for his liberal opinions and for contesting the views of President Hoar at faculty meetings. Mulcahy considers his firing "a personal vendetta."[70] He is being made a scapegoat "to satisfy the reactionary trustees."[71] This occurs in a context of the Alger Hiss inquiry, the confession of Karl Fuchs to selling nuclear secrets, and Senator Joe McCarthy's hearings in the U.S. Congress. Henry, for all his flaws, is a sympathetic character whose liberal thought and outspoken demeanor are unpardonable transgressions. He tells Sheila, a student who visits his office, that he has been let go by the university. She is as sympathetic as a reader might be and raises an important personal question: "How to tell your wife?"[72] On a snowy day, Henry Mulcahy pouts with wounded pride. He decides that Hoar expects silence. He will create publicity. He is willing "to make trouble, to be inconvenient."[73]

NEIL KLUGMAN IN *GOODBYE, COLUMBUS* BY PHILIP ROTH

Neil Klugman is the self-reflective narrator of Philip Roth's lighthearted comic realism and probing of contemporary society. The novelette raises questions of cultural identity, often in comic fashion. Neil's summer romance with Brenda Patimkin brings him from the streets of Newark to the promised land of the suburbs and into a test to be acceptable to her newly upper-middle-class family. His grand infatuation with Brenda is marked by optimism and anxieties. He is the outsider, living with his Aunt Gladys and Uncle Max, working in the Newark Public Library, and making the drive from Newark to Short Hills.

We first meet Neil while he is in the kitchen conversing with his Aunt Gladys, who is urging him to eat and complicating another simple meal as if it was a gustatory delight. Her personality jumps off the page at us. Her motherly fuss, her care, and her Jewishness are marked by unmistakable qualities of voice and phrasing. "Since when do Jewish people live in Short Hills?"[74]

Neil meets Brenda at a swimming pool, stammers excitedly and tumbles over his words on the telephone, then arranges to see her while she plays tennis with her rather snooty friend. Brenda may look good to Neil in her tennis shorts or her bathing suit and add a sparkle to his life, but she is a self-centered and sheltered girl. "I had my nose fixed. I was pretty. Now I'm prettier," she says.[75] She is petulant, continually in conflict with her mother, and tries to make Neil acceptable. She wants what she wants—and her father provides most everything for her.

Ben Patimkin has created a suburban home for his family and has joined a consumer-land American dream of sporting goods, appliances, and fruit in the basement refrigerator. The Patimkins have become a success through Ben's business, Patimkin Kitchen and Bathroom Sinks in Newark. He has joined the exodus to Short Hills and Livingston and the quest for respectability. Ben is driven to acquire and to fit in. He strives to overcome the outsider status of immigrant Jewishness. He encourages his athletic son, Ron, who has played basketball at Millburn High School and will also play in college. He plays with his youngest daughter Julie, shooting basketballs up from the driveway. The sporting tree in the yard is surrounded by baseball mitts, balls, and other signs of their numerous trips to the sporting goods store. The living room is graced by photographs of the family. The basement refrigerator is stocked with a variety of fruits yet to be washed and consumed. Mrs. Patimkin putters amid her appliances like a displaced princess. She seems to miss the Hadassah in Newark. In the photos in the living room, her hair appears to be "in a halo." Yet there is an ongoing tension between her and Brenda.

Short Hills, rose-colored at dusk, becomes "like a Gaugin stream," Neil tells us.[76] The thought emerges from his interactions with a young black boy who he has guided to photos of Gaugin's images of Tahiti in the art books on the third floor of the Newark Library. Neil's world has become focused on two people: Brenda and the little black boy who talks to the lion statues outside the library and escapes from his urban life and into the photos of Gaugin's art. At the library, Neil tells a patron who expresses interest in the book that the book is already checked out on reserve. He tries to keep the book available for the boy. Some ladies have been "motored down from Upper Montclair" to look at the society pages.[77] When Neil asks the boy if he would like a library card so he can take the book home, the boy from the hard streets of Newark tells him that the book would only get ruined if he did that. Neil's prejudiced coworker grumbles about the black boy, and Neil is protective of him.

The economic distance between Neil and the Patimkins becomes clear. He "vacations" at their home. He is asked questions about his job at the library and his education at Rutgers-Newark. Neil has to explain that his parents went to live in Arizona because of their asthma. Mrs. Patimkin asks him about his family, the temple in Newark, and Jewish organizations. He asks her whether she knows Martin Buber's work, and she is not familiar with the Jewish philosopher. Neil visits and helps out at Patimkin Kitchen and Bathroom Sinks. The company building is in a formerly Jewish section of Newark that has now become an African American section. The kosher delis, fish stores, stickball games, and scents of corned beef and whitefish have given way to auto yards, grease, a brewery, and a leather factory. In private conversations with Brenda, he insists that she get a diaphragm: a suggestion she rejects. Her brother Ron is now engaged to his girlfriend Harriet, who to Neil seems "all surfaces." The family has Mantovani records, and Ron's Columbus record plays patriotic music, bells, and the voice of Edward R. Murrow. It intones the words "And so, goodbye Columbus."[78]

Like Neil we are on a voyage of discovery. We have walked up the steps into the library, where a boy waits, a lively young person whose life is bound by racism and poverty. The world stretches before him in a picture book that touches his imagination but not his reality. We are traveling like Neil from the streets of Newark to the suburbs of America, imagining the breadth and possibility of a new continent, a new century. With Neil, we sense that there is something more to life than a well-stocked refrigerator, the football on the lawn, sunset dwindling over the hill, and the commuter train bringing a woman or man in a gray flannel suit home. The world is round, and the horizon of history stretches out before us. Goodbye, Columbus. The light is changing.

NOTES

1. INTRODUCTION

1. Leslie Fiedler, *Love and Death in the American Novel* (New York: Stein and Day, 1956, rpt. 1960), 31; Robert Lowell, "Memories of West Street and Lepke," in *Selected Poems* (New York: Farrar, Straus & Giroux, 1976). Richard Chase is quoted by Martin Halliwell in *American Culture in the 1950s* (Edinburgh: Edinburgh University Press, 2007), 53. Leonard Cassuto, in *Hard-Boiled Sentimentality: The Secret History of American Crime Stories* (New York: Columbia University Press, 2009), points out that literary study has increasingly given attention to the "bottom up" history, "stressing that literature is of its time, and that writers do not (and cannot) transcend their context" (3). Here attention is given to the 1950s contexts and its themes, the book market, minority literature, collapsing high (literary) and low (pop formula) novels, and recognizing an intertextual and dialogical sense of the interplay between novels.

2. In 1817, Samuel Taylor Coleridge, in *Biographia Literaria*, vol. 7 of *The Collected Works of Samuel Taylor Coleridge*, ed. James Engell and W. Jackson Bate (Princeton, NJ: Princeton University Press, 1985), contributed thoughts on what he called "the willing suspension of disbelief."

3. Richard Lea, "Fictional Characters Make Experiential Crossings into Real Life Study Finds," *Guardian*, February 14, 2017.

4. Cody C. Debistraty, "The Psychological Comforts of Storytelling," *Atlantic*, November 2, 2014.

5. Wayne Booth, *The Rhetoric of Fiction* (Chicago: University of Chicago Press, 1961), 130. Of fictional characters, Bernard J. Paris writes: "Psychological analysis has shown that they are complex characters who are portrayed with

considerable subtlety." Imagined psychological analysis enables us to enter into the character's life. Perception and perspective are emphasized. Bernard J. Paris, *Imagined Human Beings* (New Brunswick, NJ: Transaction, 2010).

6. Roland Barthes, *Writing Degree Zero*, trans. Annette Lavers and Colin Smith (New York: Hill & Wang, 1953, rpt. 1977). Also see Roland Barthes, *S/Z: An Essay*, trans. Richard Miller (New York: Hill & Wang, 1970, rpt. 1975). In the semiotic approach to characters, Jaan Valsiner writes in *Transforming the Semiotic Object* that "[f]ictional characters live in an incomplete handicapped world" (99). Quoted in Jaan Valsiner, "Between Fiction and Reality: Transforming the Semiotic Object," *Sign Systems* 37 (2009): 99–112. "We are participant observers in the fixed lives of the fictional characters," said Umberto Eco (Valsiner, "Between Fiction and Reality," 107).

7. Richard J. Gerrig, *Experiencing Narrative Worlds: On the Psychological Activities of Reading* (New Haven, CT: Yale University Press, 1993), 170; Richard Marback, review of *Experiencing Narrative Worlds: On the Psychological Activities of Reading*, by Richard J. Gerrig, *Criticism* 37, no. 1 (Winter 1995): 172–74.

8. Stephen Davies, "Responding Emotionally to Fictions," *Journal of Aesthetics and Art Criticism* 67, no. 3 (June 1, 2009): 269–84. Similarly, Jaan Valsiner writes: "We respond emotionally to scenarios that are hypothetical or counterfactual as to ones that are actual" (Valsiner, "Between Fiction and Reality," 99).

9. Keith Oatley, *Such Stuff as Dreams: The Psychology of Fiction* (New York: Wiley, 2011). Matthew Pelowski and Fuminori Akibo concur in "A Model of Art Perception, Evaluation and Emotion in Transformative Aesthetic Experience," *New Ideas Psychology* 29 (2011): 80–97. Raymond A. Mar, Keith Oatley, and Jordan B. Peterson, "Exploring the Link between Reading Fiction and Empathy: Ruling Out Individual Differences and Examining Outcomes," *Communications* 34 (2009): 407–38. Mar, Oatley, and Peterson are researchers in a combined study from the University of York and the University of Toronto. Ten years earlier Oatley wrote "Why Fiction May Be Twice as True as Fact: Fiction as Cognitive and Emotional Simulation," *Review of General Psychology* 2 (1999): 101–17. In a Dutch study, researchers affirmed that fiction has to project "believability" and that readers must feel a sense of being transported into the fictional world. P. Matthijs and Martijn Veltkamp, "How Does Fiction Influence Empathy? An Experiential Investigation on the Role of Emotional Transportation," *PLoS* ONE 8, no. 1 (2013). See also M. C. Green, "Transportation into Narrative: The Role of Prior Knowledge and Perceived Realism," *Discourse Processes* 38 (2004): 247–66.

10. David Reisman, *The Lonely Crowd: A Study of the Changing American Character* (New Haven, CT: Yale University Press, 1950); C. Wright Mills, *The*

Power Elite (Oxford: Oxford University Press, 1956); William Whyte, *The Organization Man* (New York: Simon & Schuster, 1955); Norman Mailer, *Advertisements for Myself* (New York: Putnam, 1959).

11. Lisa Zunshine, *Why We Read Fiction: Theory of Mind and the Novel* (Columbus: Ohio State University Press, 2006), 132.

12. Umberto Eco, "The Narrative Structures in Fleming," introduction to *The Bond Affair*, ed. Orestes Buono and Umberto Eco (London: Macdonald, 1966). See also Lila Azam Zanganeli, "Umberto Eco, the Art of Fiction, No. 197," *Paris Review* 185 (Summer 2008).

13. Gregory F. Tague, *Evolution and Human Culture* (Amsterdam and New York: Rodopi, 2016), 131–32, 140.

14. Gregory F. Tague, *Making Mind: Moral Sense and Consciousness in Philosophy, Science, and Literature* (Amsterdam and New York: Rodopi, 2014), 226.

15. Norman N. Holland, *Literature and the Brain* (Gainesville, FL: PsyArt Foundation, 2009), 182, 183.

16. Holland, *Literature and the Brain*, 182.

17. Holland, *Literature and the Brain*, 182.

18. Holland, *Literature and the Brain*, 184.

19. Holland, *Literature and the Brain*, 357.

20. Holland, *Literature and the Brain*, 358.

21. Holland, *Literature and the Brain*, 237.

22. Holland, *Literature and the Brain*, 123.

23. Holland, *Literature and the Brain*, 124. Our brains have separate "what" and "where" systems. Holland says: "we can know that a character has and does not have a location" (Holland, *Literature and the Brain*, 124). See also Holland, *Literature and the Brain*, 108–24.

24. Davies, "Responding Emotionally to Fictions," 271.

25. Morris Dickstein, *Leopards in the Temple: The Transformation of American Fiction, 1945–1970* (Cambridge, MA: Harvard University Press, 2002), 158.

26. Dickstein, *Leopards in the Temple*, 156.

27. "Three Literary Prizes," *New York Times*, January 22, 1950, 12. The National Book Awards began in 1936 ("Books and Authors," *New York Times*, April 12, 1936, BR 12). They were discontinued during the Second World War. In 1950, the awards were reinstituted. The winners included Nelson Algren for *The Man with the Golden Gun*, Ralph Rusk for his biography of Ralph Waldo Emerson, and William Carlos Williams for Book Three of *Paterson* and for his *Selected Poems*.

28. See the divide between high and low culture discussed by Andreas Huyssen and by Lawrence Levine. Andreas Huyssen, *After the Great Divide:*

Modernism, Mass Culture, Postmodernism (Bloomington: Indiana University Press, 1987); Lawrence Levine, *Highbrow/Lowbrow: The Emergence of Cultural Hierarchy in America* (Cambridge, MA: Harvard University Press, 1988, rpt. 1990). See also Joan Shelley Rubin's discussion of middlebrow in Joan Shelley Rubin, *The Making of Middlebrow Culture* (Chapel Hill and London: University of North Carolina Press, 1992).

29. See the National Book Foundation website at https://www.nationalbook.org.

30. Ian Ballantine created his paperback publishing company in May 1952. He had worked for Allen Lane at Penguin in Britain as they attempted to compete with Pocket Books, which was backed by Simon & Schuster in New York. Ballantine had been president of Bantam Books.

31. George M. Marsden, *The Twilight of the American Enlightenment: The 1950s and the Crisis of Liberal Belief* (New York: Basic, 2014), xii. Marsden has asserted that religion ought to continue to have a significant role in public discourse. For another discussion of this perspective, see Stephen L. Carter, *The Culture of Disbelief: How American Law and Politics Trivializes Religious Devotion* (New York: Basic, 1993).

32. The "Our Country and Our Culture" discussion in *Partisan Review* (1952) is considered in Stephen Schryer, *Fantasies of the New Class: Ideologies of Professionalism in Post–World War II American Fiction* (New York: Columbia University Press, 2015), 5. John Kenneth Galbraith, *The New Industrial State* (Boston and New York: Houghton Mifflin, 1967); Lionel Trilling, "Science, Literature and Culture: A Comment on the Leavis-Snow Controversy," *Commentary*, June 1962, 462.

33. Hiram Hayden et al., "What's Wrong with the American Novel?" *American Scholar* 24, no. 4 (Autumn 1955): 464–503. Also see Ralph Ellison, "*Invisible Man*: Prologue to a Novel," *Partisan Review* 19, no. 1 (January–February 1952): 31–40.

34. Ellison, "*Invisible Man*: Prologue to a Novel," 36.

35. Louis Menand is cited by Tim Lacy, *The Dream of a Democratic Culture: Mortimer J. Adler and the Great Books Idea* (New York and Basingstoke: Palgrave Macmillan, 2013), 16.

36. Lacy, *The Dream of a Democratic Culture*, 3.

37. Lacy, *The Dream of a Democratic Culture*, 5.

38. Lacy, *The Dream of a Democratic Culture*, 6.

39. Lacy, *The Dream of a Democratic Culture*, 6–7.

40. Robert A. Ferguson, *Alone in America: The Stories That Matter* (Cambridge, MA: Harvard University Press, 2013), 1.

41. Alfred Kazin saw in Melville "man's separateness on earth" (*A Walker in the City* [New York: Harcourt Brace, 1951], 146). Also see Alfred Kazin, "Melville the New Yorker," *New York Review of Books*, April 5, 1973.

42. Ferguson, *Alone in America*, 3.

43. Alexis de Tocqueville, cited in Ferguson, *Alone in America*, 4.

44. X (George Frost Kennan), "The Sources of Soviet Conduct," *Foreign Affairs* 25 (July 1947): 575.

45. David Halberstam, *The Coldest Winter* (New York: Hachette, Hyperion, 2007), 71.

46. John Lewis Gaddis, *The Cold War* (New York: Penguin, 2005), 58.

47. Halberstam, *The Coldest Winter*, 90–91.

48. The North Korean leader Kim Il-sung was the grandfather of Kim Jong-un, North Korea's present leader.

49. Arthur Schlesinger discussed issues like this in his study, *The Imperial Presidency* (New York: Houghton Mifflin Harcourt, 1973). He argued that the formation of the executive office under Franklin Delano Roosevelt and executive agencies during the New Deal were factors that increased presidential powers.

50. The *New York Times* reported this in Roy Cohn's obituary on August 3, 1986.

51. Justice Earl Warren wrote the opinion for Brown v. Board of Education of Topeka, 347, US 483, May 17, 1954.

52. Evan Brier, *A Novel Marketplace: Mass Culture, the Book Trade, and Postwar American Fiction* (Philadelphia: University of Pennsylvania Press, 2010).

53. Shirley Brice Heath is referenced by Jonathan Rose in *Readers' Liberation: The Literary Agenda* (New York and Oxford: Oxford University Press, 2018), 193, 195.

54. Dwight Macdonald's "Masscult and Midcult" (1959) appeared as a pamphlet from *Partisan Review* in 1961. The essay is reprinted in Dwight Macdonald, *Mass Cult and Midcult: Essays against the American Grain*, ed. John Summers (New York: New York Review of Books, 2011), 3–71; quote appears on page 25. Janice Radway, *A Feeling for Books: The Book of the Month Club, Literary Taste, and Middle-Class Desire* (Chapel Hill: University of North Carolina Press, 1997, rpt. 1999).

2. WISTFUL WARRIORS

1. Don Whitehead, "AP Was There: D-Day Correspondent Returns Ten Years Later," Associated Press, June 3, 2019. The Associated Press on June 3,

2019, republished journalist Don Whitehead's June 8, 1944, account of the landing and his article on his visit to the beaches of Normandy ten years later on June 5–6, 1954.

2. John Hersey, *The Wall* (New York: Knopf, 1950). The descriptions of Noach Levinson all appear in the first chapter.

3. Martin Gilbert, *The Holocaust* (London: Folio, 2012), 110.

4. Gilbert, *The Holocaust*, 108.

5. Gilbert, *The Holocaust*, 111.

6. Hersey, *The Wall*, 25.

7. Hersey, *The Wall*, 40.

8. Hersey, *The Wall*, 42.

9. Hersey, *The Wall*, 73.

10. Hersey, *The Wall*, 75.

11. Hersey, *The Wall*, 82.

12. Hersey, *The Wall*, 97.

13. Hersey, *The Wall*, 99.

14. Hersey, *The Wall*, 101.

15. Hersey, *The Wall*, 113.

16. Hersey, *The Wall*, 114.

17. Hersey, *The Wall*, 119.

18. Hersey, *The Wall*, 123.

19. Hersey, *The Wall*, 123.

20. Hersey, *The Wall*, 153.

21. James Jones, *From Here to Eternity* (New York: Scribner, 1951), 68.

22. Jones, *From Here to Eternity*, 73

23. Jones, *From Here to Eternity*, 85.

24. Jones, *From Here to Eternity*, 87.

25. For Hanson W. Baldwin, a *New York Times* editor on military issues, the central focus of *The Caine Mutiny* is "the issue of unreasoning unquestioning acceptance of orders." "*The Caine Mutiny* Issue," *New York Times*, March 21, 1954, SM 12. John Keegan, introduction to *The Face of Battle: A Study of Agincourt, Waterloo and the Somme* (New York: Viking, 1976).

26. Herman Wouk, *The Caine Mutiny* (Garden City, NY: Doubleday, 1951).

27. Queeg is considered mentally ill in Jacqueline Noll Zimmerman's *People Like Ourselves: Portrayals of Mental Illness in the Movies* (Lanham, MD: Scarecrow Press, 2003). Philosopher Alan Donagan (1993) argued Queeg's case by making use of a command-based view of ethics, charging "incoherency." A distinction is made between irrationality and "unreasonableness" (17–18). Alan Donagan, "Moral Dilemmas, Genuine and Spurious: A Comparative Anatomy," *Ethics* 104, no. 1 (1993): 7–21. See also Patricia S. Greenspan,

Practical Guilt: Moral Dilemmas, Emotions and Social Norms (Oxford and New York: Oxford University Press, 1995).

28. Meghan Flynn, "How *The Caine Mutiny* and the Paranoid Capt. Queeg Influenced the 25th Amendment's Drafters, Making It Harder to Sideline a President," *Washington Post*, September 10, 2018.

29. Baldwin, "*The Caine Mutiny* Issue," SM 12.

30. Thomas J. Cutler, "Lest We Forget: Wouk's Gift to the Navy," *U.S. Naval Institute Proceedings* 143, no. 7 (July 2017); Jeffrey Butler, *Change Leadership in Higher Education: A Practical Guide to Academic Transformation* (San Francisco, CA: Jossey-Bass, 2014); "*The Caine Mutiny*: A Lesson in Leadership," *Army Lawyer* 26, no. 2 (February 2010); Richard D. Chessick, "Critique: *The Caine Mutiny*," review of *The Caine Mutiny*, by Herman Wouk, *American Journal of Psychotherapy* (October 1, 1975): 604–5; David Machiowitz, "Lawyer on the Aisle: Captain Queeg Is Back on Broadway," *American Bar Association Journal* 69, no. 6 (June 1, 1983): 833.

31. Mark Thompson, "10 Questions: An Interview with Herman Wouk," *Time*, February 1, 2016. *The Caine Mutiny* has become part of "the essential film library" of naval stories, along with 1950s films like *Victory at Sea* (1952) and *Mister Roberts* (1955). There was a television production of *The Caine Mutiny* in 1956, with actor Lloyd Nolan as Queeg. A new *Caine Mutiny* stage revival at the Gerald Schoenfeld Theatre in Chicago was discussed in *USA Today* on May 8, 2006. A U.S. Navy reading list was compiled that included *The Caine Mutiny*, Herman Melville's *Billy Budd*, Robert Heinlein's *Starship Trooper*, E. M. Forster's *A Passage to India*, and Stephen Covey's *The 7 Habits of Highly Effective People*. "By the Books," *Career World* 36, no. 1 (September 2007). Editions of *Naval History* select books and films in "Our Pics: Great WWII Books and Movies," *Naval History* 19, no. 4 (August 2005).

32. Malcolm Cowley, "Nightmare and Ritual in Hemingway," in *Hemingway: A Collection of Critical Essays*, Twentieth Century Views, ed. Robert Weeks (Englewood Cliffs, NJ: Prentice Hall, 1962), 1.

33. Ernest Hemingway, *Across the River and into the Trees* (New York: Scribner, 1950), 222–24.

34. Jackson J. Benson, *Hemingway: The Writer's Art of Self-Defense* (Minneapolis: University of Minnesota Press, 1969), 126.

35. Benson, *Hemingway*, 126.

36. Reviews of Hemingway's *Across the River and into the Trees* written by Maxwell Geismer (187), Alfred Kazin (379), and Philip Rahv (400) are cited in Jeffrey Meyers, ed., *Hemingway: The Critical Heritage* ed. (New York and London: Routledge, 1982). Michael S. Reynolds, *Hemingway: The Final Years* (New York: Norton, 2000), 211.

37. Benson, *Hemingway*, 126.

38. William Faulkner, *A Fable*, in *Faulkner: Novels 1942–1954*, ed. Noel Polk and Joseph Blotner (New York: Library of America, 1994), 669.

39. Faulkner, *A Fable*, 680.

40. Faulkner, *A Fable*, 988.

41. Faulkner, *A Fable*, 988.

42. William Faulkner, letter to Harold Ober, October 30, 1943, in *Selected Letters of William Faulkner*, ed. Joseph Blotner (New York: Random House, 1977), 178, 180. On May 25, 1945, he wrote to Ober: "It's a novel now" (Faulkner, *Selected Letters*, 192). In 1948–1949, Faulkner wrote *Intruder in the Dust*. He then wrote *Requiem for a Nun*, which was published in 1951. He returned to *A Fable* in 1952–1953.

43. Joseph Urgo, *Faulkner's Apocrypha: A Fable, Snopes, and the Spirit of Human Rebellion* (Jackson: University of Mississippi Press, 1989), 95; Giorgio Mariani, *Waging War on War: Peacefighting in American Literature* (Urbana: University of Illinois Press, 2015), 149. Mariani refers to the work of Rene Girard regarding sacrifices that arise from the "scapegoat mechanism": a response to the marginalized one who threatens the community's "monstrous features" that attempt to maintain stability.

44. Faulkner, *A Fable*, 857.

45. Joseph Blotner, *William Faulkner: A Biography* (New York: Random House, 1974, rpt. 1984), 1:494.

46. Willard Waller claims that 30 percent of war casualties had psychosis or had psycho-neurotic issues caused by war experience. Waller claims that this was "America's gravest social problem." He anticipated postwar veteran issues in *The Veteran Comes Back* (New York: Dryden, 1944), 13, 166.

47. Mark Osteen, *Nightmare Alley: Film Noir and the American Dream* (Baltimore: Johns Hopkins University Press, 2013). Roger Luckhurst, cited in Osteen, *Nightmare Alley*, 80. In his study of film noir, Osteen peers into noir nightmares, dream sequences, amnesia, and lost identities, and its critique of individualism and self-making.

48. Waller, *The Veteran Comes Back*, 180, 77.

49. Alfred Kazin, "Last of the Leftists?," review of *Barbary Shore*, *Time*, May 28, 1951. See also Alfred Kazin, "The Trouble He's Seen," review of *Armies of the Night*, by Norman Mailer, *New York Times*, May 5, 1968.

50. Alfred Kazin, "Last of the Leftists?"

51. J. Michael Lennon, *Norman Mailer: A Double Life* (New York: Simon & Schuster, 2013).

52. William Barrett, "Lapse of a Novelist," review of *Barbary Shore*, by Norman Mailer, *Commentary*, June 1, 1951, 603.

53. Norman Mailer, *Barbary Shore* (New York: Rinehart, 1951), 6.

54. J. Michael Lennon points out that McLeod's name came from the name of a labor organizer (Lennon, *Norman Mailer: A Double Life*, 115). Mailer, *Barbary Shore*, 217.

55. Mailer, *Barbary Shore*, 217.

56. Norman Mailer, *Advertisements for Myself* (New York: Putnam, 1959), 94.

57. Mailer, *Advertisements for Myself*, 94.

58. Andrew Gordon, *An American Dreamer: A Psychoanalytic Study of the Fiction of Norman Mailer* (Madison: Fairleigh Dickinson University Press, 1980), 32.

59. Norman Mailer, *Selected Letters*, ed. J. Michael Lennon (New York: Random House, 2014), 111.

60. Mailer, *Selected Letters*, 95.

61. Diana Trilling, cited in Gordon, *An American Dreamer*, 34.

62. See C. Fuhrman and Steven T. Levy, *Influential Papers from the 1950s* (London: Routledge, 2018).

63. Michel Foucault, *Madness and Civilization: A History of Insanity in the Age of Reason*, trans. Richard Howard (New York: Vintage, 1988), 59; Philip Rieff, *Freud: The Mind of the Moralist* (New York: Viking, 1959, rpt. 1961); Christopher Lasch, *The Culture of Narcissism: American Life in an Age of Diminishing Expectations* (New York: Norton, 1979), 13; T. J. Jackson Lears, *Fables of Abundance: A Cultural History of Advertising in America* (New York: Basic, 1995); Rachel Mykkanen, "Militarized Desires: Consumerism in American Culture, 1939–1955" (PhD diss., University of California–Irvine, 2014); Maggie McKinley, *Understanding Norman Mailer* (Columbia: University of South Carolina Press, 2016).

3. ALIENATED DREAMERS

1. J. D. Salinger, *The Catcher in the Rye* (New York: Little, Brown, 1951), 111, 122. Richard Locke provides an interesting comparison of Holden Caulfield with David Copperfield. Richard Locke, *Critical Children: The Use of Childhood in Ten Great Novels* (New York: Columbia University Press, 2011).

2. J. D. Salinger's short stories "I'm Crazy" and "Slight Rebellion Off Madison" have been viewed as precursors to *The Catcher in the Rye*.

3. S. N. Behrman, "The Vision of the Innocent," *New Yorker*, August 11, 1951, 71.

4. Richard and Carol Ohman argue that Holden is not a universal adolescent figure but is situated in the 1940s–1950s period. Their essay appears in

Joel Salzburg, ed., *Critical Essays on Salinger's* The Catcher in the Rye (Boston: GK Hall, 1990).

5. Robert Coles, "Anna Freud and J. D. Salinger's Holden Caulfield," *Virginia Quarterly Review* 76, no. 2 (2000): 215.

6. David D. Cooper, *Secular Days, Sacred Moments: The America Columns of Robert Coles* (East Lansing: Michigan State University Press, 2013), 103.

7. David Rachels quotes Kazin in "Holden Caulfield: A Hero for All Ages," *Chronicle of Higher Education* 47, no. 29 (March 30, 2001). For reader responses to *Catcher in the Rye*, see Chris Kubica and Will Hochman, eds., *Letters to J. D. Salinger* (Madison: University of Wisconsin Press, 2002).

8. John R. Huber and Gail Ledbetter, "Holden Caulfield, Self-Appointed Catcher in the Rye: Some Additional Thoughts," *Journal of Individual Psychology* 33, 2 (1977): 250–56; Benjamin Priest, "*The Catcher and the Rye* and the Ill Member of the Group: Holden Caulfield and Adolescent Development," *Psychodynamic Practice* 22, no. 3 (2016): 210.

9. Sarah Graham, *Salinger's* The Catcher in the Rye (New York: Bloomsbury, 2007); Kubica and Hochman, *Letters to J. D. Salinger*. See Dorothy Day, *The Duty of Delight: The Diaries of Dorothy Day* (Milwaukee, WI: Marquette University Press, 2008, rpt. New York: Image, 2011). Dorothy Day, one of Salinger's readers, wrote in her diary on July 14, 1959: "I have been getting some writing done since reading Salinger's latest story—a strange technique of starting and stopping" (264). On April 12, 1977, there were prayers for Salinger. Day wrote, "We owe him a debt" (577). The Dorothy Day Papers are at Marquette University, Raynor Library Archives, Milwaukee, Wisconsin.

10. Bryce A. Taylor, "Holden Caulfield: Sort of a Christian," *Religion and the Arts* 18, no. 5 (2014).

11. Salinger, *The Catcher in the Rye*, 99. See also Josef Benson, *J. D. Salinger's* Catcher in the Rye*: A Cultural History* (Lanham, MD: Rowman & Littlefield, 2014).

12. Louis Menand, "Holden at Fifty," *New Yorker*, September 21, 2001; Dennis McCort, "Hyakujo's Geese, Amban's Doughnuts and Rilke's Carrousel: Sources East and West for Salinger's *Catcher*," in *Bloom's Modern Critical Interpretations: J. D. Salinger's* The Catcher in the Rye, ed. Harold Bloom (New York: Infobase, 2014), 45–62; Harold Bloom, introduction to *Bloom's Modern Critical Interpretations: J. D. Salinger's* The Catcher in the Rye, ed. Harold Bloom (New York: Infobase, 2014), 1–4.

13. Rachels, "Holden Caulfield: A Hero for All Ages."

14. Clifton Fadiman, review of *The Catcher in the Rye*, by J. D. Salinger, *Book-of-the-Month Club News*, July 1951.

15. Virgilia Peterson, "Three Days in the Bewildering Life of an Adolescent," *New York Herald Tribune*, July 15, 1951, 3; Nash K. Burger, "Books of the Times," *New York Times*, July 16, 1951; Anne L. Goodman, "Mad about Children," *New Republic* 125, no. 3 (July 16, 1951): 20–21; Paul Engle, "Honest Tale of Distraught Adolescent," *Chicago Sunday Tribune Magazine of Books*, July 15, 1951, 3; T. Morris Longstreth, "New Novels in the News," *Christian Science Monitor*, July 19, 1951.

16. Mary McGrory, "Story of Adolescent Steers from Mawkish into Something New," *Evening Star*, July 15, 1951, C-3; William Poster, "Tomorrow's Child: *The Catcher in the Rye*," *Commentary* 13 (1952): 90–92.

17. George Steiner, "The Salinger Industry," *Nation*, November 14, 1959, 360; Granville Hicks, "J. D. Salinger: Search for Wisdom," *Saturday Review*, July 25, 1959; Alfred Kazin, "Everybody's Favorite," *Atlantic* 208, no. 2 (August 1961); Arthur Heiserman and James E. Miller Jr. "J. D. Salinger: Some Crazy Cliff," *Western Humanities Review* 10 (1956); Warren French, *J. D. Salinger* (Boston: Twayne, 1963).

18. Ralph Ellison, *Invisible Man* (New York: Random House, 1952), 37. Ellison spent seven years working on *Invisible Man*. His editor was Albert Erskine. Erskine's wife Fanny, Stanley Edgar Hyman, Harry Ford, and Albert Murray were part of his readers' circle. Hyman was married to author Shirley Jackson.

19. Ellison, *Invisible Man*, 46, 54.

20. Ellison, *Invisible Man*, 57.

21. Ellison, *Invisible Man*, 217.

22. Ellison, *Invisible Man*, xv–xvi.

23. Ellison, *Invisible Man*, 381–82.

24. Ellison, *Invisible Man*, 270.

25. Ellison, *Invisible Man*, 291.

26. Ellison, *Invisible Man*, 284.

27. Ralph Ellison, "The Novel as a Function of Democracy" (originally published June 1967), in *The Collected Essays of Ralph Ellison*, ed. John F. Callahan (New York: Modern Library, 1995, rpt. 2003), 755–65; Ralph Ellison, "The World and the Jug Part II" (originally published in *New Leader*, February 3, 1964), in *The Collected Essays of Ralph Ellison*, ed. John F. Callahan (New York: Modern Library, 1995, rpt. 2003), 183.

28. Morris Dickstein, *Leopards in the Temple: The Transformation of American Fiction, 1945–1970* (Cambridge, MA: Harvard University Press, 2002), 210; Ellison, *Invisible Man*, 6.

29. Horace A. Porter, *Jazz Country: Ralph Ellison in America* (Iowa City: University of Iowa Press, 2001), 72, 74; Eric Sundquist, *Cultural Contexts for Ralph Ellison's* Invisible Man (New York: Bedford/St. Martin's, 1995.

30. Henry Louis Gates, *The Signifying Monkey: A Theory of African American Literary Criticism*(New York: Oxford University Press, 1989, rpt. 2014), 131.

31. Ralph Ellison, *Living with Music: The Jazz Writings of Ralph Ellison*, ed. Robert O'Meally (New York: Modern Library, 2001), 36. See Horace A. Porter, "Jazz Beginnings: Charlie Christian and Ralph Ellison in Oklahoma City," *Antioch Review* 57, no. 3 (Summer 1999): 277–95.

32. Ralph Ellison, *Shadow and Act* (New York: Random House, 1964), 217.

33. Adam Bradley, *Ralph Ellison in Progress: From* Invisible Man *to* Three Days before the Shooting (New Haven, CT: Yale University Press, 2010), 8.

34. Bradley, *Ralph Ellison in Progress*, 10.

35. Robert Penn Warren, *Band of Angels* (New York: Random House, 1955), 134.

36. Robert Penn Warren interview by John Baker is cited by William Bedford Clark, *The American Vision of Robert Penn Warren* (Lexington: University Press of Kentucky, 1991), 178. The story may be considered a romance, in Nathaniel Hawthorne's sense, as William Bedford Clark observes.

37. John Crowe Ransom et al., *I'll Take My Stand*, introduction by Louis D. Rubin Jr. (Baton Rouge: Louisiana State University Press, 1978), xxix, 263.

38. Robert Penn Warren, "Segregation: The Inner Conflict in the South," in *Reporting Civil Rights*, vol. 1, *American Journalism, 1941–1963*, comp. Clayborne Carson et al. (New York: Library of America, 2003), 285.

39. Warren, "Segregation," 286.

40. Warren, "Segregation," 286.

41. Warren, "Segregation," 291.

42. Warren, "Segregation," 290.

43. Warren, "Segregation," 291.

44. Warren, "Segregation," 295.

45. Warren, "Segregation," 307.

46. Warren, "Segregation," 312.

47. Warren, "Segregation," 312.

48. Warren, "Segregation," 313.

49. Warren, "Segregation," 316–19.

50. Warren, "Segregation," 321.

51. Warren, "Segregation," 319.

52. Warren, "Segregation," 320.

53. Warren, "Segregation," 286.

54. E. T. A. Hoffmann, "Beethoven's Instrumental Music," 1813, in *E.T.A. Hoffmann Samliche Werke*, ed. C. G. von Massen (Munich: Muller, 1908).

55. James Baldwin, "The Price of the Ticket," in *Baldwin: Collected Essays*, ed. Toni Morrison (New York: Library of America, 1998).

56. James Baldwin, *Creative America* (Washington, DC: National Cultural Center; New York: Ridge Press, 1962).

57. James Baldwin, "Sonny's Blues," in *Going to Meet the Man*, collected in *Baldwin: Early Novels and Stories*, ed. Toni Morrison (New York: Library of America, 1998), 832.

58. These are insights from neuroscience articulated by William Benzon in *Beethoven's Anvil* (New York: Basic, 2001), and William McNeill in *Keeping Together in Time* (Cambridge, MA: Harvard University Press, 1995).

59. Benzon, *Beethoven's Anvil*, 20–22.

60. Antonio Damasio, *Descartes' Error* (New York: Putnam, 1994); Nils Wallin, *Biomusicology* (Hillsdale, NY: Pendragon, 1992).

61. Leonard Meyer, *Emotion and Meaning in Music* (Chicago: University of Chicago Press, 1956).

62. Lawrence Kramer, *Music and Poetry: The Nineteenth Century and After* (Berkeley: University of California Press, 1984).

63. Baldwin, "Sonny's Blues," 834.

64. Kramer, *Music and Poetry*. "Romantic Repetition" is chapter 2.

65. Kramer, *Music and Poetry*. The phrase "transit of identity" occurs across the entire chapter and is the title of the chapter, as in the accompanying note that follows. Sigmund Freud, *Beyond the Pleasure Principle*, "a compulsion to repeat" (New York: Norton, 1920), 38, see also 54–55. A clear explanation of repetition compulsion appears in the Introduction, xiv.

66. Kramer, *Music and Poetry*, 16.

67. Baldwin, "Sonny's Blues," 843.

68. Baldwin, "Sonny's Blues," 850.

69. Baldwin, "Sonny's Blues," 850.

70. Baldwin, "Sonny's Blues," 850.

71. Baldwin, "Sonny's Blues," 857.

72. Baldwin, "Sonny's Blues," 856.

73. Baldwin, "Sonny's Blues," 854.

74. Baldwin, "Sonny's Blues," 855.

75. Baldwin, "Sonny's Blues," 855.

76. Baldwin, "Sonny's Blues," 856.

77. James Baldwin, "Down at the Cross," in *The Fire Next Time*, collected in *Baldwin: Collected Essays*, ed. Toni Morrison (New York: Library of America, 1998).

78. James Baldwin, "The Creative Process," in *Creative America* (Washington, DC: National Cultural Center; New York: Ridge Press, 1962).

79. James Baldwin, "On Catfish Row," *Commentary*, September 1959.

80. Baldwin, "Sonny's Blues," 859.

81. Baldwin, "Sonny's Blues," 861.

82. Baldwin, "Sonny's Blues," 861.
83. Baldwin, "Sonny's Blues," 861.
84. Baldwin, "Sonny's Blues," 861.
85. Baldwin, "Sonny's Blues," 862.
86. Baldwin, "Sonny's Blues," 862.
87. Baldwin, "Sonny's Blues," 862.
88. Baldwin, "Sonny's Blues," 863.

4. HEROES AND ANTIHEROES

1. Ernest Hemingway, *The Old Man and the Sea* (New York: Charles Scribner's Sons, 1952), 92, 95, 105. *The Old Man and the Sea* first appeared in *Life* magazine (September 1, 1952), which sold some 5.3 million copies. Scribner's published the novel the next week. The Book of the Month Club distributed 153,000 copies.

2. Hemingway, *The Old Man and the Sea*, 23.

3. There has been a wide range of critical perspectives across the years. Jeffrey Meyers, Kenneth Lynn, Carlos Baker, Philip Young, and Leo Gurko have read *The Old Man and the Sea* as an allegory or parable. See Jeffrey Meyers, *Hemingway: A Biography* (New York: Da Capo, 1987); Kenneth Lynn, *Hemingway* (New York: Simon & Schuster, 1987); Carlos Baker, *Hemingway: The Writer as Artist* (Princeton, NJ: Princeton University Press, 1956). Leo Gurko, in "The Heroic Impulse in *The Old Man and the Sea*," *English Journal* 44, no. 7 (October 1955), affirms that this story presents a world where "heroic deeds are possible" (377). Allen C. Jones takes a deep ecology or biocentric approach to *The Old Man and the Sea*. He sees "a story of nature rather than a story about Santiago" (104). See Allen C. Jones, "Man or Fish? An Ecocritical Reading of *The Old Man and the Sea*," in *Hemingway and the Natural World*, ed. Robert Fleming (Moscow: University of Idaho Press, 1999), 102–13. Harold Bloom views story as "involuntary parody" that is saved only by "a gentleness, a nuanced tenderness." He claims that the story is "tiresomely repetitive" (1–2). Hemingway makes use of repetition as a structural device. Harold Bloom, introduction to *Bloom's Modern Critical Interpretations: Ernest Hemingway's* The Old Man and the Sea, ed. Harold Bloom (New York: Infobase, 2018).

4. "Dom Di Maggio, Almost Victim, Five Men Drown in Heavy Surf at Golden Gate," *Madeira Tribune*, February 19, 1951.

5. Hemingway, *The Old Man and the Sea*, 13.

6. Hemingway, *The Old Man and the Sea*, 26.

7. Hemingway, *The Old Man and the Sea*, 26.

8. G. B. Wilson Jr., "Incarnation and Redemption in *The Old Man and the Sea*," *Studies in Short Fiction* 14 (September 1977): 372. Dwight Eddino refers to the myth of the Sisyphus connection in "Of Rocks and Marlin: The Existentialist Agon in Camus' *Sisyphus* and Hemingway's *Old Man and the Sea*," in *Bloom's Modern Critical Interpretations: Ernest Hemingway's* The Old Man and the Sea, ed. Harold Bloom (New York: Infobase, 2018).

9. Hemingway, *The Old Man and the Sea*, 114. Carlos Baker connects the lions with Manolin, who, he suggests, recalls Santiago's youth (307). See Baker, *Hemingway: The Writer as Artist*. Susan Beegel sees in them a return to peacefulness in nature and some resolution or rest (75). See Susan Beegel, "Hemingway's Education as a Naturalist," in *A Historical Guide to Ernest Hemingway*, ed. Linda Wagner-Martin (Oxford and New York: Oxford University Press, 1999). See also Susan Beegel, "A Guide to the Marine Life in Ernest Hemingway's *The Old Man and the Sea*," *Resources for American Literary Study* 30 (2006): 236–315.

10. Ray Bradbury, *Fahrenheit 451* (New York: Ballantine, 1953, rpt. New York: Simon & Schuster, 1967), 4.

11. Bradbury, *Fahrenheit 451*, 105–6.

12. Bradbury, *Fahrenheit 451*, 100.

13. Bradbury, *Fahrenheit 451*, 132.

14. Bradbury, *Fahrenheit 451*, 152.

15. Bradbury, *Fahrenheit 451*, 104.

16. Bradbury, *Fahrenheit 451*, 87, 58.

17. Jonathan R. Eller, *Ray Bradbury Unbound* (Urbana: University of Illinois Press, 2014), 156. *Fahrenheit 451* is dedicated to Don Congdon, Bradbury's literary agent. Bradbury regarded Congdon as instrumental in the book's development. In "Burning Bright," a foreword to the fortieth anniversary edition of the novel (*Fahrenheit 451: 40th Anniversary Edition* [New York: Simon & Schuster, 1993]), Bradbury tells us that Congdon was contacted by Ballantine with a request that Bradbury lengthen and expand his short story "The Fireman." Congdon had been a Simon & Schuster editor. He was able to secure a contract for Bradbury with an advance of $5,000.

18. This episode is from the first season of *The Twilight Zone* in 1959.

19. Ray Bradbury, "The Pedestrian," *Reporter*, August 7, 1951, 40.

20. Ray Bradbury, "The Veldt." In *The Vintage Bradbury* (New York: Vintage, Random House, 1965).

21. Eller, *Ray Bradbury Unbound*, 11. Eller effectively traces Bradbury's reading. Evan Brier, *A Novel Marketplace: Mass Culture, the Book Trade, and Postwar American Fiction* (Philadelphia: University of Pennsylvania Press, 2010).

22. Bradbury in Eller, *Ray Bradbury Unbound*,

23. Eller, *Ray Bradbury Unbound.*

24. Brier, *A Novel Marketplace*, 272.

25. Ayn Rand, *Atlas Shrugged* (New York: Random House, 1957), 1029.

26. Rand, *Atlas Shrugged*, 1020. Rand argues for individualism. She rejects the man in the gray flannel suit's conformity and the "frantic parade to nowhere." See Sloan Wilson, *The Man in the Gray Flannel Suit* (New York: Simon & Schuster, 1956), 42.

27. Rand, *Atlas Shrugged*, 1012.

28. Rand, *Atlas Shrugged*, 1018.

29. Rand, *Atlas Shrugged*, 1020.

30. Rand, *Atlas Shrugged*, 1012.

31. Rand, *Atlas Shrugged*, 1014.

32. Ayn Rand, *The Virtue of Selfishness: A New Concept of Egoism* (New York: Signet, New American Library, 1964), 28.

33. Rand, *Atlas Shrugged*, 1017–18.

34. Rand, *The Virtue of Selfishness*, 37.

35. Rand, *The Virtue of Selfishness*, 28.

36. Rand, *The Virtue of Selfishness*, 28.

37. Rand, *Atlas Shrugged*, 1029.

38. Rand, *Atlas Shrugged*, 1018.

39. Rand, *Atlas Shrugged*, 1012.

40. Rand, *Atlas Shrugged*, 1012–13.

41. Rand, *Atlas Shrugged*, 1014. Galt always makes use of the male pronoun *he*.

42. Rand, *Atlas Shrugged*, 1012–13.

43. Rand, *Atlas Shrugged*, 1014.

44. Rand, *Atlas Shrugged*, 1029.

45. Philip Davis, *Bernard Malamud: A Writer's Life* (New York and Oxford: Oxford University Press, 2007), 179.

46. Michiko Kakutani, "Malamud Still Seeks Balance and Solitude," *New York Times*, July 15, 1980.

47. Robert Montgomery Bird Diary, Robert Montgomery Bird Collection, University of Pennsylvania Kislak Center Special Collections, file 182, 5–6. *The Gladiator*, produced in Philadelphia in 1831, was not published in his lifetime. The play appears in Allan Gates Halline, ed., *American Plays* (New York: American Book Company, 1935), 153–98. Edwin Forrest is referred to in "Old Time Minstrel: He Has Gone Out of Vogue but the Public Recollects Him with Pleasure," *New York Times*, May 9, 1897. George Bancroft, "Review of 'The Influence of Slavery in the Political Revolution in Rome': A Lecture Delivered before a Society of Young Men in Massachusetts," *North American Review* 39 (1834): 413–47.

48. Gerald Sorin, *Howard Fast: Life and Literature in the Left Lane* (Bloomington: Indiana University Press, 2012).

49. "Robeson Says US Negroes Won't Fight against Russia," *Peekskill Evening Star*, April 21, 1949; "Loves Soviet Best, Robeson Declares," *New York Times*, June 20, 1949. See also James Rorty, "The Lessons of the Peekskill Riots," *Commentary*, October 1950, 309–23; Joseph Walwik, *The Peekskill, New York Anti-communist Riots* (Lewiston, NY: Edwin Mellen, 2002). Pete Seeger was interviewed by Steve Courtney in 1999. Steve Courtney, "Peekskill's Days of Infamy: The Robeson Riots of 1949," *Reporter Dispatch*, September 5, 1982. See also the Westchester County Grand Jury Report (June 1958) on "Violence in Peekskill"; Howard Fast, *Peekskill USA: A Personal Experience* (New York: Civil Rights Congress, 1951).

50. Sorin, *Howard Fast: Life and Literature in the Left Lane*, 183–84.

51. "Concert Planned by Left-Wing Activists, Area Conservatives Vow to Stop It," *Peekskill Evening Star*, August 27, 1949; "Violence Ends Robeson Meet, Dewey Asks County Probe," *Peekskill Evening Star*, September 6, 1949.

52. T. C. Boyle, *World's End* (Norwalk, CT: Easton, 2014), 406.

53. Boyle, *World's End*, 402.

54. Hedda Hopper, in her nationally syndicated column, criticized actor Kirk Douglas for the hiring of blacklisted screenwriter Dalton Trumbo to cowrite the film *Spartacus* with Howard Fast. In the film *Trumbo* (2015), Helen Mirren played Hedda Hopper, and Bryan Cranston played Dalton Trumbo. The film was directed by Jay Roach, and the screenplay was written by John McNamara.

55. Howard Fast, *Spartacus* (London: North Castle; Routledge, 1996; originally published by the author in 1951). The Stanley Kubrick film was released in October 1960. It featured Kirk Douglas (Spartacus), Laurence Olivier (Crassus), Peter Ustinov (slave trader Lentius Batiatus), Jean Simmons, Charles Laughton, Tony Curtis, and John Gavin. The script was written by Dalton Trumbo and Howard Fast, who was not credited. The film received four Academy Awards and was the biggest money-making film in Hollywood until *Airport*, which was based on a novel by Alex Hailey.

56. William Faulkner, *The Hamlet*, in *Faulkner: Novels 1957–1962*, ed. Noel Polk (New York: Library of America, 1999), 6.

57. Faulkner, *The Hamlet*, 77.

58. Faulkner, *The Hamlet*, Part II, "Eula." Also see William Faulkner, *The Hamlet* (New York: Modern Library, 1940), 95.

59. Faulkner, *The Hamlet*, Part II, "Eula." The description of Eula appears at the beginning of Part II.

60. Faulkner, *The Mansion*, in *Faulkner: Novels, 1957–1962*, ed. Noel Polk (New York: Library of America, 1999), , 294.

61. Faulkner, *The Mansion*, 419.

62. Faulkner, *The Mansion*, 419.

63. Faulkner, *The Mansion*, 6.

64. Faulkner, *The Town*, in *Faulkner: Novels 1957–1962*, ed. Noel Polk (New York: Library of America, 1999), 276.

65. See John Matthews's perceptive essay, "Many Mansions: Faulkner's Cold War Conflicts," in *Global Faulkner*, ed. Annette Tefzer and Ann J. Abalie (Jackson: University Press of Mississippi, 2009), 3–23. "Faulkner uses the vulnerability of the South to criticize capitalist certitudes" (11).

66. Faulkner, *The Mansion*, 7–8.

67. Faulkner, *The Mansion*, 243–44.

68. Faulkner, *The Mansion*, 89–90.

69. Noel Polk, *Faulkner and Welty and the Southern Literary Tradition* (Jackson: University Press of Mississippi, 2010; originally published in 1983), 125.

5. SAINTS, SINNERS, AND NOTORIOUS NARCISSISTS

1. James Baldwin, *Go Tell It on the Mountain*, in *Baldwin: Early Novels and Stories*, ed. Toni Morrison (New York: Library of America, 1998), 19.

2. Baldwin, *Go Tell It on the Mountain*, 193–94.

3. Baldwin, *Go Tell It on the Mountain*, 92.

4. Baldwin, *Go Tell It on the Mountain*, 73.

5. Baldwin, *Go Tell It on the Mountain*, 208.

6. James Baldwin, *The Devil Finds Work*, in *Baldwin: Collected Essays*, ed. Toni Morrison (New York: Library of America, 1998), 477. For the first print edition, see James Baldwin, *The Devil Finds Work* (New York: Dial, 1976).

7. William Giraldi, *American Audacity* (New York: Liveright, 2018), 293.

8. Giraldi, *American Audacity*, 306.

9. James Baldwin, "The Harlem Ghetto," in *Notes of a Native Son*, collected in *Baldwin: Collected Essays*, ed. Toni Morrison (New York: Library of America, 1998), 47.

10. Baldwin, "The Harlem Ghetto," 49.

11. Flannery O'Connor, *Wise Blood*, in *O'Connor: Collected Works* (New York: Library of America, 1988), 1. In O'Connor's story, "all the characters are symbols," Harvey C. Webster, an early reviewer, recognized. Harvey C. Webster, "Nihilism as a New Faith," review of *Wise Blood*, by Flannery O'Connor, *New Leader*, June 23, 1952, 23. This is also a desert experience that critic

Richard Giannone, in *Flannery O'Connor, Hermit Novelist* (Chicago: University of Illinois Press, 2000, rpt. Columbia: University of South Carolina Press, 2010) likens to the asceticism and spiritual quest of the anchorites. Richard Giannone sees the desert fathers in this novel. How is this sacramental? For Giannone, Hazel acts in an ascetic fashion (3). He points to the self-flagellation toward "denial and self-injury" (4) However, are Motes's actions the same as this self-abnegation of the desert fathers? Gene Kellogg, in *The Vital Tradition: The Catholic Novel in a Period of Convergence* (Chicago: Loyola University Press, 1970), sees in this story "criticism of the secular world and criticism of the religious community" (188).

12. O'Connor, *Wise Blood*, 16.
13. O'Connor, *Wise Blood*, 19.
14. O'Connor, *Wise Blood*, 128.
15. O'Connor, *Wise Blood*, 125, 131.
16. O'Connor, *Wise Blood*, 43.
17. Frederick Assals, *Flannery O'Connor: The Imagination of Extremity* (Athens: University of Georgia Press, 1982), 48.
18. O'Connor, *Wise Blood*, 130. Some critics have pointed out that O'Connor's grotesques are parallel to the dark humor of Franz Kafka whose Joseph K. suggests the search for meaning and the alienation of modern people. Frederick Hoffman observes that Hazel's story reminds one somewhat of Franz Kafka, at least in its violation of normal expectations" (33). Frederick Hoffman, "The Search for Redemption: Flannery O'Connor's Fiction," in *The Added Dimension: The Art and Mind of Flannery O'Connor*, ed. Melvin J. Friedman and Lewis A. Lawson (New York: Fordham University Press, 1978). R. W. B. Lewis also saw in the story "the Kafkaesque village removed to the American South." Lewis saw "a curious tension in the novel between a rather surrealistic set of characters and incidents and a remarkably pure, luminous prose" (150). R. W. B. Lewis, "Eccentric's Pilgrimage," *Hudson Review* 6, no. 1 (Spring 1953): 144–50.
19. Debra Cumberland, "Flannery O'Connor and the Question of the Christian Novel," in *Wise Blood: A Re-Consideration*, ed. John J. Han (Amsterdam and New York: Rodopi, 2018), 7, 10.
20. Vladimir Nabokov, *Lolita* (Paris: Olympia, 1955, rpt. New York: Vintage, 1989), 32.
21. Nabokov, *Lolita*, 1.
22. Nabokov, *Lolita*, 13.
23. Lionel Trilling, "The Last Lover: Vladimir Nabokov's *Lolita*," *Encounter* 11, no. 4 (1958): 11. Trilling's essay was collected in Leon Wieseltier, ed., *The Moral Obligation to Be Intelligent* (Chicago: Northwestern University Press,

2008), 358. Martin Green, "The Morality of *Lolita*," *Kenyon Review* 28, no. 3 (1966): 365.

24. Dorothy Day, *The Duty of Delight: The Diaries of Dorothy Day* (Milwaukee, WI: Marquette University Press, 2008, rpt. New York: Image, 2011), 245.

25. Nabokov, *Lolita*, 25.

26. Ellen Pifer, introduction to *Vladimir Nabokov's* Lolita*: A Casebook* (Oxford: Oxford University Press, 2003), 10; Richard Rorty, *Contingency, Irony, Solidarity* (Cambridge: Cambridge University Press, 1989).

27. Chapter 33, part 2 of *Lolita* only shows that he was released from prison, pretended to be police, and tricked her. The story is recounted in Sarah Weinman's *The Real Lolita: The Kidnapping of Sally Horner and the Novel That Scandalized the World* (New York: HarperCollins, 2018). Horner was approached in a Woolworth's store. Woolworth's discontinued business and closed its stores July 17, 1997.

28. Nabokov, *Lolita*, 150.

29. Paul McCarthy, *John Steinbeck* (New York: Frederick Ungar, 1980), 120.

30. Truman Capote, *Breakfast at Tiffany's* (New York: Random House, 1958), 12.

31. Capote, *Breakfast at Tiffany's*, 141.

32. Patricia Highsmith, *The Talented Mr. Ripley* (London and New York: Coward McCann, 1955), 78.

33. Graham Greene, *The End of the Affair* (London: Heinemann, 1951, rpt. New York: Penguin, 1991), 25, 91. Upon reading *The End of the Affair*, Paul Theroux wrote : "Bendrix, a lonely man, capable of great sympathy, but with a sliver of ice in his heart" (Paul Theroux, "Graham Greene as I Knew Him," *New York Times Book Review*, April 21, 1991). Biographer Norman Sherry asserted that Greene could be identified with his characters. Norman Sherry, *The Life of Graham Greene*, vol. 1 (New York: Penguin, 1989).

34. Greene, *The End of the Affair*, 12. Sarah is to Bendrix as a sainted Beatrice was to Dante, although she is adulterous like Dante's Francesca de Rimini.

35. Greene, *The End of the Affair*, 50–51.

36. Greene, *The End of the Affair*, 47.

37. Graham Greene, *The Quiet American* (London: Heinemann, 1955, rpt. New York: Penguin, 2002), 20.

38. Greene, *The Quiet American*, 77.

39. Greene, *The Quiet American*, 52.

40. Greene, *The Quiet American*, 36.

41. Greene, *The Quiet American*, 86.

42. Greene, *The Quiet American*, 89.

43. Norman Mailer, *The Deer Park* (New York: Putnam, 1955), 4. Stanley Rinehart said that he would publish Mailer's novel then backed away from doing so because of concerns about obscenity and vulgarity. Putnam then published *The Deer Park*.

44. Mailer, *The Deer Park*, 19.

45. Mailer, *The Deer Park*, 22.

46. Mailer, *The Deer Park*, 45–46.

47. Mailer, *The Deer Park*, 46.

48. Mailer, *The Deer Park*, 45.

49. Mailer, *The Deer Park*, 5.

50. Mailer, *The Deer Park*, 9.

51. Mailer, *The Deer Park*, 18–19.

52. Mailer, *The Deer Park*, 9.

53. Mailer, *The Deer Park*, 13.

54. Mailer, *The Deer Park*, 23.

55. Mailer, *The Deer Park*, 24.

56. Mailer, *The Deer Park*, 26. In 2018, when the Library of America issued a collection of Mailer's writings of the 1960s, Peter Tonquette recalled Mailer in "Mailer's Sixties Slump" (*National Review*, April 12, 2018). A writer need not be "a nice guy" to write a good novel, he observed. However, "Norman Mailer displayed some of the least attractive traits and completed some of his least credible work in the ten years from 1960 to 1969." The decade began infamously with his stabbing of his wife Adele at a drunken party: an incident he later claimed prevented his nomination for a Nobel Prize. (See his conversation with Gunter Grass at the New York Public Library in 2007. See also J. Michael Lennon, ed., *Norman Mailer: The Sixties*, 2 vols. [New York: Library of America, 2018].) Mailer wrote two novels in the 1960s: *Why Are We in Vietnam?* (1967) and *American Dream* (1965), featuring the rather mad congressman Stephen Rojack.

57. Joan Shelley Rubin, *Cultural Considerations: Essays on Readers, Writers and Musicians in Postwar America* (Amherst: University of Massachusetts Press, 2013), 73.

58. Dwight Macdonald, "By Cozzens Possessed," *Commentary* 25 (January 1958): 36–47.

59. Rubin, *Cultural Considerations*, 65.

60. "Novelist Cozzens," *Time*, September 2, 1957; Rubin, *Cultural Considerations*, 67.

61. Frederick Bracher, introduction to *The Novels of James Gould Cozzens* (New York: Harcourt Brace Jovanovich, 1959).

6. THE HAUNTED AND THE TERRIFIED

1. John Knowles, *A Separate Peace* (New York: Macmillan, 1959, rpt. New York: Bantam, 1960), 1–2.

2. John A. Farrell, *Richard Nixon: The Life* (New York: Vintage, 2017), 210.

3. Knowles, *A Separate Peace*, 6.

4. H. P. Lovecraft is quoted in *Supernatural Horror in Literature*, which ran in the *Recluse* from November 1925 to May 1927. See E. F. Bleiler, ed., *Supernatural Horror in Literature* (New York: Dover, 1973) and http://www.hplovecraft.com/writings/textessays/shil.aspx.

5. William March, *The Bad Seed* (New York: Rinehart, 1954, rpt. New York: Knopf/Doubleday, 2015), 29.

6. W. H. Auden, *The Age of Anxiety: A Baroque Ecologue* (Princeton, NJ: Princeton University Press, 2011; originally published in 1947); William Faulkner, Nobel Prize speech, December 10, 1950, American Rhetoric, https://www.americanrhetoric.com/speeches/williamfaulknernobelprizeaddress.htm; Norman Mailer, "The White Negro: Superficial Reflections on the Hipster," in *Advertisements for Myself* (New York: Putnam, 1959); Søren Kierkegaard, *The Concept of Dread*, ed. Walter Lowrie (Princeton, NJ: Princeton University Press, 1968). See also Sigmund Freud, "Das Unheimlich" [The Uncanny], *Imago* 5 (1919).

7. Shirley Jackson, *The Haunting of Hill House* (New York: Viking, 1959), 16. Darryl Hattenhauser sees Jackson as a precursor to postmodernism. Darryl Hattenhauser, *Shirley Jackson's American Gothic* (Albany: State University of New York Press, 2003). Lenemaja Friedman's biography, *Shirley Jackson*, appeared in 1973. Ruth Franklin's biography, *Shirley Jackson: A Rather Haunted Life* (Liveright), appeared more recently. Joan Wylie Hall offered a critical analysis in *Shirley Jackson: The Short Fiction* (1993). Bernice M. Murphy has collected essays on Jackson in *Shirley Jackson: Essays on the Literary Legacy* (2005). Judie Newman, for example, provides an interesting analysis in "Shirley Jackson: The Reproduction of Mothering: *The Haunting of Hill House*," in *Shirley Jackson: Essays on the Literary Legacy*, ed. Bernice M. Murphy (Jefferson, NC: McFarland, 2005), 169–82.

8. Jackson, *The Haunting of Hill House*, 24.

9. Jackson, *The Haunting of Hill House*, 73.

10. Jackson, *The Haunting of Hill House*, 36.

11. Jackson, *The Haunting of Hill House*, 155.

12. Jackson, *The Haunting of Hill House*, 212.

13. Jackson, *The Haunting of Hill House*, 232.

14. Jackson, *The Haunting of Hill House*, 78.

15. Dale Bailey, *American Nightmares: The Haunted House Formula in American Popular Fiction* (Bowling Green, OH: Bowling Green University Popular Press; Madison: University of Wisconsin Press, 1999), 28. For feminist views on the restriction of women, see Sandra Gilbert and Susan Gubar, *The Madwoman in the Attic* (New Haven, CT: Yale University Press, 1979, rpt. 1997); Charlotte Perkins Gilman, *The Yellow Wallpaper* (New York: Feminist Press, 1996). Irving Malin, in *The New American Gothic* (Carbondale: Southern Illinois University Press, 1962, rpt. 1968), has viewed the Gothic as a turning inward.

16. The 1950s housewife-writer comments: "Our house is old and noisy and full. When we moved into it, we had two children and about five thousand books." Shirley Jackson, *Life among the Savages* (New York: Farrar, Straus & Giroux, 1953), 1.

17. Lenemaja Friedman, *Shirley Jackson* (Cincinnati: Bobbs-Merrill, 1973), 161.

18. Ruth Franklin, *Shirley Jackson: A Rather Haunted Life* (Philadelphia: Liveright, 2016), ii; Harold Bloom, introduction to *Bloom's Major Short Story Writers: Shirley Jackson*, ed. Harold Bloom (New York: Infobase, 2009), 10.

19. Lynnette Carpenter and Wendy Kolmar, introduction to *Haunting the House of Fiction: Feminist Perspectives on Ghost Stories by American Women*, ed. Lynnette Carpenter and Wendy Kolmar (Knoxville: University of Tennessee Press, 1991), 145. Lynnette Carpenter and Wendy K. Kolmar point to the women's domestic sphere and home associations with the haunted house (14). See also Carpenter and Kolmar, *Haunting the House of Fiction*, 25.

20. Edmund Fuller, "Terror Lived There Too: Review of *The Haunting of Hill House*," *New York Times Book Review*, October 18, 1959, 4.

21. Robert Bloch, *Psycho* (New York: Harry Abrams, 2010; originally published in 1959), 93.

22. Randall D. Larson points to these stories in *The Robert Bloch Companion: Collected Interviews 1969–1986* (San Bernardino, CA: Borgo, 1990), 59, 82. See Richard Matheson, who calls "Lucy" a forerunner of *Psycho*, in Richard Matheson, introduction to *The Twilight Zone: The Original Stories*, ed. Martin Harry Greenberg, Richard Matheson, and Charles G. Waugh (New York: Avon, 1985), 72.

23. See the 1995 David J. Schow interview with Robert Bloch in David J. Schow, ed., *The Lost Bloch* (Burton, MI: Subterranean, 2002), 113.

24. William H. Chafe, *The Unfinished Journey: America since World War II* (New York and Oxford: Oxford University Press, 2011), 7:123.

25. Chafe, *The Unfinished Journey*, 7:127.

26. Chafe, *The Unfinished Journey*, 7:138.

27. Chafe, *The Unfinished Journey*, 7:115.

28. See Robert Ellwood, *The Fifties Spiritual Marketplace: American Religion in a Decade of Conflict* (New Brunswick, NJ: Rutgers University Press, 1997).

29. Ellwood, *The Fifties Spiritual Marketplace*.

30. Albert Einstein, *Einstein on Politics*, ed. David E. Rowe and Robert Shulman (Princeton, NJ: Princeton University Press, 2007), 477.

31. Einstein, *Einstein on Politics*, 404.

32. Einstein, *Einstein on Politics*, 403–4.

33. Albert Einstein, *Ideas and Opinions* (Norwalk, CT: Easton, 2004), 161.

34. Einstein, *Ideas and Opinions*, 164.

35. Einstein, *Einstein on Politics*, 497–98.

36. John Carey, *The Intellectuals and the Masses: Pride and Prejudice among the Literary Intelligentsia, 1880–1939* (Chicago: Chicago Review Press, 2005).

37. See the discussion of this novel by Michael Bliss, *Invasions USA: The Essential Science Fiction Films of the 1950s* (Lanham, MD: Rowman & Littlefield, 2014), 16–18.

38. Richard Matheson, *I Am Legend* (New York: Gold Medal, 1954, rpt. New York: Tor, 2003), 7. See Agnieszka Soltysik Monnet, "They Are Legend: The Popular American Gothic of Ambrose Bierce and Richard Matheson," in *A Companion to American Gothic*, ed. Charles L. Grow (New York: Wiley-Blackwell, 2014); Richard Matheson, *Collected Stories*, vol. 1, ed. Stanley Wiater (Colorado Springs, CO: Gauntlet, 2003); M. R. Bradley, *Richard Matheson on Screen: A History of the Filmed Works* (Jefferson, NC: McFarland, 2010).

39. Rollo May, "Reflections on Anxiety," *Psychology Today* (1978). Cassette recording transcription. www.existentialanalysis.org.uk/assets/articles/Understanding-Anxiety-and-Coping-with-Anxiety-Rollo-May-transcription-Martin-Adams-pdf. See also Rollo May, *The Meaning of Anxiety* (New York: Ronald Press, 1950, rpt. New York: Norton, 2018).

40. Leslie Dale Feldman, *Spaceships and Politics: The Political Theory of Rod Serling* (Lanham, MD: Lexington Books, 2010), 6.

41. Paula Rabinowitz, *American Pulp: How Paperbacks Brought Modernism to Main Street* (Princeton, NJ: Princeton University Press, 2014), 3.

42. Ray B. Browne and Gary Hoppenstand, *The Defective Detective in the Pulps* (Bowling Green, OH: Bowling Green Popular Press, 1983).

43. Nevil Shute, *On the Beach* (London: Heinemann, 1957), 5. The 1957 story is set in the near future. We learn that Peter and Mary Holmes were married in 1961.

44. Shute, *On the Beach*, 17.

45. Claire P. Curtis, *Postapocalyptic Fiction and the Social Contract* (Lanham, MD: Lexington Books, 2010), 20.

46. Curtis, *Postapocalyptic Fiction and the Social Contract*, 21.

47. Curtis, *Postapocalyptic Fiction and the Social Contract*, 20.

48. Pat Frank, *Alas, Babylon* (Philadelphia: Lippincott, 1959), 91.

49. Frank, *Alas, Babylon*, 123.

50. Frank, *Alas, Babylon*, 258.

51. Frank, *Alas, Babylon*, 312.

52. Robert Heilbroner, *The Future as History* (New York: Grove, 1959, rpt. 1961), 61.

53. Heilbroner, *The Future as History*, 63–64.

54. Heilbroner, *The Future as History*, 67.

55. Heilbroner, *The Future as History*, 68.

56. Heilbroner, *The Future as History*, 72.

57. Heilbroner, *The Future as History*, 74; Susanne Langer, *Philosophy in a New Key* (New York: Mentor, 1951), 238.

58. Jonathan Schell, *The Fate of the Earth* (New York: Knopf, 1982), 6. Jonathan Schell points to studies on the potential impact of nuclear war: "The Effects of Nuclear War" (1979) by the Office of Technology Assessment appeared twenty years after Pat Frank's *Alas, Babylon*. "The Effects of Nuclear Weapons" by Samuel Gladstone and Philip J. Dolan was published by the Department of Defense and the Energy Research and Development Administration. The aftermath of the nuclear bombs in Japan was studied. Among other studies noted by Schell was "Longterm Worldwide Effects of Multiple Nuclear Detonations" (1975) by the National Academy of Sciences. See Schell, *The Fate of the Earth*, 5.

59. Dwight D. Eisenhower, letter to Richard L. Simon of Simon & Schuster, April 4, 1956, in *The Papers of Dwight D. Eisenhower*, vol. 4, *The War Years*, ed. Alfred D. Chandler and Stephen Ambrose (Baltimore: Johns Hopkins University Press, 1970). The original letter is in the Dwight David Eisenhower Diaries Series, Box 14, April 1956, in the Presidential Papers in the Eisenhower Library.

60. William Golding, *Lord of the Flies* (London: Faber and Faber, 1954), 62.

61. Jack I. Biles wrote that there was little study of literary "characters as representations of human beings" (219). Quoted in Maurice L. McCullen, "*Lord of the Flies*: The Critical Quest," in *William Golding: Some Critical Considerations*, ed. Jack I. Biles and Robert O. Evans (Lexington: University Press of Kentucky, 1978), 203, 219.

62. Peter Green, "The Stranger Within," *New Republic*, September 2, 2010, 33–34. Biographer John Carey cites the interview with Golding in "*Lord of the*

Flies Goes to College," *New Republic*, May 4, 1963, 28–29. See also John Carey, *William Golding: The Man Who Wrote* Lord of the Flies (New York: Free Press, 2012).

63. Green, "The Stranger Within," 34.

7. DEMOCRACY'S DEFENDERS

1. Frank Desmond, "M'Carthy Charges Reds Hold U.S. Jobs," *Wheeling Intelligencer*, February 10, 1950. The number "on the list" indicated by Joseph McCarthy varies across different reports. See https://www.ohiocountylibrary.org/history/U.S.-se.-joseph-r-mccarthy-speaks-in-wheeling/5655.

2. William F. Buckley, *The Redhunter* (Boston: Little, Brown, 1999), 118.

3. Buckley, *The Redhunter*, 20.

4. Margaret Chase Smith's criticism of McCarthy, "Declaration of Conscience," appears in the *Congressional Record*, June 1, 1950.

5. Joseph McCarthy, remarks in a speech at a Manitowac, Wisconsin, fundraiser, March 15, 1954. Joseph McCarthy Archives, Marquette University, Raynor Library, Milwaukee, Wisconsin. Recordings of Senator McCarthy's statements are available online from the Marquette University collection. See audio excerpts at http://cdm16280.contentdm.oclc.org/cdm/search/searchterm/mccarthy/field/ab/mode/all/conn/and/order/title/as/asc/cosuppress/1. (See Marquette University, Raynor Library, Milwaukee, Wisconsin, http://www.marquette.edu/library/archives/News/McCarthy.php.) The library houses the papers of Wisconsin Senator Joseph McCarthy, who graduated from the Marquette Law School in 1935.

6. McCarthy, remarks, March 15, 1954.

7. McCarthy specifically cited the communist affiliation of Wendell Furry, a Harvard physics professor, who contributed to quantum field theory with Robert Oppenheimer. Joseph McCarthy, remarks in Houston, Texas, on April 21, 1954 (McCarthy Archives, Marquette University, Raynor Library, Milwaukee, Wisconsin).

8. McCarthy's address in Wausau, Wisconsin, May 8, 1954, occurred during the U.S. Army hearings, and G. David Schine, as an aide to McCarthy, had been implicated in the issues. The heir of a hotel chain fortune, Schine was introduced to Roy Cohn, counsel for McCarthy. Schine was drafted into the army, and McCarthy claimed the army was leaning on him with pressure on Schine. Schine later became the producer of the film *The French Connection* (1971) and head of a music company that distributed recordings by Lou Rawls and Bobby Sherman. He died in an airplane crash near Burbank, California.

9. The statement by Joseph Welch, often quoted in critical commentaries, appears in the *Congressional Record* (June 9, 1954) and McCarthy hearing documents.

10. Henry S. Reuss, *When Government Was Good: Memories of a Life in Politics* (Madison: University of Wisconsin Press, 1999), 38. Poet and librarian of Congress Archibald MacLeish observed that dissent was restricted in a McCarthyist environment. See Archibald MacLeish, "Loyalty and Freedom," *American Scholar* 22, no. 4 (Autumn 1953): 393–98.

11. Reuss, *When Government Was Good*, xiii.

12. Kingsley Amis, *The James Bond Dossier* (London: Jonathan Cape, 1965), 46.

13. Ian Fleming, *Dr. No* (London: Jonathan Cape, 1958; New York: Macmillan, 1958), 224.

14. Amis, *The James Bond Dossier*, 144.

15. Bernard Bergonzi, review of *Dr. No*, by Ian Fleming, *Twentieth Century Magazine*, March 1958, 220.

16. Ian Fleming, *Casino Royale* (London: Jonathan Cape, 1953), 27.

17. Michael Denning, *Cover Stories: Narrative and Ideology in the British Spy Thriller* (London and New York: Routledge and Kegan Paul, 1987), 109–10. Also see Lisa Funnell, *For His Eyes Only: The Women of James Bond* (London: Wallflower / Columbia University Press, 2015), 13.

18. When Honeychile Rider in *Dr. No* is first seen by Bond (and presumably by the male reader), we read: "It was a naked girl, her back to him. She was not quite naked" (Fleming, *Dr. No*, 79).

19. James Chapman, *Licence to Thrill: A Cultural History of James Bond* (London: Tauris, 2008), 9.

20. These statistics are provided by Tony Bennett and Janet Woolacott, *Bond and Beyond: The Political Career of a Popular Hero* (New York and London: Macmillan, 1987), 214. The spy genre flourished in 1960s television with *I Spy*, *Mission Impossible*, and *The Man from U.N.C.L.E.*, as well as the situation comedy *Get Smart*.

21. Thomas H. Eliot, "Robin Hood in Boston," *New Republic*, March 12, 1956, 28.

22. Allen Drury, *Advise and Consent* (Garden City, NY: Doubleday, 1959), 3.

23. John J. Miller, "The Great Washington Novel," *National Review*, February 9, 2015. The comment about Washington appears in chapter 2 of Drury, *Advise and Consent*.

24. Arthur Schlesinger, *The Imperial Presidency* (New York: Houghton Mifflin Harcourt, 1973).

25. Thomas Mallon, "*Advise and Consent* at 50," *New York Times Book Review*, June 25, 2009. On presidential rhetoric, see Elvin T. Lim, *The Anti-Intellectual Presidency: The Decline of Presidential Rhetoric from George Washington to George W. Bush* (New York and Oxford: Oxford University Press, 2008). Arthur Schlesinger, *The Imperial Presidency* (New York: Houghton Mifflin Harcourt, 1973).

26. David Reisman, *The Lonely Crowd: A Study of the Changing American Character* (New Haven, CT: Yale University Press, 1950), 46, 176. David Reisman, in *American Scholar*, referred to *ethnicity*: one of the first uses of the term. He wrote of "our ethnic diversity, our regional and religious pluralism." David Reisman, "Some Observations on Intellectual Freedom," *American Scholar* 23, no. 1 (Winter 1953–1954): 14. Will Herberg explored ethnicity and religious thought in *Protestant, Catholic, Jew* (1955). To be ethnic was to be marginal. If ethnicity meant separation, this was not helpful to *e pluribus unum*: a vision of a united nation that is open to embracing diversity.

27. Scott Simon, "At 50: A D.C. Novel with Legs," *Wall Street Journal*, September 2, 2009; Roger Kaplan, "Allen Drury and the Washington Novel," *Policy Review* 97 (October/November 1999); *New Yorker*, May 2019.

28. For an anthology of 1950s civil rights journalism, see Clayborne Carson, David J. Garrow, Bill Kovach, and Carol Polsgrove, comps., *Reporting Civil Rights, 1941–1963*, vol. 1, *American Journalism 1941–1963* (New York: Library of America, 2003).

29. Martin Luther King Jr., "A Knock at Midnight," in *Voices from the Dexter Pulpit*, ed. Michael Thurman (Montgomery, AL: New South, 2001), 50–51. Leon Sullivan provided the introduction for this collection of sermons from the Dexter Avenue Memorial Baptist Church. Also see Clayborne Carson, ed., *A Knock at Midnight: Inspiration from the Great Sermons of Martin Luther King, Jr.* (New York: IPM, Warner, 1998). The Martin Luther King, Jr., Research Institute at Stanford University publishes the King Papers Project initiated by the King Center of Atlanta, Georgia. King served at the Dexter Memorial Baptist Church, 1954–1960. Vernon John preceded Martin Luther King Jr. in the Dexter pulpit (1947–1952). King was elected president of the Montgomery Improvement Association, December 5, 1955.

30. King, "A Knock at Midnight," 53.

31. King, "A Knock at Midnight," 53.

32. King, "A Knock at Midnight," 51.

33. Martin Luther King Jr., address concerning the Montgomery bus boycott, Holt Street Baptist Church, December 5, 1955.

34. President Ulysses S. Grant was from Galen, Ohio.

35. Mark Osteen, *Nightmare Alley: Film Noir and the American Dream* (Baltimore: Johns Hopkins University Press, 2013), 2.

36. Osteen, *Nightmare Alley*, 4, 11.

37. Krutnik is cited by Osteen, *Nightmare Alley*, 54–55. Krutnik's comments appear in Frank Krutnik, *In a Lonely Street: Film Noir, Genre, Masculinity* (London and New York: Routledge, 1991), 54–55. The psychoanalytic approach of Sigmund Freud called attention to the repression of disturbing memories or impulses. He theorized that dreams hide the latent content of emotional memories and wishes and that dreams operated by condensation or displacement. See Sigmund Freud, *The Interpretation of Dreams*, trans. A. A. Brill (London: Macmillan, 1913, rpt. New York: Basic, 2010), 312–44.

38. Leonard Cassuto, *Hard-Boiled Sentimentality: The Secret History of American Crime Stories* (New York: Columbia University Press, 2009), 3.

39. Cassuto, *Hard-Boiled Sentimentality*, 10; Jane Tompkins, *Sensational Designs: The Cultural Work of American Fiction, 1790–1860* (Oxford and New York: Oxford University Press, 1986).

40. Wright, cited by John T. Irwin, *Unless the Threat Is behind Them: Hard-Boiled Fiction and Film Noir* (Baltimore: Johns Hopkins University Press, 2006), 172–73; Dorothy Sayers, introduction to *The Omnibus of Crime: Great Short Stories of Detection* (London: Payson and Clarke, 1929); Sayers's statement on the Detection Club guidelines is cited by Irwin, *Unless the Threat Is behind Them*, 172.

41. Raymond Chandler's comment to Alfred Hitchcock is quoted by Jerry Speir in *Raymond Chandler* (New York: Frederick Ungar, 1981), 15.

42. The titles of all Perry Mason novels of the 1950s begin with the phrase "The Case of the . . ." They include *The Case of the Neglected Nymph*, *The Case of the One-Eyed Witness*, *The Case of the Fiery Fingers*, *The Case of the Angry Mariner*, *The Case of the Moth-Eaten Mink*, *The Case of the Grinning Gorilla*, *The Case of the Hesitant Hostess*, *The Case of the Green-Eyed Sister*, *The Case of the Fugitive Nurse*, *The Case of the Runaway Corpse*, *The Case of the Restless Redhead*, *The Case of the Glamorous Ghost*, *The Case of the Sun Bather's Diary*, *The Case of the Nervous Accomplice*, *The Case of the Terrified Typist*, *The Case of the Demure Defendant*, *The Case of the Gilded Lily*, *The Case of the Lucky Loser*, *The Case of the Long-Legged Models*, *The Case of the Screaming Woman*, *The Case of the Footloose Doll*, *The Case of the Calendar Girl*, *The Case of the Daring Decoy*, *The Case of the Deadly Toy*, *The Case of the Mythical Monkey*, and *The Case of the Singing Skirt*, among others.

43. Mickey Spillane, *Kiss Me Deadly*, in *The Mike Hammer Collection* (New York: New American Library, 2001), 2:124; cited by Roland K. Vegso, *The Naked Communist: Cold War Modernism and the Politics of Popular Culture* (Bronx, NY: Fordham University Press, 2013), 164. After *Kiss Me Deadly*, Spillane paused in his Mike Hammer series until 1962. Spillane's spy fiction also emerged in the 1960s.

44. Philip Wylie, "The Crime of Mickey Spillane," *Good Housekeeping*, February 1955, 54.

45. Charles J. Rolo, "Simenon and Spillane: Metaphysics of Murder for the Millions," in *Mass Culture: The Popular Arts in America*, ed. Bernard Rosenberg and David M. White (Glencoe, IL: Free Press, 1957), 91.

46. Amy Benfer, "Girl Revised," *New York Times*, March 6, 2004.

47. Benfer, "Girl Revised."

48. Ross Macdonald, *Moving Target* (New York: Random House, 1949), 111, 127.

49. These novels have recently been made available in a new edition by the Library of America. Another volume collects Ross Macdonald novels from the early 1960s. The Library of America has also published a boxed set of eleven Lew Archer novels by Ross Macdonald (whose given name was Kenneth Millar). Ross Macdonald, *Four Novels of the 1950s* (New York: Library of America, 2015). *Moving Target* and *The Long Goodbye* appear in the Vintage Crime series of Ross Macdonald novels from Random House.

50. William F. Buckley, "My Friend E. Howard Hunt," *Los Angeles Times*, March 4, 2007.

8. ADVENTURERS

1. James Michener, "The Conscience of the Contemporary Novel," in *The Arts in Renewal*, ed. Lewis Mumford (Philadelphia: University of Pennsylvania Press, 1951), 123.

2. James Michener, *The Voice of Asia* (New York: Random House, 1951), 118.

3. Michener, "The Conscience of the Contemporary Novel," 117.

4. Saul Bellow, *The Adventures of Augie March*, in *Saul Bellow: Novels 1944–1953* (New York: Library of America, 2003), 1. Augie March narrates his story, beginning with "I am an American, Chicago born." In that "somber city," he "knocks" at the door of life. Augie March lives in the Humboldt Park area. Einhorn, who owns a pool room, says, "In the end you can't save your life by thought" (117). David Dempsey, Leon Edel, Mary McCarthy, Arthur Mizener, and Gerald Sykes were the judges for the National Book Award for 1954 won by *The Adventures of Augie March*.

5. Bellow, *The Adventures of Augie March*, 383. Bellow suggests that the insights of the heart are deeper and often truer than rational thought.

6. Bellow, *The Adventures of Augie March*, 385.

7. Bellow, *The Adventures of Augie March*, 384.

8. Bellow, *The Adventures of Augie March*, 387.

9. Bellow, *The Adventures of Augie March*, 392–93.
10. Bellow, *The Adventures of Augie March*, 394.
11. Bellow, *The Adventures of Augie March*, 396.
12. Bellow, *The Adventures of Augie March*, 430.
13. Bellow, *The Adventures of Augie March*, 421.
14. Bellow, *The Adventures of Augie March*, 431–33.
15. Bellow, *The Adventures of Augie March*, 434–35.
16. Bellow, *The Adventures of Augie March*, 438–39.
17. Bellow, *The Adventures of Augie March*, 449, 494.
18. Bellow, *The Adventures of Augie March*, 453–54.
19. Bellow, *The Adventures of Augie March*, 499.
20. Bellow, *The Adventures of Augie March*, 495.
21. Bellow, *The Adventures of Augie March*, 473.
22. Bellow, *The Adventures of Augie March*, 466.
23. Bellow, *The Adventures of Augie March*, 477.
24. Bellow, *The Adventures of Augie March*, 475.
25. Robert Penn Warren, "The Man with No Commitments," review of *The Adventures of Augie March*, by Saul Bellow, *New Republic* 129, no. 14 (November 1953): 22–23; Steven M. Gerson, "The New American Adam in the Adventures of Augie March," *Modern Fiction* 25, no. 1 (1979): 128. Also see Christopher Hitchens, "The Great American Augie," *Wilson Quarterly* 25, no. 1 (Winter 2001): 22–29. Christopher Borelli, in "Diving into Saul Bellow's Archives" (*Chicago Tribune*, May 16, 2019), mentions that in Box 80 in the University of Chicago Bellow archive can be found correspondence from each presidential administration from Kennedy to Clinton. He also wrote "Walking through Bellow's Chicago," *Chicago Tribune*, June 7, 2015, when Bellow would have turned one hundred.
26. Delmore Schwartz, "Adventures in America," *Partisan Review* 21, no. 1 (January–February 1954); Leonard Kriegel, "Wrestling with Augie March," *Nation*, June 23, 2003.
27. Jack Kerouac, *On the Road*, in *Kerouac: Road Novels 1957–1960*, ed. Douglas G. Brinkley (New York: Library of America, 2007), 25.
28. Timothy Hunt, *Kerouac's Cracked Road* (Carbondale: Southern Illinois University Press, 1981), xxxi, xxvii. John Clellan Holmes differentiated the Beat Generation from the Lost Generation of the 1920s. He wrote that the Beat Generation took the ruins for granted. "They were brought up in these ruins and no longer notice them," he wrote. "The wild boys of today are not lost, often scoffing, always intent faces elude the word and it would sound phony to them." John Clellon Holmes, "This Is the Beat Generation," *New York Times Magazine*, November 16, 1952.
29. Kerouac, *On the Road*, 53.

30. Kerouac, *On the Road*, 175.
31. Kerouac, *On the Road*, 174.
32. Kerouac, *On the Road*, 226.
33. Kerouac, *On the Road*, 231.
34. Kerouac, *On the Road*, 243.
35. Sal encounters boxcars (Kerouac, *On the Road*, 40–41), hitchhikers (22), and hobos (104).
36. Kerouac, *On the Road*, 173.
37. David Brooks, "Sal Paradise at 50," *New York Times*, October 6, 2007.
38. Kerouac, *On the Road*, 15.
39. Kerouac, *On the Road*, 278. Poet Allen Ginsberg and Jack Kerouac were central to the development of Beat poetry, and Ginsberg was influenced by Kerouac's spontaneous prose style. In 1956, Allen Ginsberg's "Howl" was published by Lawrence Ferlinghetti's City Lights Books. Kerouac started *Desolation Angels*. He visited William S. Burroughs upon sailing to Tangier, where he helped to type *Naked Lunch*.
40. William S. Burroughs, *Naked Lunch* (New York: Grove, 1959), 6.
41. Burroughs, *Naked Lunch*, 13–14.
42. Burroughs, *Naked Lunch*, 14.
43. Richard Goldstein, "Go the Way Your Blood Beats: An Interview with James Baldwin," in *James Baldwin: The Legacy*, ed. Quincy Troupe (New York: Simon & Schuster, 1989), 173–85.
44. James Baldwin, *Giovanni's Room*, in *Baldwin: Early Novels and Stories*, ed. Toni Morrison (New York: Library of America, 1998), 90, 5. One might read the novel in a poststructuralist manner and ask whether gender categories and identity are socially constructed and consider how nationhood is imagined.
45. Baldwin, *Giovanni's Room*, 92.
46. Baldwin, *Giovanni's Room*, 62.
47. Baldwin, *Giovanni's Room*, 58.
48. Baldwin, *Giovanni's Room*, 57.
49. Grace Metalious, *Peyton Place* (New York: Julian Messner, 1956), 15. The 1953 Kinsey report on female sexual behavior underscored the passions of *Peyton Place*. See Alfred Kinsey, Wardell Pomeroy, Clyde Martin, and Paul Gebhard, *Sexual Behavior in the Human Female* (Philadelphia: Saunders, 1953). Some feminists have argued for the liberating power of imagination and fantasy that encourages female action. Scholarly studies of popular fiction and reading include Elizabeth Long, *Book Clubs: Women and the Uses of Reading in Everyday Life* (Chicago: University of Chicago Press, 2003); Janice Radway, *A Feeling for Books: The Book of the Month Club, Literary Taste, and Middle-Class Desire* (Chapel Hill: University of North Carolina Press, 1997); Michael Denning, *Mechanic Accents: Dime Novels and Working-Class Culture in*

America (London: Verso, 1987); and Joan Shelley Rubin, *The Making of Middlebrow Culture* (Chapel Hill and London: University of North Carolina Press, 1992).

50. Metalious, *Peyton Place*, 16.

51. Metalious, *Peyton Place*, 15, 17.

52. Malcolm Bradbury and James McFarlane, eds., *Modernism: A Guide to European Literature, 1890–1930* (New York: Penguin, 1991).

53. C. P. Snow, *The New Men* (London: Macmillan, 1954, rpt. 1960), 301.

54. Stefan Collini, introduction to *The Two Cultures*, by C. P. Snow (Cambridge: Cambridge University Press, 1993), lxx.

55. Collini, introduction to *The Two Cultures*, lxiii.

56. J. H. Plumb, ed., *The Crisis of the Humanities* (London: Penguin, 1964).

57. Collini, introduction to *The Two Cultures*, xliii.

58. Thomas Kuhn, *The Structure of Scientific Revolutions* (Chicago: University of Chicago Press, 1962). The history of science was a limited field in Snow's time, as Collini reminds us (Collini, introduction to *The Two Cultures*, xviii). Matthew Arnold's own Rede Lecture at the Senate House in 1882 was on "Literature and Science." For Arnold, "literature" meant all the great books, including those of science as well as novels, essays, and poetry. His grandnephew Aldous Huxley wrote his reflections on the "two cultures" in *Literature and Science* (New York: Harper & Row, 1963).

59. F. R. Leavis, "Two Cultures? The Significance of C. P. Snow," *Spectator*, March 9, 1962, 297–303. Leavis's comments were published in book form by Chatto and Windus in 1962. See also Lionel Trilling, "Science, Literature and Culture: A Comment on the Leavis-Snow Controversy," *Commentary*, June 1962, 461–77.

60. Collini, introduction to *The Two Cultures*, ix.

61. Collini, introduction to *The Two Cultures*, ix.

62. Reinhold Niebuhr, *The Irony of American History* (1952), in *Reinhold Niebuhr: Major Works on Religion and Politics*, ed. Elisabeth Sifton (New York: Library of America, 2015), 507.

63. Niebuhr, *The Irony of American History*, 508.

64. Niebuhr, *The Irony of American History*, 508.

65. For further reading on C. P. Snow, you may consult Cynthia Crossen, "Studying Arts and Sciences in C. P. Snow's *The Masters*," *Wall Street Journal*, September 20, 2007. In *C. P. Snow: The Politics of Conscience* (Carbondale: Southern Illinois University Press, 1965), Frederick Karl viewed Snow as a late Victorian realist. He sees *homo faber*, man the maker, in Snow's stories: a man defined in his roles and his jobs (20–21). Also see John De La Mothe, *C. P. Snow and the Struggle of Modernity* (Montreal and Kingston: McGill-Queen's University Press, 1992, rpt. Austin: University of Texas Press, 2011); C. P.

Snow, *The Two Cultures*, with an introduction by Stefan Collini (Cambridge: Cambridge University Press, 1998).

66. F. R. Leavis, *Education and the University* (Cambridge: Cambridge University Press, 1943, rpt. 1979).

67. Mary McCarthy, *The Groves of Academe* (New York: Harcourt Brace, 1952), 17.

68. McCarthy, *The Groves of Academe*, 14.

69. McCarthy, *The Groves of Academe*, 15.

70. McCarthy, *The Groves of Academe*, 25.

71. McCarthy, *The Groves of Academe*, 28.

72. McCarthy, *The Groves of Academe*, 38.

73. McCarthy, *The Groves of Academe*, 23.

74. Philip Roth, *Goodbye, Columbus*, in *Philip Roth: Novels and Stories 1959–1962*, ed. Ross Miller (New York: Library of America, 2005), 48.

75. Roth, *Goodbye, Columbus*, 13.

76. Roth, *Goodbye, Columbus*, 33.

77. Roth, *Goodbye, Columbus*, 28.

78. Roth, *Goodbye, Columbus*, 61.

BIBLIOGRAPHY

Amis, Kingsley. *The James Bond Dossier*. London: Jonathan Cape; New York: New American Library, 1965.

———. *Lucky Jim*. Garden City, NY: Doubleday, 1954.

Assals, Frederick. *Flannery O'Connor: The Imagination of Extremity*. Athens: University of Georgia Press, 1982.

Auden, W. H. *The Age of Anxiety: A Baroque Ecologue*. Princeton, NJ: Princeton University Press, 2011. Originally published in 1947.

Bailey, Dale. *American Nightmares: The Haunted House Formula in American Popular Fiction*. Bowling Green, OH: Bowling Green University Popular Press; Madison: University of Wisconsin Press, 1999.

Baker, Carlos. *Hemingway: The Writer as Artist*. Princeton, NJ: Princeton University Press, 1956.

Baldwin, Hanson W. "*The Caine Mutiny* Issue." *New York Times*, March 21, 1954, SM 12.

Baldwin, James. *Creative America*. Washington, DC: National Cultural Center; New York: Ridge Press, 1962.

———. "The Creative Process." In *Creative America*. Washington, DC: National Cultural Center; New York: Ridge Press, 1962.

———. *The Devil Finds Work*. New York: Dial, 1976.

———. *The Devil Finds Work*. In *Baldwin: Collected Essays*, edited by Toni Morrison. New York: Library of America, 1998.

———. "Down at the Cross." In *The Fire Next Time*, collected in *Baldwin: Collected Essays*, edited by Toni Morrison. New York: Library of America, 1998.

———. *Giovanni's Room*. In *Baldwin: Early Novels and Stories*, edited by Toni Morrison. New York: Library of America, 1998.

———. *Go Tell It on the Mountain*. In *Baldwin: Early Novels and Stories*, edited by Toni Morrison. New York: Library of America, 1998.

———. "The Harlem Ghetto." In *Notes of a Native Son*, collected in *Baldwin: Collected Essays*, edited by Toni Morrison. New York: Library of America, 1998.

———. *Notes of a Native Son*. In *Baldwin: Collected Essays*, edited by Toni Morrison. New York: Library of America, 1998.

———. "On Catfish Row." *Commentary*, September 1959.

———. "The Price of the Ticket." In *Baldwin: Collected Essays*, edited by Toni Morrison. New York: Library of America, 1998.

———. "Sonny's Blues." In *Going to Meet the Man*, collected in *Baldwin: Early Novels and Stories*, edited by Toni Morrison. New York: Library of America, 1998.

Barrett, William. "Lapse of a Novelist." *Commentary*, June 1, 1951, 602–4.

Barthes, Roland. *S/Z: An Essay*. Translated by Richard Miller. New York: Hill & Wang, 1970. Reprint, 1975.

———. *Writing Degree Zero*. Translated by Annette Lavers and Colin Smith. New York: Hill & Wang, 1953. Reprint, 1977.

Beegel, Susan. "A Guide to the Marine Life in Ernest Hemingway's *The Old Man and the Sea*." *Resources for American Literary Study* 30 (2006): 236–315.

———. "Hemingway's Education as a Naturalist." In *A Historical Guide to Ernest Hemingway*, edited by Linda Wagner-Martin. Oxford and New York: Oxford University Press, 1999.

Behrman, S. N. "The Vision of the Innocent." *New Yorker*, August 11, 1951, 71–76.

Bell, Daniel. *The End of Ideology: On the Exhaustion of Political Ideas in the Fifties*. Glencoe, IL and New York: Free Press, 1960.

Belletto, Steven, ed. *American Literature in Transition, 1950–1960*. Cambridge: Cambridge University Press, 2017.

Bellow, Saul. *The Adventures of Augie March*. In *Saul Bellow: Novels 1944–1953*. New York: Library of America, 2003.

———. *Henderson the Rain King*. In *Saul Bellow: Novels 1956–1964*. New York: Library of America, 2007.

———. *Seize the Day*. In *Saul Bellow: Novels 1956–1964*. New York: Library of America, 2007.

Benet, Stephen Vincent. "By the Waters of Babylon." In *Twenty-Five Stories by Stephen Vincent Benet*. New York: Sundial, 1943.

Benfer, Amy. "Girl Revised." *New York Times*, March 6, 2004.

Bennett, Tony, and Janet Woolacott. *Bond and Beyond: The Political Career of a Popular Hero*. New York and London: Macmillan, 1987.

Benson, Jackson J. *Hemingway: The Writer's Art of Self-Defense*. Minneapolis: University of Minnesota Press, 1969.

Benson, Josef. *J. D. Salinger's* Catcher in the Rye*: A Cultural History*. Lanham, MD: Rowman & Littlefield, 2014.

Benzon, William. *Beethoven's Anvil*. New York: Basic, 2001.

Bergonzi, Bernard. Review of *Dr. No*, by Ian Fleming. *Twentieth Century Magazine*, March 1958, 220.

Biles, Jack I., and Robert O. Evans, eds. *William Golding: Some Critical Considerations*. Lexington: University Press of Kentucky, 1978.

Bird, Robert Montgomery. *The Gladiator: A Tragedy in Five Acts* (Philadelphia, 1831). In *American Plays*, edited by Alan Gates Halline. New York: American Book Company, 1935.

———. Robert Montgomery Bird Diary. Robert Montgomery Bird Collection, University of Pennsylvania Kislak Center Special Collections.

Bleiler, E. F., ed. *Supernatural Horror in Literature*. New York: Dover, 1973.

Bliss, Michael. *Invasions USA: The Essential Science Fiction Films of the 1950s*. Lanham, MD: Rowman & Littlefield, 2014.

Bloch, Robert. *Psycho*. New York: Harry Abrams, 2010. Originally published in 1959.

Bloom, Harold. Introduction to *Bloom's Major Short Story Writers: Shirley Jackson*, edited by Harold Bloom. New York: Infobase, 2009.

———. Introduction to *Bloom's Modern Critical Interpretations: Ernest Hemingway's* The Old Man and the Sea, edited by Harold Bloom. New York: Infobase, 2018.

———. Introduction to *Bloom's Modern Critical Interpretations: J. D. Salinger's* The Catcher in the Rye, edited by Harold Bloom, 1–4. New York: Infobase, 2014.

Blotner, Joseph. *William Faulkner: A Biography*. 2 vols. New York: Random House, 1974. Reprint, 1984.

Bonn, Thomas L. *Heavy Traffic and High Culture: New American Library as a Literary Gatekeeper in the Paperback Revolution*. New York: Meridian, 1990.

"Books and Authors." *New York Times*, April 12, 1936, BR 12.

Boorstin, Daniel J. *The Image: A Guide to Pseudo-Events in America*. New York: Harper Colophon, 1964.

Booth, Wayne. *The Rhetoric of Fiction*. Chicago: University of Chicago Press, 1961.
Borelli, Christopher. "Diving into Saul Bellow's Archives." *Chicago Tribune*, May 16, 2019.
———. "Walking through Bellow's Chicago." *Chicago Tribune*, June 7, 2015.
Bowie, Robert R., and Richard H. Immerman. *Waging Peace: How Eisenhower Shaped an Enduring War Strategy*. New York: Oxford University Press, 1998.
Boyle, T. C. *World's End*. Norwalk, CT: Easton, 2014.
Bracher, Frederick. Introduction to *The Novels of James Gould Cozzens*. New York: Harcourt Brace Jovanovich, 1959.
Bradbury, Malcolm, and James McFarlane, eds. *Modernism: A Guide to European Literature, 1890–1930*. New York: Penguin, 1991.
Bradbury, Ray. *Fahrenheit 451*. New York: Ballantine, 1953. Reprint, New York: Simon & Schuster, 1967.
———. "The Fireman." *Galaxy* 1, no. 5 (1953): 4–61.
———. "The Pedestrian." *Reporter*, August 7, 1951, 39–42.
———. "There Will Come Soft Rains." In *The Martian Chronicles*, by Ray Bradbury. Garden City, NY: Doubleday, 1950.
———. "The Veldt." In *The Vintage Bradbury*, 13–28. New York: Vintage, Random House, 1965.
———. *The Vintage Bradbury*. New York: Vintage, Random House, 1965.
Bradley, Adam. *Ralph Ellison in Progress: From* Invisible Man *to* Three Days before the Shooting. New Haven, CT: Yale University Press, 2010.
Bradley, M. R. *Richard Matheson on Screen: A History of the Filmed Works*. Jefferson, NC: McFarland, 2010.
Brenner, Gerry. The Old Man and the Sea*: The Story of a Common Man*. New York: Twayne, 1991.
Brier, Evan. *A Novel Marketplace: Mass Culture, the Book Trade, and Postwar American Fiction*. Philadelphia: University of Pennsylvania Press, 2010.
Briet, Harvey. "Conversation with Saul Bellow, September 20, 1953." In *The Writer Observed*, 271–74. New York: World Publishers, 1956.
Brooks, David. "Sal Paradise at 50." *New York Times*, October 6, 2007.
Browne, Ray B., and Gary Hoppenstand. *The Defective Detective in the Pulps*. Bowling Green, OH: Bowling Green Popular Press, 1983.
Buckley, William F. "My Friend E. Howard Hunt." *Los Angeles Times*, March 4, 2007.
———. *The Redhunter*. Boston and New York: Little, Brown, 1999.
Burger, Nash K. "Books of the Times." *New York Times*, July 16, 1951.
Burroughs, William S. *Naked Lunch*. New York: Grove, 1959.
Butler, Jeffrey. *Change Leadership in Higher Education: A Practical Guide to Academic Transformation*. San Francisco, CA: Jossey-Bass, 2014.
Butterworth, Keen. *A Critical and Textual Study of Faulkner's* A Fable. Ann Arbor: UMI Research Press, 1983.
"*The Caine Mutiny*: A Lesson in Leadership." *Army Lawyer* 26, no. 2 (February 2010).
Cameron, Ardis. *The Unbuttoning of America: A Biography of* Peyton Place. Ithaca, NY: Cornell University Press, 2015.
Capote, Truman. *Breakfast at Tiffany's*. New York: Random House, 1958.
Carey, John. *The Intellectuals and the Masses: Pride and Prejudice among the Literary Intelligentsia, 1880–1939*. Chicago: Chicago Review Press, 2005.
———. "*Lord of the Flies* Goes to College." *New Republic*, May 4, 1963, 28–29.
———. *William Golding: The Man Who Wrote* Lord of the Flies. New York: Free Press, 2012.
Carpenter, Lynnette, and Wendy Kolmar. Introduction to *Haunting the House of Fiction: Feminist Perspectives on Ghost Stories by American Women*, edited by Lynnette Carpenter and Wendy Kolmar. Knoxville: University of Tennessee Press, 1991.
Carson, Clayborne, ed. *A Knock at Midnight: Inspiration from the Great Sermons of Martin Luther King, Jr.* New York: IPM, Warner, 1998.

Carson, Clayborne, David J. Garrow, Bill Kovach, and Carol Polsgrove, comps. *American Journalism 1941–1963*. Vol. 1 of *Reporting Civil Rights, 1941–1963*. New York: Library of America, 2003.

Carter, Stephen L. *The Culture of Disbelief: How American Law and Politics Trivializes Religious Devotion*. New York: Basic, 1993.

Cassuto, Leonard. *Hard-Boiled Sentimentality: The Secret History of American Crime Stories*. New York: Columbia University Press, 2009.

Cassuto, Leonard, Clare Virginia Eby, and Benjamin Reiss, eds. *The Cambridge History of the American Novel*. Cambridge: Cambridge University Press, 2011.

Castronovi, David. *Beyond the Gray Flannel Suit: Books from the 1950s That Made American Culture*. New York: Continuum, 2004.

Cawelti, John G. *Adventures, Mystery, and Romance: Formula Stories as Art and Popular Culture*. Chicago: University of Chicago Press, 1976.

Chafe, William H. *The Unfinished Journey: America since World War II*. 7th ed. New York and Oxford: Oxford University Press, 2011.

Chandler, Raymond. *Farewell, My Lovely*. New York: Knopf, 1940. Reprint, New York: Vintage, 1992.

———. *The Long Goodbye*. New York: Houghton Mifflin, 1953. Reprint, New York: Vintage, 1988.

Chapman, James. *Licence to Thrill: A Cultural History of James Bond*. London: Tauris, 2008.

Chatman, Seymour. "Story: Existents." In *Story and Discourse: Narrative Structure in Fiction and Film*, 96–145. Ithaca, NY: Cornell University Press, 1978.

Chessick, Richard D. "Critique: *The Caine Mutiny*." Review of *The Caine Mutiny*, by Herman Wouk. *American Journal of Psychotherapy* (October 1, 1975): 604–5.

Clark, William Bedford. *The American Vision of Robert Penn Warren*. Lexington: University Press of Kentucky, 1991.

Coleridge, Samuel Taylor. *Biographia Literaria*. Vol. 7 of *The Collected Works of Samuel Taylor Coleridge*, edited by James Engell and W. Jackson Bate. Princeton, NJ: Princeton University Press, 1985.

Coles, Robert. "Anna Freud and J. D. Salinger's Holden Caulfield." *Virginia Quarterly Review* 76, no. 2 (2000): 214–24.

Collini, Stefan. Introduction to *The Two Cultures*, by C. P. Snow. Cambridge: Cambridge University Press, 1993.

"Concert Planned by Left-Wing Activists, Area Conservatives Vow to Stop It." *Peekskill Evening Star*, August 27, 1949.

Cooper, David D. *Secular Days, Sacred Moments: The America Columns of Robert Coles*. East Lansing: Michigan State University Press, 2013.

Corstophine, Kevin. "A Search for the Father Image: Masculine Anxiety in Robert Bloch's Fiction." In *It Came from the 1950s: Popular Culture, Popular Anxieties*, edited by Darryl Jones, Elizabeth McCarthy, and Bernice M. Murphy, 158–75. New York: Palgrave Macmillan, 2011.

Courtney, Steve. "Peekskill's Days of Infamy: The Robeson Riots of 1949." *Reporter Dispatch*, September 5, 1982.

Cowley, Malcolm. "Nightmare and Ritual in Hemingway." In *Hemingway: A Collection of Critical Essays*, edited by Robert Weeks. Twentieth Century Views. Englewood Cliffs, NJ: Prentice Hall, 1962.

———. "Review of Ernest Hemingway, *Across the River and into the Trees*." *New York Herald Tribune*, September 10, 1950, 1, 16.

Cozzens, James Gould. *By Love Possessed*. New York: Harcourt Brace, 1957.

Crossen, Cynthia. "Studying Arts and Sciences in C. P. Snow's *The Masters*." *Wall Street Journal*, September 20, 2007.

Cumberland, Debra. "Flannery O'Connor and the Question of the Christian Novel." In Wise Blood*: A Re-Consideration*, edited by John J. Han, 1–23. Amsterdam and New York: Rodopi, 2018.

Curtis, Claire P. *Postapocalyptic Fiction and the Social Contract*. Lanham, MD: Lexington Books, 2010.

Cutler, Thomas J. "Lest We Forget: Wouk's Gift to the Navy." *U.S. Naval Institute Proceedings* 143, no. 7 (July 2017).

Damasio, Antonio. *Descartes' Error*. New York: Putnam, 1994.

Davies, Stephen. "Responding Emotionally to Fictions." *Journal of Aesthetics and Arts Criticisms* 67, no. 3 (June 1, 2009): 269–84.

Davis, Philip. *Bernard Malamud: A Writer's Life*. New York and Oxford: Oxford University Press, 2007.

Day, Dorothy. *The Duty of Delight: The Diaries of Dorothy Day*. Milwaukee, WI: Marquette University Press, 2008. Reprint, New York: Image, 2011.

De La Mothe, John. *C. P. Snow and the Struggle of Modernity*. Montreal and Kingston: McGill-Queen's University Press, 1992. Reprint, Austin: University of Texas Press, 2011.

Debistraty, Cody C. "The Psychological Comforts of Storytelling." *Atlantic*, November 2, 2014.

Denning, Michael. *Cover Stories: Narrative and Ideology in the British Spy Thriller*. London and New York: Routledge and Kegan Paul, 1987.

———. *Mechanic Accents: Dime Novels and Working-Class Culture in America*. London: Verso, 1987.

Desmond, Frank. "M'Carthy Charges Reds Hold U.S. Jobs." *Wheeling Intelligencer*, February 10, 1950.

Dickstein, Morris. "Between Generations: An Interview with Morris Dickstein." In *Critics at Work, Interviews 1993–2003*, edited by Jeffrey J. Williams, 154. New York: New York University Press, 2004.

———. *Leopards in the Temple: The Transformation of American Fiction, 1945–1970*. Cambridge, MA: Harvard University Press, 2002.

———. "Ralph Ellison, Race, and American Culture." *Raritan* 18, no. 4 (1999): 30–50.

"Dom Di Maggio, Almost Victim, Five Men Drown in Heavy Surf at Golden Gate." *Madeira Tribune*, February 19, 1951.

Donagan, Alan. "Moral Dilemmas, Genuine and Spurious: A Comparative Anatomy." *Ethics* 104, no. 1 (1993): 7–21.

Drury, Allen. *Advise and Consent*. Garden City, NY: Doubleday, 1959.

Du Maurier, Daphne. "The Birds." In *The Apple Tree*. London: Gollancz, 1952. Reprint, *"The Birds" and Other Stories*. New York: Penguin, 1963.

Eco, Umberto. "The Narrative Structures in Fleming." In *The Bond Affair*, edited by Oresto del Buono and Umberto Eco. London: Macdonald, 1966.

Eddino, Dwight. "Of Rocks and Marlin: The Existentialist Agon in Camus' *Sisyphus* and Hemingway's *Old Man and the Sea*." In *Bloom's Modern Critical Interpretations: Ernest Hemingway's* The Old Man and the Sea, edited by Harold Bloom. New York: Infobase, 2018.

Eder, Jens. "Understanding Characters." *Projections* 4, no. 1 (2010): 16–40.

Einstein, Albert. *Einstein on Politics*. Edited by David E. Rowe and Robert Shulman. Princeton, NJ: Princeton University Press, 2007.

———. *Ideas and Opinions*. Norwalk, CT: Easton, 2004.

Eisenhower, Dwight D. *The Papers of Dwight D. Eisenhower*. Vol. 4, *The War Years*, edited by Alfred D. Chandler and Stephen Ambrose. Baltimore: Johns Hopkins University Press, 1970.

———. *The Papers of Dwight D. Eisenhower*. Vol. 18, *The Presidency: Keeping the Peace*, edited by Louis Galambos and Daun Van Ee. Baltimore: Johns Hopkins University Press, 2001.

Eliot, Thomas H. "Robin Hood in Boston." *New Republic*, March 12, 1956, 28.

Eller, Jonathan R. *Ray Bradbury Unbound*. Urbana: University of Illinois Press, 2014.

Ellison, Ralph. *The Collected Essays of Ralph Ellison*. Edited by John F. Callahan. New York: Modern Library, 1995. Reprint, 2003.

———. *Invisible Man*. New York: Random House, 1952.

———. "*Invisible Man*: Prologue to a Novel." *Partisan Review* 19, no. 1 (January–February 1952): 31–40.

———. *Living with Music: The Jazz Writings of Ralph Ellison*. Edited by Robert O'Meally. New York: Modern Library, 2001.

———. "The Novel as a Function of Democracy." In *The Collected Essays of Ralph Ellison*, edited by John F. Callahan, 755–65. New York: Modern Library, 1995. Originally published June 1967.

———. *Shadow and Act*. New York: Random House, 1964.

———. "The World and the Jug Part II." In *The Collected Essays of Ralph Ellison*, edited by John F. Callahan. New York: Modern Library, 1995. Originally published in *New Leader*, February 3, 1964.

Ellwood, Robert. *The Fifties Spiritual Marketplace: American Religion in a Decade of Conflict*. New Brunswick, NJ: Rutgers University Press, 1997.

Engle, Paul. "Honest Tale of Distraught Adolescent." *Chicago Sunday Tribune Magazine of Books*, July 15, 1951, 3.

Fadiman, Clifton. Review of *The Catcher in the Rye*, by J. D. Salinger. *Book-of-the-Month Club News*, July 1951.

Fahy, Thomas. *Understanding Truman Capote*. Columbia: University of South Carolina Press, 2014.

Farrell, John A. *Richard Nixon: The Life*. New York: Vintage, 2017.

Fast, Howard. *Peekskill USA: A Personal Experience*. New York: Civil Rights Congress, 1951.

———. *Spartacus*. London: North Castle; Routledge, 1996. Originally published by Howard Fast in 1951.

Faulkner, William. *A Fable*. In *Faulkner:Novels 1942–1954*, edited by Noel Polk and Joseph Blotner. New York: Library of America, 1994.

———. *The Hamlet*. New York: Modern Library, 1940.

———. *The Hamlet*. In *Faulkner: Novels 1957–1962*, edited by Noel Polk. New York: Library of America, 1999.

———. *The Mansion*. In *Faulkner: Novels 1957–1962*, edited by Noel Polk. New York: Library of America, 1999.

———. Nobel Prize speech, December 10, 1950. American Rhetoric, https://www.americanrhetoric.com/speeches/williamfaulknernobelprizeaddress.htm.

———. *Selected Lettersof William Faulkner*. Edited by Joseph Blotner. New York: Random House, 1977.

———. *The Town*. In *Faulkner: Novels 1957–1962*, edited by Noel Polk. New York: Library of America, 1999.

Feldman, Leslie Dale. *Spaceships and Politics: The Political Theory of Rod Serling*. Lanham, MD: Lexington Books, 2010.

Ferguson, Robert A. *Alone in America: The Stories That Matter*. Cambridge, MA: Harvard University Press, 2013.

Fiedler, Leslie. *Love and Death in the American Novel*. New York: Stein and Day, 1956. Reprint, 1960.

———. Review of *The Assistant*, by Bernard Malamud. *Reconstructionist* 24 (February 21, 1958).

Fleming, Ian. *Casino Royale*. London: Jonathan Cape, 1953; New York: Macmillan, 1953.

———. *Dr. No*. London: Jonathan Cape, 1958; New York: Macmillan, 1958.

Flynn, Meghan. "How *The Caine Mutiny* and the Paranoid Capt. Queeg Influenced the 25th Amendment Drafters, Making It Harder to Sideline a President." *Washington Post*, September 10, 2018.

Foucault, Michel. *Madness and Civilization: A History of Insanity in the Age of Reason*. Translated by Richard Howard. New York: Vintage, 1988. Originally published as *Folie et déraison: Histoire de la folie a l'âge classique* (Paris: Plon, 1961).

Frank, Pat. *Alas, Babylon*. Philadelphia: Lippincott, 1959.

Franklin, Ruth. *Shirley Jackson: A Rather Haunted Life*. Philadelphia: Liveright, 2016.

French, Warren. *J. D. Salinger*. Boston: Twayne, 1963.

Freud, Sigmund. *Beyond the Pleasure Principle*. New York: Norton, 1920.

———. *The Interpretation of Dreams*. Translated by A. A. Brill. London: Macmillan, 1913. Reprint, New York: Basic, 2010. Originally published as *Die Traumdeutung* (Leipzig and Vienna: Franz Deuticke, 1900).

———. "Das Unheimlich" [The Uncanny]. *Imago* 5 (1919).

Friedman, Lenemaja. *Shirley Jackson*. Cincinnati: Bobbs-Merrill, 1973.

Fuhrman, C., and Steven T. Levy. *Influential Papers from the 1950s*. London: Routledge, 2018.

Fuller, Edmund. "Terror Lived There Too: Review of *The Haunting of Hill House*." *New York Times Book Review*, October 18, 1959.

Funnell, Lisa. *For His Eyes Only: The Women of James Bond*. London: Wallflower / Columbia University Press, 2015.

Gaddis, John Lewis. *The Cold War*. New York: Penguin, 2005.

Galbraith, John Kenneth. *The New Industrial State*. Boston and New York: Houghton Mifflin, 1967.

Gates, Henry Louis. *The Signifying Monkey: A Theory of African American Literary Criticism*. New York: Oxford University Press, 1989. Reprint, 2014.

Gerrig, Richard J. *Experiencing Narrative Worlds: On the Psychological Activities of Reading*. New Haven, CT: Yale University Press, 1993.

Gerson, Steven M. "The New American Adam in the Adventures of Augie March." *Modern Fiction* 25, no. 1 (1979): 117–28.

Giannone, Richard. *Flannery O'Connor, Hermit Novelist*. Chicago: University of Illinois Press, 2000. Reprint, Columbia: University of South Carolina Press, 2010.

Gilbert, Martin. *The Holocaust*. London: Folio, 2012.

Gilbert, Sandra, and Susan Gubar. *The Madwoman in the Attic*. New Haven, CT: Yale University Press, 1979. Reprint, 1997.

Gilman, Charlotte Perkins. *The Yellow Wallpaper*. New York: Feminist Press, 1996.

Giraldi, William. *American Audacity*. New York: Liveright, 2018.

Glaude, Eddie S. *In a Shade of Blue: Pragmatism and the Politics of Black America*. Chicago: University of Chicago Press, 2007.

Godden, Richard. *Fictions of Labor: William Faulkner and the South's Long Revolution*. Cambridge: Cambridge University Press, 2007.

Golding, William. *Lord of the Flies*. London: Faber and Faber, 1954.

Goldstein, Richard. "Go the Way Your Blood Beats: An Interview with James Baldwin." In *James Baldwin: The Legacy*, edited by Quincy Troupe, 173–85. New York: Simon & Schuster, 1989.

Goodman, Anne L. "Mad about Children." *New Republic* 125, no. 3 (July 16, 1951): 20–26.

Gordon, Andrew. *An American Dreamer: A Psychoanalytic Study of the Fiction of Norman Mailer*. Madison: Fairleigh Dickinson University Press, 1980.

———. "Red Scare: The Early Cold War Novels by Mailer, Doctorow and Roth." *Mailer Review* 8, no. 1 (Fall 2014).

Gordon, Avery F. *Shirley Jackson's American Gothic: Haunting and the Sociological Imagination*. Minneapolis: University of Minnesota Press, 2008.

Graham, Mayemma, and Amiritjit Singh. *Conversations with Ralph Ellison*. Jackson: University Press of Mississippi, 1995.

Graham, Sarah. *Salinger's* The Catcher in the Rye. New York: Bloomsbury, 2007.

Green, Martin. "The Morality of *Lolita*." *Kenyon Review* 28, no. 3 (1966): 365, 369–70.

Green, M. C. "Transportation into Narrative: The Role of Prior Knowledge and Perceived Realism." *Discourse Processes* 38 (2004): 247–66.

Green, Peter. "The Stranger from Within." *New Republic*, September 2, 2010, 33–34.

Greenberg, Martin Harry, Richard Matheson, and Charles G. Waugh. *The Twilight Zone: The Original Stories*. New York: MJF, 1997.

Greene, Graham. *The End of the Affair*. London: Heinemann, 1951. Reprint, New York: Penguin, 1991.

———. *The Quiet American*. London: Heinemann, 1955. Reprint, New York: Penguin, 2002.

Greenspan, Patricia S. *Practical Guilt: Moral Dilemmas, Emotions and Social Norms*. Oxford and New York: Oxford University Press, 1995.

Gurko, Leo. "The Heroic Impulse in *The Old Man and the Sea*." *English Journal* 44, no. 7 (October 1955): 377–82.

Halberstam, David. *The Coldest Winter*. New York: Hachette, Hyperion, 2007.

———. *The Fifties*. New York: Ballantine, 1994.

Hall, Joan Wylie. *Shirley Jackson: A Study of the Short Fiction*. Boston: Twayne, 1993.

Halliwell, Martin. *American Culture in the 1950s*. Edinburgh: Edinburgh University Press, 2007.

Hattenhauser, Darryl. *Shirley Jackson's American Gothic*. Albany: State University of New York Press, 2003.

Hawkes, John. "Flannery O'Connor's Devil." *Sewanee Review* 70 (1962): 395–407.

Hayden, Hiram, et al. "What's Wrong with the American Novel?" *American Scholar* 24, no. 4 (Autumn 1955): 464–503.

Heilbroner, Robert. *The Future as History*. New York: Grove, 1959. Reprint, 1961.

Heiserman, Arthur, and James E. Miller Jr. "J. D. Salinger: Some Crazy Cliff." *Western Humanities Review* 10 (1956).

Hemingway, Ernest. *Across the River and into the Trees*. New York: Scribner, 1950.

———. *The Old Man and the Sea*. New York: Charles Scribner's Sons, 1952.

Herlihy, Jeffrey. "Expatriation from Spain and Ethnic Otherness in *The Old Man and the Sea*." *Hemingway Review* 28, no. 2 (Spring 2009).

Hersey, John. *The Wall*. New York: Knopf, 1950.

Hicks, Granville. "J. D. Salinger: Search for Wisdom." *Saturday Review*, July 25, 1959.

Highsmith, Patricia. *The Talented Mr. Ripley*. London and New York: Coward McCann, 1955.

Himes, Chester. *Cast the First Stone*. New York: Coward McCann, 1952.

———. *Real Cool Killers*. New York: Avon, 1959.

Hitchens, Christopher. "The Great American Augie." *Wilson Quarterly* 25, no. 1 (Winter 2001): 22–29.

Hochman, Baruch. *Character in Literature*. Ithaca, NY: Cornell University Press, 1985.

Hoffman, Frederick. "The Search for Redemption: Flannery O'Connor's Fiction." In *The Added Dimension: The Art and Mind of Flannery O'Connor*, edited by Melvin J. Friedman and Lewis A. Lawson, 32–48. New York: Fordham University Press, 1978.

Hoffmann, E. T. A. "Beethoven's Instrumental Music." In *E. T. A. Hoffmann Samliche Werke*, edited by C. G. von Massen. Munich: Muller, 1908. Originally published in 1813.

Hofstadter, Richard. *The Age of Reform*. New York: Vintage, 1957.

Holland, Norman N. *Literature and the Brain*. Gainesville, FL: PsyArt Foundation, 2009.

Holmes, John Clellon. "This Is the Beat Generation." *New York Times Magazine*, November 16, 1952.

Horwitz, Allan V. "How an Age of Anxiety Became an Age of Depression." *Milbank Quarterly* 88, no. 1 (March 2010): 112–38.

Huber, R. John, and Gail Ledbetter. "Holden Caulfield, Self-Appointed Catcher in the Rye: Some Additional Thoughts." *Journal of Individual Psychology* 33, no. 2 (November 1977): 250.

Hunt, Timothy. *Kerouac's Cracked Road*. Carbondale: Southern Illinois University Press, 1981.

Huttenhauer, Darryl. *Shirley Jackson's American Gothic*. Albany: State University of New York Press, 2003.

Huxley, Aldous. *Literature and Science*. New York: Harper & Row, 1963.

Huyssen, Andreas. *After the Great Divide: Modernism, Mass Culture, Postmodernism*. Bloomington: Indiana University Press, 1987.

Irwin, John T. *Unless the Threat Is behind Them: Hard-Boiled Fiction and Film Noir*. Baltimore: Johns Hopkins University Press, 2006.

Iser, Wolfgang. *The Implied Reader: Patterns of Communication in Prose Fiction from Bunyan to Beckett*. Baltimore: Johns Hopkins University Press, 1974.

Jackson, Lawrence P. *Chester B. Himes: A Biography*. New York: Norton, 2017.

Jackson, Shirley. *The Haunting of Hill House*. New York: Viking, 1959.
———. *Life among the Savages*. New York: Farrar, Straus & Giroux, 1953.
———. *Raising Demons*. New York: Farrar, Straus & Giroux, 1957.
Johnson, Haynes. *The Age of Anxiety: McCarthyism to Terrorism*. New York: Harcourt, 2005.
Jones, Allen C. "Man or Fish? An Ecocritical Reading of *The Old Man and the Sea*." In *Hemingway and the Natural World*, edited by Robert Fleming, 102–13. Moscow: University of Idaho Press, 1999.
Jones, James. *From Here to Eternity*. New York: Scribner, 1951.
Joshi, S. T. "Shirley Jackson: Domestic Horror." In *Shirley Jackson: Essays on the Literary Legacy*, edited by Bernice M. Murphy, 183–98. Jefferson, NC: McFarland, 2005.
Kakutani, Michiko. "Malamud Still Seeks Balance and Solitude." *New York Times*, July 15, 1980.
Kammen, Michael. *American Culture, American Tastes: Social Change in the Twentieth Century*. New York: Knopf, 2003.
Kaplan, Carla. *The Erotics of Talk: Women's Writing and Feminist Paradigms*. New York: Oxford University Press, 1996.
Kaplan, Roger. "Allen Drury and the Washington Novel." *Policy Review* 97 (October/November 1999).
Karl, Frederick. *C. P. Snow: The Politics of Conscience*. Carbondale: Southern Illinois University Press, 1965.
Kazin, Alfred. *Alfred Kazin's Journals*. Edited by Richard M. Cook. New Haven, CT: Yale University Press, 2011.
———. "Everybody's Favorite." *Atlantic* 208, no. 2 (August 1961).
———. "Melville the New Yorker." *New York Review of Books*, April 5, 1973.
———. "The Trouble He's Seen." Review *Armies of the Night*, by Norman Mailer. *New York Times*, May 5, 1968.
———. *A Walker in the City*. New York: Harcourt Brace, 1951.
Keegan, John. Introduction to *The Face of Battle: A Study of Agincourt, Waterloo and the Somme*. New York: Viking, 1976.
Keene, Carolyn. *The Penguin Nancy Drew Complete Set*. New York: Grosset and Dunlap, Penguin, 2006.
"Kefauver Hearings: A Window into the Evolution of Money Laundering and Financial Sleuthing." *ACAMS Today*, September 3, 2013.
Kellogg, Gene. *The Vital Tradition: The Catholic Novel in a Period of Convergence*. Chicago: Loyola University Press, 1970.
Kerouac, Jack. *On the Road*. In *Kerouac: Road Novels 1957–1960*, edited by Douglas G. Brinkley. New York: Library of America, 2007.
Kierkegaard, Søren. *The Concept of Dread*. Edited by Walter Lowrie. Princeton, NJ: Princeton University Press, 1968.
King, Martin Luther, Jr. "A Knock at Midnight." In *Voices from the Dexter Pulpit*, edited by Michael Thurman. Montgomery, AL: New South, 2001.
Kinsey, Alfred, Wardell Pomeroy, Clyde Martin, and Paul Gebhard. *Sexual Behavior in the Human Female*. Philadelphia: Saunders, 1953.
Knowles, John. *A Separate Peace*. New York: Macmillan, 1959. Reprint, New York: Bantam, 1960.
Kramer, Lawrence. *Music and Poetry: The Nineteenth Century and After*. Berkeley: University of California Press, 1984.
Kriegel, Leonard. "Wrestling with Augie March." *Nation*, June 23, 2003.
Kubica, Chris, and Will Hochman, eds. *Letters to J. D. Salinger*. Madison: University of Wisconsin Press, 2002.
Kuhn, Thomas. *The Structure of Scientific Revolutions*. Chicago: University of Chicago Press, 1962.
Lacy, Tim. *The Dream of a Democratic Culture: Mortimer J. Adler and the Great Books Idea*. New York and Basingstoke: Palgrave Macmillan, 2013.
Langer, Susanne. *Philosophy in a New Key*. New York: Mentor, 1951.

Larson, Randall D. *The Robert Bloch Companion: Collected Interviews 1969–1986*. San Bernardino, CA: Borgo, 1990.

Lasch, Christopher. *The Culture of Narcissism: American Life in an Age of Diminishing Expectations*. New York: Norton, 1979.

"Last of the Leftists?" Review of *Barbary Shore*, by Norman Mailer. *Time*, May 28, 1951.

Lea, Richard. "Fictional Characters Make Experiential Crossings into Real Life Study Finds." *Guardian*, February 14, 2017.

Lears, T. J. Jackson. *Fables of Abundance: A Cultural History of Advertising in America*. New York: Basic, 1995.

Leavis, F. R. *Education and the University*. Cambridge: Cambridge University Press, 1943. Reprint, 1979.

———. "Two Cultures? The Significance of C. P. Snow." *Spectator*, March 9, 1962, 297–303.

Lennon, J. Michael. *Norman Mailer: A Double Life*. New York: Simon & Schuster, 2013.

———. *Norman Mailer: The Sixties*. 2 vols. New York: Library of America, 2018.

Levine, Lawrence. *Highbrow/Lowbrow: The Emergence of Cultural Hierarchy in America*. Cambridge, MA: Harvard University Press, 1988. Reprint, 1990.

Lewis, R. W. B. "Eccentric's Pilgrimage." *Hudson Review* 6, no. 1 (Spring 1953): 144–50.

Lim, Elvin T. *The Anti-intellectual Presidency: The Decline of Presidential Rhetoric from George Washington to George W. Bush*. New York and Oxford: Oxford University Press, 2008.

Locke, Richard. *Critical Children: The Use of Childhood in Ten Great Novels*. New York: Columbia University Press, 2011.

Long, Elizabeth. *Book Clubs: Women and the Uses of Reading in Everyday Life*. Chicago: University of Chicago Press, 2003.

Longstreth, T. Morris. "New Novels in the News." *Christian Science Monitor*, July 19, 1951.

"Loves Soviet Best, Robeson Declares." *New York Times*, June 20, 1949.

Lowell, Robert. "Memories of West Street and Lepke." In *Selected Poems*. New York: Farrar, Straus & Giroux, 1976.

Lynn, Kenneth. *Hemingway*. New York: Simon & Schuster, 1987.

Macdonald, Dwight. "By Cozzens Possessed." *Commentary* 25 (January 1958): 36–47.

———. "Masscult and Midcult." In *Mass Cult and Midcult: Essays against the American Grain*, edited by John Summers, 3–71. New York: New York Review of Books, 2011.

Macdonald, Ross. *Four Novels of the 1950s*. New York: Library of America, 2015.

———. *Moving Target*. New York: Random House, 1949.

Machiowitz, David S. "Lawyer on the Aisle: Captain Queeg Is Back on Broadway." *American Bar Association Journal* 69, no. 6 (June 1, 1983): 833.

MacLeish, Archibald. "Loyalty and Freedom." *American Scholar* 22, no. 4 (Autumn 1953): 393–98.

Mailer, Norman. *Advertisements for Myself*. New York: Putnam, 1959.

———. *Barbary Shore*. New York: Rinehart, 1951.

———. *The Deer Park*. New York: Putnam, 1955.

———. *Norman Mailer: The Sixties*. Edited by J. Michael Lennon. 2 vols. New York: Library of America, 2018.

———. *Selected Letters*. Edited by J. Michael Lennon. New York: Random House, 2014.

———. "The White Negro: Superficial Reflections on the Hipster." In *Advertisements for Myself*. New York: Putnam, 1959.

Malamud, Bernard. *The Assistant*. New York: Farrar, Straus & Giroux, 1957.

———. *The Natural*. New York: Harcourt Brace, 1952.

Malin, Irving. *The New American Gothic*. Carbondale: Southern Illinois University Press, 1962. Reprint, 1968.

Mallon, Thomas. "*Advise and Consent* at 50." *New York Times Book Review*, June 25, 2009.

Manchester, William. *The Glory and the Dream: 1932–1962*. London: Joseph, 1975.

Mar, Raymond A., Keith Oatley, and Jordan B. Peterson. "Exploring the Link between Reading Fiction and Empathy: Ruling Out Individual Differences and Examining Outcomes." *Communications* 34 (2009): 407–38.

Marback, Richard. Review of *Experiencing Narrative Worlds: On the Psychological Activities of Reading*, by Richard J. Gerrig. *Criticism* 37, no. 1 (Winter 1995): 172–74.
March, William. *The Bad Seed*. New York: Rinehart, 1954. Reprint, New York: Knopf/Doubleday, 2015.
Margolin, Uri. "Character." In *Routledge Encyclopedia of Narrative Theory*, edited by David Herman, Manfred Jahn, Marie-Laure Ryan. New York and London: Routledge, 2005.
Mariani, Giorgio. *Waging War on War: Peacefighting in American Literature*. Urbana: University of Illinois Press, 2015.
Marsden, George M. *The Twilight of the American Enlightenment: The 1950s and the Crisis of Liberal Belief*. New York: Basic, 2014.
Matheson, Richard. *Collected Stories*. Vol. 1. Edited by Stanley Wiater. Colorado Springs, CO: Gauntlet, 2003.
———. *I Am Legend*. New York: Gold Medal, 1954. Reprint, New York: Tor, 2003.
———. Introduction to *The Twilight Zone: The Original Stories*. Edited by Martin Harry Greenberg, Richard Matheson, and Charles G. Waugh. New York: Avon, 1985.
Matthews, John. "Many Mansions: Faulkner's Cold War Conflicts." In *Global Faulkner*, edited by Annette Tefzer and Ann J. Abalie, 3–23. Jackson: University Press of Mississippi, 2009.
Matthijs, P., and Martijn Veltkamp. "How Does Fiction Influence Empathy? An Experiential Investigation on the Role of Emotional Transportation." *PLoS ONE* 8, no. 1 (2013).
May, Rollo. *The Meaning of Anxiety*. New York: Ronald Press, 1950. Reprint, New York: Norton, 2018.
McCarthy, Joseph R. Joseph R. McCarthy Papers. Raynor Library, Marquette University, Milwaukee, Wisconsin. https://www.marquette.edu/library/archives/Mss/JRM/index.php.
McCarthy, Mary. *The Groves of Academe*. New York: Harcourt Brace, 1952.
McCarthy, Paul. *John Steinbeck*. New York: Frederick Ungar, 1980.
McCort, Dennis. "Hyakujo's Geese, Amban's Doughnuts and Rilke's Carrousel: Sources East and West for Salinger's *Catcher*." In *Bloom's Modern Critical Interpretations: J. D. Salinger's* The Catcher in the Rye, edited by Harold Bloom, 45–62. New York: Infobase, 2014.
McCullen, Maurice. "*Lord of the Flies*: The Critical Quest." In *William Golding: Some Critical Considerations*, edited by Jack I. Biles and Robert O. Evans. Lexington: University Press of Kentucky, 1978.
McCullers, Carson. *The Ballad of the Sad Café*. New York: Houghton Mifflin, 1951.
McGrory, Mary. "Story of Adolescent Steers from Mawkish into Something New." *Evening Star*, July 15, 1951, C-3.
McKinley, Maggie. *Understanding Norman Mailer*. Columbia: University of South Carolina Press, 2016.
McLuhan, Marshall. *Understanding Media: The Extensions of Man*. New York: McGraw-Hill, 1964.
McNeill, William. *Keeping Together in Time*. Cambridge, MA: Harvard University Press, 1995.
Medovoi, Leeran. "Democracy, Capitalism, and American Literature: The Cold War Construction of J. D. Salinger's Paperback Hero." In *The Other Fifties: Interrogating Midcentury American Icons*, edited by Joel Foreman. Urbana: University of Illinois Press, 1996.
Menand, Louis. "Holden at Fifty." *New Yorker*, September 21, 2001.
———. "True Story: The Art of Short Fiction." *New Yorker*, December 1, 2003.
Metalious, Grace. *Peyton Place*. New York: Julian Messner, 1956.
Meyer, Leonard. *Emotion and Meaning in Music*. Chicago: University of Chicago Press, 1956.
Meyers, Jeffrey. *Hemingway: A Biography*. New York: Harper & Row, 1985.
———, ed. *Hemingway: The Critical Heritage*. New York and London: Routledge, 1982.
Miall, David S. "Anticipation and Feeling in Literary Response: A Neuropsychological Perspective." *Poetics* 23 (1995): 275–98.
———. "Beyond the Schema Given: Affective Comprehension of Literary Narratives." *Cognition and Emotion* 3, no. 1 (1989): 55–78; *Poetics* 23 (August 1995): 275–98.

Michener, James. "The Conscience of the Contemporary Novel." In *The Arts in Renewal*, edited by Lewis Mumford, 107–40. Philadelphia: University of Pennsylvania Press, 1951.

———. *The Voice of Asia*. New York: Random House, 1951.

Miller, Douglas, and Marion Nowak. *The Fifties: The Way We Really Were*. Garden City, NY: Doubleday, 1977.

Miller, J. Hillis. "Character in the Novel: A 'Real Illusion.'" In *From Smollett to James: Studies in the Novel and Other Essays Presented to Edgar Johnson*, edited by Samuel I. Mintz, Alice Chandler, and Christopher Mulvey. Charlottesville: University of Virginia Press, 2008.

Miller, John J. "The Great Washington Novel." *National Review*, February 9, 2015.

Mills, C. Wright. *The Power Elite*. Oxford: Oxford University Press, 1956.

Monnet, Agnieszka Soltysik. "They Are Legend: The Popular American Gothic of Ambrose Bierce and Richard Matheson." In *A Companion to American Gothic*, edited by Charles L. Grow. New York: Wiley-Blackwell, 2014.

Mudrick, Marvin. "Character and Event in Fiction." *Yale Review* 50 (1961): 202–18.

Murphy, Bernice M. *Shirley Jackson: Essays on the Literary Legacy*. Jefferson, NC: McFarland, 2005.

Mykannen, Rachel. "Militarized Desires: Consumerism in American Culture, 1939–1955." PhD diss., University of California–Irvine, 2014.

Nabokov, Vladimir. *Lolita*. Paris: Olympia, 1955. Reprint, New York: Vintage, 1989.

Nadel, Alan. *Invisible Criticism*. Iowa City: University of Iowa Press, 1988.

Nell, Victor. *Lost in a Book: The Psychology of Reading for Pleasure*. New Haven, CT, and London: Yale University Press, 1988.

Newman, Judie. "Shirley Jackson and the Reproduction of Mothering: *The Haunting of Hill House*." In *Shirley Jackson: Essays on the Literary Legacy*, edited by Bernice M. Murphy, 169–82. Jefferson, NC: McFarland, 2005.

Niebuhr, Reinhold. *The Irony of American History*. In *Reinhold Niebuhr: Major Works on Religion and Politics*, edited by Elisabeth Sifton. New York: Library of America, 2015. Originally published in 1952.

"Novelist Cozzens." *Time*, September 2, 1957.

Oatley, Keith. *Such Stuff as Dreams: The Psychology of Fiction*. New York: Wiley, 2011.

———. "Why Fiction May Be Twice as True as Fact: Fiction as Cognitive and Emotional Simulation." *Review of General Psychology* 2 (June 1999): 101–17.

O'Connor, Edwin. *The Last Hurrah*. Boston: Little, Brown, 1956.

O'Connor, Flannery. *Wise Blood*. In *O'Connor: Collected Works*. New York: Library of America, 1988.

"Old Time Minstrel: He Has Gone Out of Vogue but the Public Recollects Him with Pleasure." *New York Times*, May 9, 1897.

Oppenheimer, Judy. *Private Demons: The Life of Shirley Jackson*. New York: Ballantine, 1988.

Osteen, Mark. *Nightmare Alley: Film Noir and the American Dream*. Baltimore: Johns Hopkins University Press, 2013.

Paris, Bernard J. *Imagined Human Beings*. New Brunswick, NJ: Transaction, 2010.

Pelowski, Matthew, and Fuminori Akibo. "A Model of Art Perception, Evaluation and Emotion in Transformative Aesthetic Experience." *New Ideas Psychology* 29 (2011): 80–97.

Peterson, Virgilia. "Three Days in the Bewildering World of an Adolescent." *New York Herald Tribune*, July 15, 1951, 3.

Phelan, James. *Living to Tell about It: A Rhetoric and Ethics of Character and Event in Fiction*. Ithaca, NY: Cornell University Press, 2005.

Pifer, Ellen. Introduction to *Vladimir Nabokov's* Lolita*: A Casebook*. Edited by Ellen Pifer. Oxford: Oxford University Press, 2003.

Plumb, J. H., ed. *The Crisis of the Humanities*. London: Penguin, 1964.

Polk, Noel. *Children of the Dark Home: Text and Context in Faulkner*. Jackson: University Press of Mississippi, 1996.

———. *Faulkner and Welty and the Southern Literary Tradition*. Jackson: University Press of Mississippi, 2010. Originally published in 1983.

Porter, Horace A. "Jazz Beginnings: Charlie Christian and Ralph Ellison in Oklahoma City." *Antioch Review* 57, no. 3 (Summer 1999): 277–95.

———. *Jazz Country: Ralph Ellison in America*. Iowa City: University of Iowa Press, 2001.

Poster, William. "Tomorrow's Child: *The Catcher in the Rye*." *Commentary* 13 (1952): 90–92.

Priest, Benjamin. "*The Catcher in the Rye* and the Ill Member of the Group: Holden Caulfield and Adolescent Development." *Psychodynamic Practice* 22, no. 3 (2016): 209–22.

Rabinowitz, Paula. *American Pulp: How Paperbacks Brought Modernism to Main Street*. Princeton, NJ: Princeton University Press, 2014.

Rachels, David. "Holden Caulfield: A Hero for All Ages." *Chronicle of Higher Education* 47, no. 29 (March 30, 2001).

Radway, Janice. *A Feeling for Books: The Book-of-the-Month Club, Literary Taste, and Middle-Class Desire*. Chapel Hill: University of North Carolina Press, 1997. Reprint, 1999.

Raine, Adrian. *The Anatomy of Violence: The Biological Roots of Crime*. New York: Vintage, 2013.

Rand, Ayn. *Atlas Shrugged*. New York: Random House, 1957.

———. *The Virtue of Selfishness: A New Concept of Egoism*. New York: Signet, New American Library, 1964.

Ransom, John Crowe, et al. *I'll Take My Stand*. Introduction by Louis D. Rubin Jr. Baton Rouge: Louisiana State University Press, 1978.

Reisman, David. *The Lonely Crowd: A Study of the Changing American Character*. New Haven, CT: Yale University Press, 1950.

———. "Some Observations on Intellectual Freedom." *American Scholar* 23, no. 1 (Winter 1953–1954): 9–25.

Reuss, Henry S. *When Government Was Good: Memories of a Life in Politics*. Madison: University of Wisconsin Press, 1999.

Reynolds, Michael S. *Hemingway: The Final Years*. New York: Norton, 2000.

Rhodes, Richard. *The Making of the Hydrogen Bomb*. New York: Simon & Schuster, 1995.

Rieff, Philip. *Freud: The Mind of the Moralist*. New York: Viking, 1959. Reprint, 1961.

"Robeson Says U.S. Negroes Won't Fight against Russia." *Peekskill Evening Star*, April 21, 1949.

Rolo, Charles J. "Simenon and Spillane: Metaphysics of Murder for the Millions." In *Mass Culture: The Popular Arts in America*, edited by Bernard Rosenberg and David M. White. Glencoe, IL: Free Press, 1957.

Rorty, James. "The Lessons of the Peekskill Riots." *Commentary*, October 1950, 309–23.

Rorty, Richard. *Contingency, Irony, Solidarity*. Cambridge: Cambridge University Press, 1989.

Rose, Jonathan. *Readers' Liberation: The Literary Agenda*. New York and Oxford: Oxford University Press, 2018.

Roth, Philip. *Goodbye, Columbus*. In *Philip Roth: Novels and Stories 1959–1962*, edited by Ross Miller. New York: Library of America, 2005.

Rubin, Joan Shelley. *Cultural Considerations: Essays on Readers, Writers and Musicians in Postwar America*. Amherst: University of Massachusetts Press, 2013.

———. *The Making of Middlebrow Culture*. Chapel Hill and London: University of North Carolina Press, 1992.

Salinger, J. D. *The Catcher in the Rye*. New York: Little, Brown, 1951.

Salzburg, Joel, ed. *Critical Essays on Salinger's* The Catcher in the Rye. Boston: GK Hall, 1990.

Sayers, Dorothy. Introduction to *The Omnibus of Crime: Great Short Stories of Detection*. London: Payson and Clarke, 1929.

Schell, Jonathan. *The Fate of the Earth*. New York: Knopf, 1982.

Schlesinger, Arthur. *The Imperial Presidency*. New York: Houghton Mifflin Harcourt, 1973.

———. *The Vital Center: The Politics of Freedom*. New York: Houghton Mifflin, 1949.

Schow, David J., ed. *The Lost Bloch*. Burton, MI: Subterranean, 2002.

Schryer, Stephen. *Fantasies of the New Class: Ideologies of Professionalism in Post–World War II American Fiction*. New York: Columbia University Press, 2011.
Schwartz, Delmore. "Adventures in America." *Partisan Review* 21, no. 1 (January–February 1954).
Serling, Rod. *The Twilight Zone*. Los Angeles, CA: CBS Productions, 1959–1963.
Sherry, Norman. *The Life of Graham Greene*. Vol. 1. New York: Penguin, 1989.
Shute, Nevil. *On the Beach*. London: Heinemann, 1957.
Simon, Scott. "At 50: A D.C. Novel with Legs." *Wall Street Journal*, September 2, 2009.
Sklar, Howard. *Art of Sympathy in Fiction*. Amsterdam: John Benjamins, 2013.
Smith, Erin A. *Hard-Boiled: Working-Class Readers and Pulp Magazines*. Philadelphia: Temple University Press, 2000.
Smith, Margaret Chase. "Declaration of Conscience." *Congressional Record*, June 1, 1950.
Snow, C. P. *The Masters*. London, Macmillan, 1950.
———. *The New Men*. London: Macmillan, 1954. Reprint, 1960.
———. *The Two Cultures*. With an introduction by Stefan Collini. Cambridge: Cambridge University Press, 1998.
Sorin, Gerald. *Howard Fast: Life and Literature in the Left Lane*. Bloomington: Indiana University Press, 2012.
Speir, Jerry. *Raymond Chandler*. New York: Frederick Ungar, 1981.
Spillane, Mickey. *Kiss Me Deadly*. New York: Signet, 1953.
———. *Kiss Me Deadly*. In *The Mike Hammer Collection*. Vol. 2. New York: New American Library, 2001.
———. *One Lonely Night*. New York: Signet, 1951.
———. *One Lonely Night*. In *The Mike Hammer Collection*. Vol. 2. New York: New American Library, 2001.
Steiner, George. "The Salinger Industry." *Nation*, November 14, 1959, 360–63.
Stern, James. "Aw, the World's a Crumby Place." *New York Herald Book Review*, July 15, 1951, 5.
Sundquist, Eric. *Cultural Contexts for Ralph Ellison's* Invisible Man. New York: Bedford/St. Martin's, 1995.
Tague, Gregory F. *Evolution and Human Culture*. Amsterdam and New York: Rodopi, 2016.
———. *Making Mind: Moral Sense and Consciousness in Philosophy, Science, and Literature*. Amsterdam and New York: Rodopi, 2014.
Taylor, Bryce A. "Holden Caulfield: Sort of a Christian." *Religion and the Arts* 18, no. 5 (2014).
Theroux, Paul. "Graham Greene as I Knew Him." *New York Times Book Review*, April 21, 1991.
Thompson, Mark. "10 Questions: An Interview with Herman Wouk." *Time*, February 1, 2016.
"Three Literary Prizes." *New York Times*, January 22, 1950, 12.
Tocqueville, Alexis de. *Democracy in America*. London: Folio, 2014.
Tompkins, Jane. *Sensational Designs: The Cultural Work of American Fiction, 1790–1860*. Oxford and New York: Oxford University Press, 1986.
Tonquette, Peter. "Mailer's Sixties Slump." *National Review*, April 12, 2018.
Trilling, Lionel. "The Last Lover: Vladimir Nabokov's *Lolita*." *Encounter* 11, no. 4 (1958): 9–19.
———. "Science, Literature and Culture: A Comment on the Leavis-Snow Controversy." *Commentary*, June 1962, 461–77.
Urgo, Joseph. *Faulkner's Apocrypha: A Fable, Snopes, and the Spirit of Human Rebellion*. Jackson: University Press of Mississippi, 1989.
Valsiner, Jaan. "Between Fiction and Reality: Transforming the Semiotic Object." *Sign Systems* 37 (2009): 99–112.
Vegso, Roland K. *The Naked Communist: Cold War Modernism and the Politics of Popular Culture*. Bronx, NY: Fordham University Press, 2013.
Vermeule, Blakey. *Why Do We Care about Literary Characters?* Baltimore: Johns Hopkins University Press, 2010.

"Violence Ends Robeson Meet, Dewey Asks County Probe." *Peekskill Evening Star*, September 6, 1949.

Vonnegut, Kurt. *Player Piano*. London: Flamingo; New York: Simon & Schuster, 1952.

Walcutt, Charles Child. *Man's Changing Mask: Modes and Methods in Characterization in Fiction*. Minneapolis: University of Minnesota Press, 1966.

Waller, Willard. *The Veteran Comes Back*. New York: Dryden, 1944.

Wallin, Nils. *Biomusicology*. Hillsdale, NY: Pendragon, 1992.

Walwik, Joseph. *The Peekskill, New York Anti-communist Riots*. Lewiston, NY: Edwin Mellen, 2002.

Warren, Robert Penn. *Band of Angels*. New York: Random House, 1955.

———. "The Man with No Commitments." Review of *The Adventures of Augie March*, by Saul Bellow. *New Republic* 129, no. 14 (November 1953): 22–23.

———. "Segregation: The Inner Conflict of the South." In *American Journalism, 1941–1963*. Vol. 1 of *Reporting Civil Rights*, comp. Clayborne Carson et al., 284–330. New York: Library of America, 2003.

Webster, Harvey C. "Nihilism as a New Faith." Review of *Wise Blood*, by Flannery O'Connor. *New Leader*, June 23, 1952, 23.

Weibel, Kay. "Mickey Spillane, Fifties Phenomenon." In *Dimensions of Detective Fiction*, edited by Pat Browne, Larry N. Lundren, and Ray B. Browne. Bowling Green, OH: Bowling Green State University Press, 1976.

Weinman, Sarah. *The Real Lolita: The Kidnapping of Sally Horner and the Novel That Scandalized the World*. New York: HarperCollins, 2018.

Whitehead, Don. "AP Was There: D-Day Correspondent Returns Ten Years Later." Associated Press, June 3, 2019.

Whyte, William. *The Organization Man*. New York: Simon & Schuster, 1955.

Wilson, Colin. *The Outsider*. New York: Houghton Mifflin, 1956.

Wilson, G. B., Jr. "Incarnation and Redemption in *The Old Man and the Sea*." *Studies in Short Fiction* 14 (September 1977): 369–73.

Wilson, Sloan. *The Man in the Gray Flannel Suit*. New York: Simon & Schuster, 1956.

Wouk, Herman. *The Caine Mutiny*. Garden City, NY: Doubleday, 1951.

Wright, Richard. *The Outsider*. New York: Harper, 1953.

Wylie, Philip. "The Crime of Mickey Spillane." *Good Housekeeping*, February 1955, 54–55.

X (George Frost Kennan). "The Sources of Soviet Conduct." *Foreign Affairs* 25 (July 1947): 566–82.

Zanganeli, Lila Azam. "Umberto Eco, the Art of Fiction, No 197." *Paris Review* 185 (Summer 2008).

Zimmerman, Jacqueline Noll. *People Like Ourselves: Portrayals of Mental Illness in the Movies*. Lanham, MD: Scarecrow Press, 2003.

Zunshine, Lisa. *Why We Read Fiction: Theory of Mind and the Novel*. Columbus: Ohio State University Press, 2006.

INDEX